"Reflecting on illicit business is important for detecting and preventing criminal entrepreneurship. This book applies the terminology from regular business to understand motives, opportunities, and willingness to operate on the wrong side of the law. Simply stated, you cannot fight something you don't understand, and you cannot fight someone you don't understand. That is why this book is so important."

Petter Gottschalk, *Professor Emeritus, Department of Leadership and Organizational Behaviour, Norwegian Business School*

ILLICIT BUSINESS

Illicit business is big business. It covers a diverse range of activities from money laundering, drug trafficking and human trafficking through to the manufacture of counterfeit goods and multiple activities in the informal and shadow economies. This book introduces the world of illegal business.

The authors contextualize the evolution in practices of illegal business around the world, highlighting the importance of organized crime, shadow economies and informal sectors. Incorporating scholarly insights with real-world examples, the book provides a much-needed business and economics analysis of a subject that is otherwise dominated by criminologists.

With a range of case studies, this book provides a global approach that will be valuable reading for students seeking to understand the business of crime.

Anthea McCarthy-Jones is Senior Lecturer in Business at the University of New South Wales Canberra, Australia.

Mark Turner is Honorary Professor of Business at the University of New South Wales Canberra, Australia.

ILLICIT BUSINESS

Anthea McCarthy-Jones and Mark Turner

Routledge
Taylor & Francis Group

LONDON AND NEW YORK

Designed cover image: Hafiyya Syafa/iStock

First published 2025
by Routledge
4 Park Square, Milton Park, Abingdon, Oxon OX14 4RN

and by Routledge
605 Third Avenue, New York, NY 10158

Routledge is an imprint of the Taylor & Francis Group, an informa business

© 2025 Anthea McCarthy-Jones and Mark Turner

The right of Anthea McCarthy-Jones and Mark Turner to be identified as authors of this work has been asserted in accordance with sections 77 and 78 of the Copyright, Designs and Patents Act 1988.

British Library Cataloguing-in-Publication Data
A catalogue record for this book is available from the British Library

Library of Congress Cataloging-in-Publication Data
A catalog record has been requested for this book

ISBN: 978-1-032-27666-3 (hbk)
ISBN: 978-1-032-27664-9 (pbk)
ISBN: 978-1-003-29362-0 (ebk)

DOI: 10.4324/9781003293620

Typeset in Sabon
by Taylor & Francis Books

For Anthony, Luca, Lucia and Estelle

CONTENTS

ILLUSTRATIONS

ABBREVIATIONS AND ACRONYMS

AI	Artificial Intelligence
AML	Anti-Money Laundering
APT	Advanced Persistent Threat
ASD	Australian Signals Directorate
ASEAN	Association of Southeast Asian Nations
ASG	Abu Sayyaf Group
ATS	Amphetamine-Type Stimulant
AUSTRAC	Australian Transaction Reports and Analysis Centre
CaaS	Cybercrime as a Service
CITES	Convention on International Trade in Endangered Species of Wild Fauna and Flora
CTF	Counter-Terrorism Financing
DDoS	Distributed Denial-of-Service
DEA	Drug Enforcement Administration
DOJ	Department of Justice
ELN	Ejército de Liberación Nacional
EU	European Union
FAO	Food and Agriculture Organization of the United Nations
FARC	Fuerzas Armadas Revolucionarias de Colombia
FATF	Financial Action Task Force
FIU	Financial Intelligence Unit
G7	Group of Seven
GDP	Gross Domestic Product
GI-TOC	Global Initiative Against Transnational Organized Crime
GOCI	Global Organized Crime Index
HDI	Human Development Index
IAT	Illegal Antiquities Trade

ICT	Information and Communications Technology
IFI	International Financial Institution
ILO	International Labour Organization
IMF	International Monetary Fund
IUCN	International Union for the Conservation of Nature
IUU	Illegal, Unreported and Unregulated
MaaS	Malware as a Service
MILF	Moro Islamic Liberation Front
ML	Machine Learning
MLaaS	Money Laundering as a Service
MMRaaS	Money Mule Recruitment as a Service
MNLF	Moro National Liberation Front
MVTS	Money or Value Transfer Services
NATO	North Atlantic Treaty Organization
NGO	Non-governmental Organization
NHS	National Health Service
OCG	Organized Crime Group
OECD	Organisation for Economic Co-operation and Development
OFC	Offshore Financial Centre
OHS	Occupational Health and Safety
PDVSA	Petróleos de Venezuela S.A.
PLA	People's Liberation Army
POGO	Philippine Offshore Gambling Operations
RaaS	Ransomware as a Service
RFMO	Regional Fisheries Management Organisation
RUF	Revolutionary United Front
SALW	Small Arms and Light Weapons
SIPRI	Stockholm International Peace Research Institute
SME	Small and Medium-Sized Enterprise
TBML	Trade-Based Money Laundering
UAE	United Arab Emirates
UN	United Nations
UNDP	United Nations Development Programme
UNITA	União Nacional para a Independência Total de Angola
UNODC	United Nations Office on Drugs and Crime
VUCA	Volatility, Uncertainty, Complexity and Ambiguity
WEF	World Economic Forum
WHO	World Health Organization
WWF	World Wildlife Fund

PREFACE

The genesis of this book can be traced back to 2017 when I was appointed to an academic position in the School of Business at UNSW Canberra. After a few of years of teaching in the School of Business it became apparent that a large and increasingly important part of business in the modern world – illicit forms of business – were not included in the offerings of business schools at most universities in Australia and abroad. This seemed to be a missed opportunity and one that I discussed with Mark Turner, the co-author of this book, on many occasions. With Mark's encouragement, I took this issue to my Head of School at the time (Prof. Michael O'Donnell) and asked whether there would be scope to develop a course on illicit business that could be offered as an elective to undergraduate business students. To my delight the idea was warmly welcomed, and so I set to work on developing the course Illicit Business in the Modern World which was first run in 2020. Since then, the course has grown in popularity so much so that it is now the largest undergraduate elective in the School of Business at UNSW Canberra. I distinctly remember a phone call in late 2021 when Mark pointed out that if I could develop a course on illicit business, I really ought to write a book on the topic. At the time I was eight months pregnant with my son, and so the thought of writing a book did seem like an impossible task. This is why I was incredibly grateful to Mark for agreeing to co-author this book. The writing process has involved many enjoyable meetings in Canberra at Tilley's for coffee and endless discussions about the book's structure, content and overarching narrative. It has been an extremely enjoyable and collaborative effort that has been reminiscent of a similar journey we embarked upon many years ago when I was a PhD student and Mark was my supervisor.

In this book, we have sought unequivocally to place a business perspective at the centre of our approach and analysis. Indeed, much of the content presented in this book has only ever been examined through a criminology lens. Yet, as we demonstrate, the drivers of illicit business share many similarities with legal businesses. The adoption of a business lens has allowed us to explain the expansion of illicit businesses across a diverse range of case studies that span continents, countries, religions, languages and cultures. It has also allowed us to identify differences in illicit business models used around the world as well as significant commonalities. This has led us to highlight the importance of network explanations and significant actors within network arrangements such as brokers. As the United Nations has identified, illicit business is big business, and therefore we hope that this book will provide a useful starting point to understand the impact of illicit business in the modern world.

This book would not have been possible without the guidance and support of a number of people. First, we would like to thank Terry Clague and Naomi Round Cahalin at Routledge. Their encouragement and support during this long process has been an important part of our ability to progress and complete this project. Also, special thanks to Alison Phillips for her excellent editorial work on our manuscript. We are particularly grateful to our families for their ongoing patience while we spent many hours toiling over our work. Anthea would like to acknowledge the unwavering support of her parents Joanne and Owen. To her partner in crime/husband Anthony, thank you for your patience, unconditional love and support during this endeavour. Your encouragement and advice are and always will be instrumental to my success. To my son, Luca, thank you for all the much-needed cuddles and giggles along the way. Mark would like to acknowledge the support of his wife, Lulu, who has witnessed the process of his academic book-writing on more occasions than she would care to remember. Special mention also to Mark's delightful young granddaughters who stayed with him and Lulu during the final four months of the project and provided a welcome distraction from the academic tasks at hand, so much so that he now wonders how he completed the book.

ACKNOWLEDGEMENTS

The authors would like to thank the following for permission to reproduce the copyright material:

1. Global Initiative on Transnational Organized Crime (GI-TOC) for permission to reproduce its figure (Figure 1.1) on vulnerability to organized crime that first appeared in Global Initiative Against Transnational Organized Crime (2021) *Global Organized Crime Index 2021.*
2. C. May and Global Financial Integrity for permission to reproduce their table (Table 1.1) (via CC BY) which first appeared in May, C. (2017) *Transnational Crime and the Developing World.* Washington, DC: Global Financial Integrity.
3. SpringerNature for permission to reproduce a table (Table 1.3) that first appeared in Dietzler, J. (2013) 'On "organized crime" in the illicit antiquities trade: Moving beyond the definitional debate.' *Trends in Organized Crime* 16, 329–342.
4. The World Bank for permission to reproduce a table (Table 3.1) that first appeared in World Bank (2020) 'Poverty and shared prosperity 2020: Reversals of fortune.' Washington, DC: World Bank. License: Creative Commons Attribution CC BY 3.0 IGO.
5. Elsevier to preproduce a table (Table 7.1) that first appeared in Turner, M. (1998) 'Kidnapping and Politics.' *International Journal of the Sociology of Law* 26 (2) 145–160.
6. United Nations Office on Drugs and Crime (UNODC) for permission to reproduce its table (Table 7.2) on Core Data and Indicators that first appeared in the *Global Report on Trafficking in Persons 2022.*

7.   Taylor & Francis for permission to reproduce a table (Table 9.1) that first appeared in McCarthy-Jones, A. and Turner, M. (2022) 'What is a "Mafia State" and how is one created?' *Policy Studies* 43 (6) 1195–1215.

1

FRAMING ILLICIT BUSINESS

Introduction

Illicit business is big business. It is global in its extent and involves multiple activities. Illicit business involves millions of people as entrepreneurs, workers and customers. Its turnover is reckoned to be in trillions of dollars. But nobody really knows the true figures as by definition illicit business is often hidden business in which participants and their activities stay out of the sight of law enforcement agencies or are not regulated by the state. However, we do have estimates of the scale of illicit business and the figures are staggeringly large.

One estimate places the global illegal economy as comprising 8%–15% of the world's gross domestic product (GDP) and amounting to between US $6.76 trillion and US $12.68 trillion (VOA 2016). The World Economic Forum (WEF) has reported 'leakage from illicit trade' as accounting for 3% of the world economy making it a greater amount than the GDP of countries such as Brazil, Italy or Canada (WEF 2019). Moving on to specific illicit activities, it is estimated that money laundering is equivalent to 2%–5% of global GDP or between US $800 billion and US $2 trillion annually (UNDOC 2022). According to an Organisation for Economic Co-operation and Development study, the international trade in fake products is worth US $464 billion per year or 2.5% of world trade (OECD 2021). The global black market for prohibited drugs is estimated to have a value of between US $426 billion and US $652 billion and to make up 1% of global trade annually (May 2017, xi). In the United States alone, the market for illegal drugs is worth US $150 billion (Gregory et al. 2019). Wildlife trafficking is valued at between US $5 billion and US $23 billion annually or between US $7.8 billion and US $10 billion depending on whose statistics are used (May 2017, xi; WWF Australia 2022). The informal economy – that is, the economy unregulated by the state – accounts for a staggering

DOI: 10.4324/9781003293620-1

61.2% of the world's adult labour force with Latin America and sub-Saharan Africa having the highest levels of informality and Europe and East Asia the lowest (ILO 2018, 13; IMF 2021). The informal economy involves an average of 35% of the economic activity in middle and low income countries and 15% in advanced economies (IMF 2021).

While the figures for illicit business cited above lack accuracy they nevertheless indicate the vast scale of such activities in terms of financial value and employment – but you need to accept that the numbers presented above and in Table 1.1 are estimates, often broad in range and compiled using incomplete and fuzzy data. Despite the imprecision, it cannot be denied that illicit business is big business and occurs in all countries. But in business and management textbooks and in the disciplines' journals there is barely a mention of illicit business. It appears to be a taboo subject. There is a large literature on illicit business but it is usually to be found in criminology. This discipline has produced numerous studies on a wide range of illicit business activities from money laundering to organ trafficking and illegal arms sales. But such studies are researched and written from a criminological perspective rather than a business one. By contrast, this book adopts a business approach. It places emphasis on the business aspects of these economic activities and examines them using concepts that are routinely employed in studies on licit business while maintaining awareness that there are important characteristics that separate the licit from the illicit. Inevitably we draw on the rich criminological literature and other literatures that deal with the phenomena that we are describing and analysing to provide this business perspective.

TABLE 1.1 Estimates of the Retail Value of Transnational Crime

Transnational Illicit Business	Estimated Annual Value
Drug trafficking	US $426 billion to US $652 billion
Small arms and light weapons trafficking	US $1.7 billion to US $3.5 billion
Human trafficking	US $150.2 billion
Organ trafficking	US $840 million to US $1.7 billion
Trafficking in cultural property	US $1.2 billion to US $1.6 billion
Counterfeiting	US $923 billion to US $1.3 trillion
Illegal wildlife trade	US $5 billion to US $23 billion
Illegal, unreported and unregulated fishing	US $15.5 billion to US $36.4 billion
Illegal logging	US $52 billion to US $157 billion
Illegal mining	US $12 billion to US $48 billion
Crude oil theft	US $5.2 billion to US $11.9 billion
Total	US $1.6 trillion to US $2.2 trillion

Note: This table first appeared in May, C. (2017) *Transnational Crime and the Developing World.* Washington, DC: Global Financial Integrity, p. xi.

In practical terms, this business perspective involves looking at such things as organizational structures and processes and why they have been adopted; strategies to create and maintain markets; risk management; human resource management issues such as personnel recruitment and pay; organizational change and innovation; and financial management. Such items and more are the bread and butter of business-focused analysis that can lead to enhanced understanding of the phenomena under the microscope. The book is also concerned with responses from the state and society to illicit business and what steps have been taken with what degrees of success to stop, manage or tolerate such activities.

Defining the Business Perspective

As this book on illicit business is written from a business perspective, it is necessary to clarify what this means. A fundamental starting point is to define what a business is and to follow this with a comparison of the similarities and differences between licit and illicit businesses. It will become evident that while there are shared characteristics between the two there are also some criteria which provide starkly contrasting results.

At the most basic level, a business is established to provide goods and/or services to the community in exchange for money. Moving beyond this it is possible to identify six criteria that are shared by all licit businesses:

1. *Profit motive*: The vast majority of businesses aim to make a profit although some may receive income from sources other than sales – for example, charities engaged in economic activities for which they receive payment such as second-hand shops or providing community services may also rely on donations and grants; businesses that need to take out loans to cover their expenses during difficult times such as during the COVID-19 pandemic. Generally, however, businesses need to make a profit over at least the medium term. If they don't, they are forced to cease operations.
2. *Continuity:* Businesses generally aim to produce their outputs and sell them on a continuous basis. Some businesses may have extended downtime, such as in seasonal tourism-related activities or be temporary in nature such as companies set up to make a particular movie. However, the vast majority of businesses aim to maintain continuous operations.
3. *Legality:* Businesses are set up to be legal and lawful. They need to be compliant with state laws and regulations. They need to be registered and to follow the regulatory requirements of government.
4. *Meeting needs:* Businesses respond to or help to create needs and wants for services and goods from society or some section of it. They need a market which will sustain the business. Thus, they try to achieve customer satisfaction as it increases the likelihood of repeat and new purchases of their products and thus sustains the business.

5. *Risk management*: All businesses face risks that are generated by the environment in which they operate. Events, forces and other organizations in the ever-changing environment present risks. Ideally, businesses should identify, evaluate and prioritize the risks they face and take action to address them. This may not always be possible as major upheavals in the environment may sound an unavoidable death knell for a business or a whole type of business.

6. *Resources:* All businesses need resources. These can be broadly divided into finance, physical capital (e.g. buildings, equipment), human resources (people with relevant skills and knowledge) and materials. A business can be likened to a processor that takes such resources from the environment and transforms them into an output (the product or service) that is then sold to customers who also make up an element of the environment.

Many of the generic characteristics of a business are common to both those that are licit and those which are illicit. For example, they share a profit motive. That was why they were established in the first place and that is what keeps them running. Both must respond to society's wants and needs or help to create the impression that they are doing so. This produces demand which in turn leads to profit. Licit and illicit businesses alike face risks in their organizational environments and must take action to deal with them if they want to continue operating. Both need to access resources to enable their businesses to function. Furthermore, all businesses will have organizational structures through which they divide up the work and coordinate it and there will be processes which are required to procure resources and produce outputs. Efficiency and effectiveness will be sought by leaders and managers. Such necessities apply to all businesses from one-person operations through to multinational corporations. However, there are some key differences between licit and illicit businesses.

The first difference is that illicit businesses are usually operating illegally. They are not permitted or authorized by the state. They may also meet the disapproval of large sections of society. Because of this, illicit businesses need to stay out of the sight of the organizations of the state such as the police who are tasked with stopping their operations and bringing them to court to face potentially very severe penalties including imprisonment, hefty fines and, in some countries, death. It should be noted that what is illegal and therefore illicit can vary between countries. For example, in much of the world it is legal to sell alcoholic drinks. They are available in a variety of outlets such as bars, cafes, restaurants, supermarkets and specialist shops. In Saudi Arabia, it is illegal to set up businesses selling alcohol. If there are such businesses they are illegal. In Pakistan, it is illegal for Muslims, who make up 96.5% of the population, to drink alcohol but it has been estimated that 10 million persons in Pakistan drink alcohol and that one million people have developed alcohol abuse disorders (Ghazal 2015). Thus, the 1977 ban on alcohol for Muslims in Pakistan has given rise to an illicit business catering to the hidden demand for alcoholic drinks. A second point to note is that legal businesses can be used as 'fronts' for illicit businesses. Restaurants have allegedly been used for money laundering purposes, as have casinos. These are legal businesses that behind the scenes are engaged in illicit activities.

Illegality has also led some illicit businesses to use the threat or actual exercise of violence to support their economic activities. This is coercive force not authorized by the state. Indeed, it is a direct challenge to the state's claim to the 'monopoly of the legitimate use of physical force' (Gerth and Mills 1946, 78). Illicit businesses utilize violence to secure the compliance of persons to behave in ways required by the businesses. It could be manifested in ensuring that people remain silent about illicit business operations by not reporting illegal activities to the police. It could involve injuring or even killing people as an example to others. Officials in Latin America may be threatened to accept bribes and to turn a blind eye to illegal drug cartel operations or accept the fatal consequences – *plata o plomo* ('silver or lead'; in other words a bullet). Abduction and the confinement of people against their will can also be used to exert pressure. Not all illicit businesses use such practices but they are very evident in many, especially those involved in drug trafficking and human trafficking where there have been many deaths and an enormous amount of human misery inflicted upon the innocent. As a business strategy, violence may be seen as a way to reduce risk in the organizational environment. It can be deployed to deter or co-opt the coercive forces of the state, to secure compliance among populations residing in the geographical areas in which the business operates, and to discourage, remove and take over the production facilities and markets of competitors. But developing and exercising violence carries a cost for the illicit business. There must be personnel to perpetrate the violence or the threat of it and equipment such as guns and transport to enable it. This means that the actual or perceived profits from the illicit business must be sufficient to facilitate such expenditure.

The second crucial difference between licit and illicit businesses is that the latter operate outside of the regulation of the state. This is of particular relevance to the informal sector of the economy. Typically, economic activities in the informal sector are not registered for tax, are unlicensed, do not necessarily comply with state rules on occupational health and safety, do not pay social security or national insurance for workers and are unlikely to observe minimum wage legislation. They exist outside of the purview of the state. However, they may not be illegal. For example, the ubiquitous micro retail businesses in developing countries are not generally selling illegal products. They are not engaged in illegal economic activities. Larger legitimate businesses that observe state regulations and pay taxes will be selling the same or similar items. Furthermore, in developing countries the state needs the informal sector to provide employment and the means of survival to millions of its citizens. In high-income nations, house-cleaning is a legal business activity. However, engaging in house-cleaning and not declaring the income obtained to the tax agency is illegal.

The Organizational Environment and Illicit Business

Several references have already been made to the organizational environment. But what is it, why is it so important and how does it interact with illicit business? The concept derives from applying the biological metaphor in which organizations are likened to living organisms that cannot survive or die out if they do not adjust to changes in their natural environment (Morgan 2006). Organizations are thus seen as 'open systems' operating in environments from which they derive inputs and into which they send outputs. They also receive feedback from the environment in relation to their inputs and outputs which enable them to identify and institute changes to their processes according to these signals (Rice 2013). In open systems theory, organizations are seen as being subject to equifinality; that is, they can achieve the same outcomes by different means. For example, one drug-dealing business may deploy excessive violence in an attempt to control its environment while another may favour a low-key approach which focuses on avoiding the attentions of law enforcement agencies while co-opting politicians and bureaucrats. All organizations exist in complicated and shifting relationships with their environments and the ways in which these relationships are managed have major implications for their success or failure. A business of any sort ignores its environment at its peril.

All organizations operate in an environment that affects their activities. It is comprised of forces, events, institutions and organizations. It is potentially everything that exists outside of the organization that may have some bearing on the activities, success and survival of that organization. Such a broad definition is of limited use as it incorporates everything outside of the organization, whereas for an organization the key elements of the environment are those which are pertinent to its activities. This is sometimes called the 'specific' or 'task' environment (Samson and Daft 2014). For example, a business engaged in illicit wildlife trafficking would need to take into account the priorities, activities and capacity of law enforcement agencies; the identification and understanding of markets and their structure; the activities of and threats from competitors; access to habitats where the required wildlife is located; access to appropriate means of wildlife transport; familiarity with relevant government regulations, such as penalties for illegal wildlife trading; and the ability to identify and recruit persons to catch and transport wildlife. It may be possible to influence or even control some elements of the environment such as bribing government officials or co-opting local people to assist in the illegal activities (Turner et al. 2015). But, as for all illicit businesses, it may be difficult or impossible to influence certain factors in the environment such as changes in the broader economy, demographic patterns, political decisions, culture and technological developments. This is the 'appreciated' environment that the organization must work within.

One aspect of the environment that is always stressed is that it is constantly changing. Dawson (1992) has identified three sources of environmental change. While these items were drawn up to explain the behaviours of licit businesses, as can be seen below they also apply to illicit businesses:

1. *Motion:* The constituent parts of the environment are not static. For example, a declining market for a particular illegal drug may result in a drug-dealing organization seeking new markets.
2. *Change:* The patterns of interactions between the constituent parts of the environment change. For example, increased competition in the illegal drugs trade because of new entrants to the market.
3. *Influence:* The organization can influence changes in the environment. For example, a powerful drug cartel can 'buy off' local and national officials.

Changes in the environment point to uncertainty. It is a constant for all businesses, but more so for many illicit businesses especially as they often face environmental challenges not usually encountered by licit business. These might include major problems presented by the legal environment; law enforcement agencies dedicated to the eradication of illegal business; unfriendly political leaders; hostility from significant sections of the community; and competition which is not conducted according to state regulations. Thus, the environment faced by illicit business fits the Volatility, Uncertainty, Complexity and Ambiguity (VUCA) model that was created by the US Army War College in 1987 to analyse the security environment at the height of the Cold War, although it is now widely used by a wide range of organizations. They are environmental characteristics that can be identified separately but which are also highly interrelated (see Table 1.2). Collectively they reflect high levels of turbulence or flux in the business environment. As has been demonstrated by illicit businesses, such conditions do not necessarily present insurmountable obstacles to the

TABLE 1.2 VUCA Environments and Illicit Business

Complexity	*Volatility*
What is it? 'Refers to the number of factors that need to be taken into account and the relationships between them' (Kraaijenbrink 2018).	*What is it?* 'Refers to the speed of change in an industry, market or the world in general' (Kraaijenbrink 2018).
Example: Trafficking across different national borders with a variety of partners, processes and obstacles.	*Example:* The price of an illicitly traded commodity fluctuates considerably either because of competition or changing patterns of demand.
Ambiguity	*Uncertainty*
What is it? 'Refers to a lack of clarity in how to interpret something' (Kraaijenbrink 2018).	*What is it?* 'The extent to which we can confidently predict the future' (Kraaijenbrink 2018).
Example: Traffickers move into unfamiliar new markets where they do not know the capabilities of the partners nor their trustworthiness.	*Example:* The COVID-19 pandemic restricts transport and travel and thus disrupts supply chains and it is unknown when 'normal' times will return.

Source: Adapted from Bennett and Lemoine (2014); Kraaijenbrink (2018).

conduct of their economic activities. They can be perceived as risks or threats to their operations and as such need to be managed. Risk management is a constant concern of illicit businesses operating in VUCA environments.

If businesses of all kinds are to survive and even prosper they need to devote time and energy to identifying and analysing the significant elements of their environments to determine what actions are needed and indeed are possible. They need to engage in environmental scanning. But how does a business know what to look for and look at? The environment is not a fixed thing, an objective reality. According to Weick (1977), different actors may see different constituents in the environment and attach different degrees of significance to them. For example, one drug cartel may view competition from a rival cartel as the greatest threat in its environment. However, another cartel may view its environment in terms of opportunities to move into other criminal activities. Thus, organizations construct their environments and then make strategic choices about what action to take. However, there can be dispute in the organization about desirable courses of action, although it is generally the 'dominant coalition' which holds the power in an organization and thus chooses how to enact the environment (Hatch 2018).

As already observed, all organizations have structures; that is, arrangements to divide up and coordinate the tasks the organization must perform to pursue its strategy. This applies to both licit and illicit businesses of all sizes and characteristics. It is generally held that the structure should follow strategy. This principle derived from Alfred Chandler's (1962) pioneering study of American business enterprises in which he found that organizational efficiency and effectiveness are best obtained from designing the structure to fit the chosen strategy. This rational view is reflected in contemporary prescriptions that organizations need to seek alignment between strategy, structure and environment where the strategy is conceived in response to changing events and forces in the environment and the structure is built to maximize performance in pursuit of the strategy. But reality is more complex. Structure can strongly influence the strategic choices that are made. So can organizational culture. There is in fact a complex reciprocal relationship between strategy and structure (Mintzberg et al. 2009; Frederickson 1986).

There are numerous possible structural arrangements for illicit business organizations. At one extreme we find simple structures involving family members in the informal sectors of developing countries. In strong contrast are the structures that are put in place by transnational crime groups. They have often shifted from more rigid hierarchical structures such as the traditional Italian mafia and the Japanese yakuza to loosely coupled networks in which different nodes take responsibility for performing specific tasks in the chain of value-creation (McCarthy-Jones et al. 2020). In such instances it may be better to talk about 'organizing' to more accurately reflect the prevailing structures. Furthermore, because of constant threats in the environments of these transnational arrangements, the network structure and those of its component nodes may be in a regular state of flux rather than being fixed arrangements (Morgan 2006). This is a characterization applied to the Abu Sayyaf terrorist group that became involved in the kidnap-for-ransom business in the southern Philippines (Ugarte and Turner 2011). The same authors also note the group's 'agility,' a buzzword in contemporary management for licit businesses, but it is perhaps even more of a necessity for illicit enterprises as they negotiate hostile environments to ensure their survival and profit (Worley and Lawler 2010). A final observation on structure is that there may be a variety of structures that can be utilized to achieve the same strategic goals. There is no one-size-fits-all solution. However, it is likely that enterprises in similar lines of business will opt for structures that display similarities. This is because they will monitor their competitors' operations, especially those that have been successful, and be affected by similar environmental pressures and constraints that will limit possible structural options.

The Importance of the State

One of the most important actors in the environment for illegal businesses is the state. This is a fundamental concept of political science but is of great importance to the operation of businesses. It is a contested concept which has spawned a range of overlapping definitions but for our purposes we will leave these academic debates aside and provide an outline of what a state is that is relevant to the topics covered in this book (English and Townshend 1998; Jessop 2016).

The state can be seen as a centralized political organization of society whose purposes include establishing law and order, regulating aspects of citizens' activities, such as business, and settling disputes. According to the traditional view, the state seeks a monopoly of legitimate coercive force to impose its will. It also seeks a broader legitimacy so that the citizens within a defined geographical territory generally accept and act according to the rules issued by the state. As can be seen from this definition of the state, illicit business comes into direct conflict with it. Illicit business is based on breaking or ignoring the state's rules. This can be manifested in a range of behaviours from businesses' simple avoidance of the state as practised by money launderers to violence aimed at state officials by drug cartels.

Political scientists have identified various types of states. This reflects the many possible patterns of state-society relations which are responsible for moulding different state forms. States have variously been depicted as weak, strong, soft, failed, collapsed, neo-patrimonial, kleptocratic, totalitarian, rogue and more. But we will focus on one other way of looking at the state that has most relevance for illicit business – the effectiveness of the state. At a basic level, state effectiveness refers to the 'ability to deliver the collective goods that expand the capabilities of citizens' (Evans et al. 2017, 380). Has the state got the capacity and capability to shape and deliver the policies needed to improve the lives of its citizens? (ESID 2021). One of the ways the state is supposed to achieve this is by providing its citizens with security and delivering law and order. They are foundational aspects of 'good governance' and requirements for socio-economic development that benefits the whole nation (Acemoglu and Robinson 2012).

States that are weak have only partially developed the characteristics of effectiveness. These states invariably are located in the developing world and often dominated by elites who have been unable to ensure, or indeed are not interested in doing so, that all citizens have access to the full range of basic services and that they have the opportunities that would enable them to improve their welfare. Poor people in rural and urban areas that experience such conditions are making their living in economic activities that are largely unregulated and unsupervised by the state. There may well be rules issued by the state regarding terms of employment, minimum wages, occupational health and safety, tax collection and business registration but they are avoided by people in the informal sector and are not followed up by the state. State officials also realize that the informal sector acts as a giant safety net (and perhaps safety valve) that provides its workers and their families with an income. The state can, however, have encounters with the informal economy, sometimes of a repressive kind, such as exacting illegal 'taxes' from vendors or evicting squatters for urban 'development.'

In rich countries, the state is much better at exerting its regulatory authority. Thus, the informal sector is much smaller than in poor countries. Nevertheless, it is evident in all rich countries. For example, in some advanced economies it is estimated to make up 15% of GDP with some countries exceeding 20% (Deléchat and Medina 2020). In the United Kingdom, one study found that 4.9% of the British population were involved in the 'hidden economy' (Doyle et al. 2017). In some Eastern European countries, transitioning from planned economies to capitalism, the informal economy has been described as an important source of household income (Wallace and Latcheva 2006). The losses to state treasuries are large. One UK study even put the figure of losses through non-payment of income tax, sales tax, national insurance and corporation tax as high as £35–£40 billion, although one needs to take care to distinguish between tax avoidance which is legal and tax evasion which is illegal (Partington 2021; Murphy 2014).

While there are various methodologies for measuring state effectiveness, we are especially interested in those that concern law and order as one of the fundamental obligations of the state should be to provide an environment of safety and security for its population. But this does not necessarily happen and communities can be subjected to the unwelcome attentions and depredations of organized crime and the responses from the state. A recent attempt to measure the extent of organized crime and the effectiveness or 'resilience' of the state to deal with it across all 193 United Nations countries is the Global Organized Crime Index (GI-TOC 2021). It describes organized crime as 'the most pernicious threat to human security, development and justice in the world today' (GI-TOC 2021, 4). The Global Organized Crime Index has three constituent parts:

1. *The scope, scale and impact of ten criminal markets:* Human trafficking, human smuggling, arms trafficking, flora crimes, fauna crimes, non-renewable resource crimes, heroin trade, cocaine trade, cannabis trade and synthetic drug trade.
2. *The structure and influence of criminal actors:* Mafia-style groups, criminal networks, state-embedded actors and foreign actors.
3. The resilience of a country to organized crime.

Countries are assigned a criminality score based on the prevalence of criminal markets and the structure and influence of criminal actors (a and b). This is then added to the resilience score (c) to provide a typology of countries in terms of levels of criminality and degree of resilience that identifies vulnerability to organized crime (see Figure 1.1).

The vulnerability classifications reveal that more than three-quarters of the world's population live in countries with high levels of criminality and countries with low resilience to organized crime. Of the 193 countries surveyed only 50 were designated as having low criminality and high resilience to organized crime. The nature and role of the state was identified as a leading determinant of the

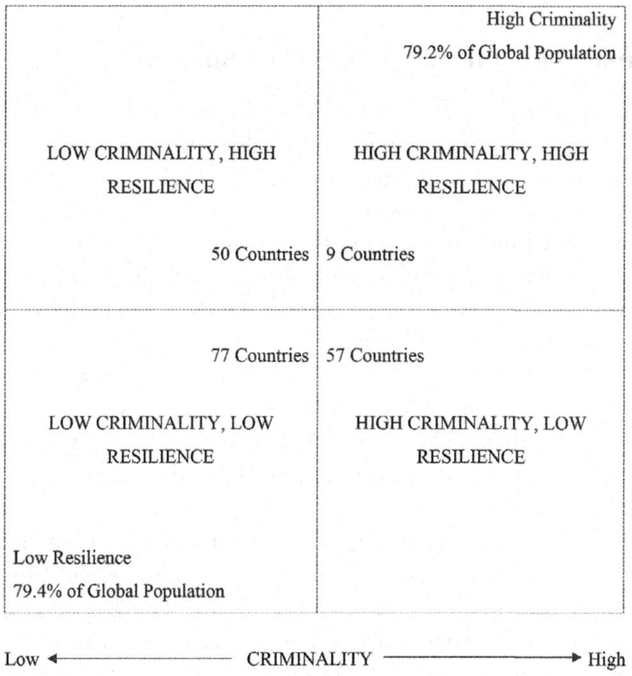

		High Criminality
		79.2% of Global Population
LOW CRIMINALITY, HIGH RESILIENCE	HIGH CRIMINALITY, HIGH RESILIENCE	
50 Countries	9 Countries	
77 Countries	57 Countries	
LOW CRIMINALITY, LOW RESILIENCE	HIGH CRIMINALITY, LOW RESILIENCE	
Low Resilience 79.4% of Global Population		

Low ◄——————— CRIMINALITY ———————► High

FIGURE 1.1 Vulnerability to Organized Crime Classifications
Note: This figure originally appeared in Global Initiative Against Transnational Organized Crime (2021) *Global Organized Crime Index 2021*, p. 13.

level of criminality and the strength of resilience. Democratic states generally demonstrated higher levels of resilience to criminality than states operating under authoritarian regimes. The centrality of the state was further emphasized in the major finding that state actors were the 'most dominant agents in facilitating illicit economies and inhibiting resilience to organized crime' (GI-TOC 2021, 17). At the extreme, state actors can become so enmeshed in criminal activities that a 'mafia state' can develop (McCarthy-Jones and Turner 2022). Such a state is characterized by a political leader who, in association with a network of relatives, friends and other allies, runs the state as a criminal enterprise.

As a final note on the relationship between the state and illicit business, it is in the interests of the latter to keep the state at low levels of effectiveness to deal with criminality. This is beneficial for illicit business as it makes the environment more predictable and thus reduces risk; for example, if state officials can be bribed to turn a blind eye to illegal activities. However, it is doubtful that illicit business wants a collapsed or failed state in which law and political order completely break down and where the government is unable to deliver any services. This would produce an extreme VUCA environment where uncertainty, volatility, instability and ambiguity could be at maximum levels – not an ideal context for conducting business. Illicit business wants the state to maintain some structure, functionality and legitimacy.

Entrepreneurship, Innovation and Illicit Business

Successful entrepreneurs are celebrated in capitalist societies for their ability to identify new business opportunities and exploit them, often for considerable financial gain. They engage in what Schumpeter (1952) terms 'creative destruction,' a process that involves old products and processes being superseded by new ones or marked improvements in the existing ones. But entrepreneurship is 'not always a wholesome and clean endeavour' (Goffschalk 2009, 1). Organized crime is often entrepreneurial in character. Like their counterparts in the legal world of business, criminals also engage in the creative and innovative behaviours that define entrepreneurship. They too start new organizations or revitalize mature ones with creativity and innovation. However, we tend to adopt an attitude of 'unconscious legalism' which makes us biased towards the judicial delimitation of the entrepreneur as being engaged in legal business activities (Rehn and Taalas 2004).

The entrepreneur, whether engaged in licit or illicit business, is essentially concerned with innovation, succinctly defined as 'the successful exploitation of new ideas' (DTI cited in Tidd and Bessant 2009, 16). For those engaged in illicit business, there is strong environmental pressure to be innovative. First, there is the incentive to increase profits, a motivation shared with legal businesses. Second, illegal businesses are in competition with other criminal organizations and need to maintain or increase their share of the market or move into new products and markets. Third, illicit businesses need to evade detection and prosecution by international and domestic law enforcement agencies to survive and prosper. Fourth, technological change can propel, necessitate or enable changes in illegal enterprises so they remain competitive and evade detection. These compelling factors have encouraged illicit businesses to be innovative. They have demonstrated the ability to be highly adaptable, agile, creative and resilient – key characteristics of successful innovation.

Illicit innovations will be in products and processes and are generally incremental in nature. For example, in Chapter 5, 'The Drug Trafficking Business,' we demonstrate how criminal organizations have, over many years, experimented with the manufacture and sale of different drugs and expanded into new markets. We also show how money launderers have embraced new technology and processes to convert 'dirty' money into clean funds. Organizational structures have also been changed from hierarchical arrangements to more loosely coupled networks that link criminals across the globe. Human traffickers have sought new methods of recruiting and transporting their illegal cargoes. Indeed, across the whole spectrum of illicit business, criminals have been engaged in innovation and continue to do so in response to opportunities and threats in the environment.

From Local to Global

Much illicit business involves networks of actors that operate in different countries performing different tasks in the division of labour along supply chains that start in one country and can move through several more before ending up at their final destinations where the products are sold to end-users. This is the globalization of illicit business. The way in which it operates can be best understood from the example of the illegal antiquities trade (IAT) as set out by Jessica Dietzler (2013) (see Table 1.3). It is both global and local with its structure resembling those associated with other types of networked transnational crime.

Dietzler (2013) is especially concerned with the structures and processes of the IAT and has developed an analytical framework that combines Routine Activity Theory (RAT) and insights derived from the work of Felson (2006) involving 'events, sequences and settings.' RAT is comprised of three components: (1) suitable targets, in this case antiquities; (2) motivated offenders, those making rational decisions to be involved in the various criminal activities in the IAT; and (3) the absence of capable guardianship; that is, where the target lacks surveillance by actors such as the police, registration authorities and witnesses. Thus, in Table 1.3 we see the sequence of events involved in the IAT – theft, transit, facilitation and sales/purchase. For each of these events, particular roles are played by motivated offenders – looters and smugglers in the first two stages but potentially a large cast in the complex business of facilitation. Moving on to spatial considerations, there are the micro-settings or task environments in which these events take place and the motivated offenders operate. These range from the sources of the antiquities at archaeological sites (theft) through border checkpoints (transit)

TABLE 1.3 Actors, Processes and Locales in the Illegal Antiquities Trade

Sequence	Stage 1 Theft	Stage 2 Transit	Stage 3 Facilitation	Stage 4 Sales/ Purchase
Role Motivated offender	Looters	Smugglers	Document forgers Government officials Curators Academics Launderers Appraisers Valuers	Dealers Buyers Collectors
Micro-setting Suitable target and absence of capable guardianship	Archae-ological site	Border checkpoint Maritime port Airport Customs	University Museum Embassy Border Checkpoint Maritime port Airport Customs Internet	Private residence Museum Hotel Internet
Macro-setting Absence of capable guardianship	Source country	Transit country	Source country Transit country Market country Internet	Market country Internet

Note: This table first appeared in Dietzler, J. (2013) 'On "organized crime" in the illicit antiquities trade: Moving beyond the definitional debate.' *Trends in Organized Crime* 16, 329–342. https://crea tivecommons.org/licenses/by/4.0/

to ports, museums and customs to the final destinations (sales/purchases) that may be private residences, museums or hotels. Finally, there is the macro-setting or general environment which includes broad categories for the events such as source country, transit country and market country. In the complex network of IAT actors and processes there is potential for instability because relationships between different actors can break down from occurrences like arrests or lack of trust. There is also differential profit-sharing among those engaged in the IAT. According to one study, the local people commissioned by middlemen or dealers to do the 'looting' received only an estimated 1% of the overall profits, while middlemen took 98% (Brodie 1998).

This analytical framework for the IAT draws attention to various concepts introduced and observations made throughout this introductory chapter. First, understanding is aided by thinking about illicit business in terms of organizing but not necessarily organizations. Second, transnational crime can be best visualized, analysed and comprehended in terms of networks which can be more or less loosely connected. They are not hierarchical forms of organization. Third, it is vital to consider the environments in which particular events or crimes take place and that at different points in the chain of events the actors involved are operating in different environments performing specific tasks that enable the antiquities to get from source to destination. Fourth, the diverse cast of actors take their profits along the sequence of events. There is no central organization that coordinates and administers payments. Market forces and the relative power of the actors are what matter most. Fifth, in most of the stages success involves evading the formal rules of the state and their application by state officials. Finally, during the sequence of events it is possible for actors such as academics, border officials and dealers to engage in a sleight of hand that transforms the illicit into the licit, a demonstration that licit business enterprises may also be involved in illicit dealings.

The IAT example clearly illustrates how the globalization of crime has led to new structural arrangements among the actors involved. In order to span borders, spread risk, avoid detection and access new customers, suppliers and skills, criminal groups from across the world have moved away from hierarchical structures and entered collaborative relationships. They engage in network forms of organization which are loosely coupled (McCarthy-Jones et al. 2020). However, there are two kinds of networks – 'bright' and 'dark' (Raab and Milward 2003). Bright networks are covert and legal, whereas dark networks are 'mostly illegal' and 'contrary to the law' and typically comprise criminal and terrorist groups (Raab and Milward 2003, 430).

The IAT example of a dark network showed a division of labour involving persons doing specialized tasks in the illicit business chain ranging from stealing antiquities to transporting them across international borders to dealers and customers. But, such networks do not come together by some natural process. Human agency is required to make the connections between the actors or nodes. There are 'structural holes' separating disconnected nodes and it requires brokers to establish the links between these disconnected others (Burt 1992; Morselli 2009). Brokers occupy the structural holes and facilitate the relationships between the previously disconnected nodes. There are two types of broker – transactional and transformational (McCarthy-Jones and Turner 2024). Transactional brokers bring together the nodes and then provide services to make the network function. Transformational brokers bring about significant network changes. They are entrepreneurial and innovate to lead the network into such things as new markets or products or new ways of operating. Network modes of transnational criminal organization have been seen to have resilience (Ayling 2009; Catanese and Fiumara 2016). They have demonstrated the ability to adapt and reconfigure when disrupted. However, brokers represent vulnerable points in dark networks because they are so important for network operations. The capture and prosecution of brokers would likely cause significant damage to dark networks.

Conclusion

Illicit business is big business. It is valued in the trillions of dollars and takes place across the globe. It can bring misery, exploitation and suffering to some and provide the necessary means of survival to millions in developing countries. This introductory chapter has established some of the fundamental ideas and concepts involved in taking a business perspective for the description and analysis of illicit business. It has been demonstrated that there are many characteristics that are shared by licit and illicit businesses, starting with the profit motive, and that the advice given by management gurus, consultants and academics for business success in legal enterprises often also applies to illicit ones. However, there are striking differences, notably that illicit businesses are engaged in illegal activities which may also be seen as unethical by a large number of citizens. Also, illicit businesses may perceive the need to use or threaten to use violence to achieve their goals. This is a challenge to the state which is oriented to the control of the activities of residents – including business activities – of the territory over which the state claims jurisdiction. But many states do not have resilience to organized crime and so provide environments in which organized crime can prosper. Illicit business is often transnational in nature involving both the local and the global in networks of activities populated by actors who perform different tasks in the process of getting the product to the market.

References

Acemoglu, D. and Robinson, J. (2012) *Why Nations Fail: The Origins of Power, Prosperity and Poverty.* New York: Crown Business.

Ayling, J. (2009) 'Criminal organizations and resilience.' *International Journal of Law Crime and Justice* 37 (4) 182–196.

Bennett, N. and Lemoine, G.J. (2014) 'What does VUCA really mean for you?' *Harvard Business Review* 92 (1/2) 27.

Brodie, N. (1998) 'Pity the poor middlemen.' *Culture Without Context: The Newsletter of the Near Eastern Project of the Illicit Antiquities Research Centre* 3, 7–9.

Burt, R. (1992) *Structural Holes.* Cambridge, MA: Harvard University Press.

Catanese, S. and Fiumara, G. (2016) 'Resilience in criminal networks.' *Atti Della Accademia Pelotoritana del Pericolanti Classe di Scienze Fische, Matematiche e Naturali* 94 (2) A1.

Chandler, A. (1962) *Strategy and Structure: Chapters in the History of the American Industrial Enterprise.* Washington, DC: Beard Books.

Dawson, A. (1992) *Analyzing Organizations.* London: Macmillan.

Deléchat, C. and Medina, L. (2020) 'What is the informal economy?' *Finance and Development* (December) 54–55.

Dietzler, J. (2013) 'On "organized crime" in the illicit antiquities trade: Moving beyond the definitional debate,' *Trends in Organized Crime* 15 (4) 329–342.

Doyle, M., Lepanjuuri, K. and Toomsie-Smith, M. (2017) *The Hidden Economy in Great Britain.* London: HM Revenue and Customs.

Effective States in Development (ESID) (2021) ESID website. Available at https://www.effective-states.org.

English, R. and Townshend, C. (eds) (1998) *The State: Historical and Political Dimensions.* London: Routledge.

Evans, P., Huber, E. and Stephens, J. (2017) 'The political foundations of state effectiveness.' In M. Centeneo, A. Kohli and D. Yasher (eds) *States in the Developing World*, pp. 380–408. Cambridge: Cambridge University Press.

Felson, M. (2006) 'The ecosystem for organized crime.' In *HEUNI 25th Anniversary Lecture, 7th Inkiri Antilla Lecture, HEUNI Paper No. 26 (October)*. Helsinki: The European Institute for Crime Prevention and Control, affiliated with the United Nations.

Frederickson, J. (1986) 'The strategic decision process and organizational structure.' *Academy of Management Review* 11 (2) 280–297.

Gerth, H.H. and Mills, C.W. (1946) *From Max Weber: Essays in Sociology*. New York: Oxford University Press.

Ghazal, P. (2015) 'The growing problem of alcoholism in Pakistan: An overview of current situation and treatment options.' *International Journal of Endorsing Health Science Research* 3 (3) 15–21.

Global Initiative Against Transnational Organized Crime (GI-TOC) (2021) *Global Organized Crime Index 2021*. GI-TOC.

Goffschalk, P. (2009) *Entrepreneurship and Organized Crime: Entrepreneurs in Illegal Business*. Cheltenham: Edward Elgar.

Gregory, M., Davenport, S., Caulkins, J. and Kilmer, B. (2019) *What America's Users Spend on Illegal Drugs, 2006–2016*. Santa Monica, CA: RAND Corporation. Available at https://www.rand.org/pubs/research_reports/RR3140.html.

Hatch, M.J. (2018) *Organization Theory: Modern, Symbolic, and Postmodern Perspectives*. Oxford: Oxford University Press.

International Labour Organization (ILO) (2018) *Women and Men in the Informal Economy: A Statistical Picture*, 3rd edition. Geneva: ILO.

International Monetary Fund (IMF) (2021) 'Five things to know about the informal economy.' *IMF News*, 23 July. Available at https://www.imf.org/en/News/Articles/2021/07/28/na-072821-five-things-to-know-about-the-informal-economy.

Jessop, B. (2016) *The State: Past, Present and Future*. Cambridge: Polity Press.

Kraaijenbrink, J. (2018) 'What does VUCA really mean?' *Forbes*, 19 December. Available at https://www.forbes.com/sites/jeroenkraaijenbrink/2018/12/19/what-does-vuca-really-mean/.

May, C. (2017) *Transnational Crime and the Developing World*. Washington, DC: Global Financial Integrity.

McCarthy-Jones, A., Doyle, C. and Turner, M. (2020) 'From hierarchies to networks: The organizational evolution of the international drug trade.' *International Journal of Crime, Law and Justice* 63 (December) 100436.

McCarthy-Jones, A. and Turner, M. (2022) 'What is a "mafia state" and how is one created?' *Policy Studies* 43 (6) 1195–1215.

McCarthy-Jones, A. and Turner, M. (2024) 'Dark networks, transnational crime and security: The critical role of brokers.' *Journal of Illicit Economies and Development* 5 (1) 58–69.

Mintzberg, H., Ahlstrand, B. and Lampel, J. (2009) *Strategy Safari: The Complete Guide through the Wilds of Strategic Management*, 2nd edition. Harlow: FT Press/Prentice Hall.

Morgan, G. (2006) *Images of Organization*, updated edition. Thousand Oaks, CA: SAGE.

Morselli, C. (2009) *Inside Criminal Networks*. New York: Springer.

Murphy, R. (2014) *In the Shade: Research on the UK's Missing Economy*. Downham Market: Tax Research.

Organisation for Co-operation and Development (OECD) (2021) *Global Trade in Fakes: A Worrying Threat*. Paris: OECD Publishing.

Partington, R. (2021) 'Tax lost in UK amounts to 35 billion pounds – almost half due to fraud.' *The Guardian*, 17 September. Available at https://www.theguardian.com/politics/2021/sep/16/tax-lost-in-uk-amounts-to-35bn-almost-half-say-campaigners-due-to.

Raab, J. and Milward, H. (2003) 'Dark networks as problems.' *Journal of Public Administration Research and Theory* 13 (4) 413–439.

Rehn, A. and Taalas, S. (2004) 'Crime and assumptions in entrepreneurship bias as literary form of "heroic drama".' In D. Hjorth and C. Steyaert (eds) *Narrative and Discursive Approaches in Entrepreneurship*, pp. 144–159. Cheltenham: Edward Elgar.

Rice, A. (ed.) (2013) *The Enterprise and its Environment: A System Theory of Management Organization*. London: Routledge.

Samson, D. and Daft, R. (2014) *Fundamentals of Management*, 5th Asia-Pacific edition. South Melbourne: Cengage Learning Australia.

Schumpeter, J. (1952) *Capitalism, Socialism and Democracy*, 4th edition. London: George Allen & Unwin.

Tidd, J. and Bessant, J. (2009) *Managing Innovation: Integrating Technological, Market and Organizational Change*, 4th edition. Chichester: John Wiley and Sons.

Turner, M., Hulme, D. and McCourt, W. (2015) *Governance, Management and Development: Making the State Work*. London: Palgrave Macmillan.

Ugarte, E. and Turner, M. (2011) 'What is the Abu Sayyaf? How labels shape reality.' *Pacific Review* 24 (4) 397–420.

United Nations Office on Drugs and Crime (UNDOC) (2022) 'Money laundering.' Available at https://www.unodc.org/unodc/en/money-laundering/overview.html.

Voice of America (VOA) (2016) 'Fighting the global illegal economy.' 12 October. Available at https://editorials.voa.gov/a/fighting-global-illegal-economy/3547560.html.

Wallace, C. and Latcheva, R. (2006) 'Economic transformation outside the law: Corruption, trust in public institutions and the informal economy in transition countries of Central and Eastern Europe.' *Europe-Asia Studies* 58 (1) 81–102.

Weick, K. (1977) 'Enactment processes in organizations.' In B. Stay and G. Salancik (eds) *New Directions in Organizational Behavior*, pp. 267–300. Chicago: St. Clair Press.

World Economic Forum (WEF) (2019) 'Illicit trade endangers the environment and SDGs. We need a global response.' 18 July. Available at https://www.weforum.org/agenda/2019/07/illicit-trade-sdgs-environment-global-danger/.

World Wildlife Fund (WWF) Australia (2022) 'Illegal wildlife trade and poaching.' Available at https://www.wwf.org.au/what-we-do/species/illegal-wildlife-trade-and-poaching#gs.9yjnja.

Worley, C. and LawlerIII, E. (2010) 'Agility and organizational design: A diagnostic framework.' *Organizational Dynamics* 39 (2) 194–204.

2

A HISTORY OF ILLICIT BUSINESS

Introduction

To understand the present requires reaching back into the past to provide historical context, identify events that are the cause of change and chart the development of phenomena over time. While it is impossible to pinpoint an exact date and time that can be attributed to the beginning of the phenomenon of illicit business, we do find examples of it stretching back to ancient times. One characteristic they all have in common is that the history of illicit business is one of symbiosis with authority – the authority claimed by a state or proto-state over a particular geographical area and its inhabitants. Illicit business challenges that centralization of authority. As this chapter will explore, while forms of authority have changed significantly over time, the dynamic nature of the symbiotic illicit business-authority relationship has not. Over the years a range of different actors all around the world have sought to pursue their profit-driven enterprises that have come into conflict with the dominant authority of the time.

It is important to note that research on illicit business, largely drawn from criminology, sociology and political science, is heavily weighted towards the more modern experiences of Europe and the United States. Thus, Fijnaut (2019, 54) notes that

> the existing research is unevenly divided, geographically speaking. For example, a relatively large body of literature on organized crime exists in western Europe (Italy, Germany, the Netherlands) and the United States, but very little on organized crime in Africa, South America, Asia and Eastern Europe.

However, this is not to say that these regions of the world have not experienced similar levels of illicit business activity over time, rather it reveals a persistent gap in current research. To address this issue, this chapter presents an overview

DOI: 10.4324/9781003293620-2

of the growth of illicit business activities over different times and geographical spaces in diverse parts of the world. Because it is impossible to cover all times and places, our aim is to give the reader a taste of the divergent places, times and illegal enterprises in demonstrating the ubiquity of illicit business.

Illicit Business in Antiquity

Ancient civilizations represent the earliest appearance of the centralized state. The rulers generally legitimated their power through religious ideologies that justified the social order and the rulers' control of the economy and society. Coercive force could be exercised by the emperors, kings and pharaohs to maintain adherence to the rules of the state. Crime rates appear to have been low, although draconian punishments could be meted out to offenders and served as a disincentive to breaking the rules imposed by the state. However, there was crime and there is evidence of illicit business.

An early example of centralized authority can be found in ancient Rome where the creation of a functioning legal system had its foundations in a written code of law (Kehoe 2011). Offences such as treason, sedition, corruption as well as murder, poisoning, rape and adultery were considered to be serious crimes that were dealt with by state officials and institutions. Forgery was also considered to be one of the more egregious crimes that could be committed against members of the citizenry and the state and is one of the earliest examples of illicit business activity (Bauman 1996). The Roman authorities made explicit attempts to counter the impact of illicit business activities in manufacturing and commerce through a system of trademarks that were used to verify the authenticity of goods in Roman markets. For example, Shelley (2018, 18) points out that these strategies were also applied to the sale and consumption of pharmaceuticals in ancient Rome 'to ensure that individuals consumed only drugs that met standards.' Another example of the state's attempts to regulate economic affairs and hence forestall, curtail or wipe out illicit business can be seen in ancient India where wide-ranging codes of law were utilized by the state (see Box 2.1).

BOX 2.1 DEALING WITH ILLICIT BUSINESS IN ANCIENT INDIA

Going back more than 2,000 years ago we can find law books that identified crimes associated with illicit business practices and recommended penalties for those citizens who were engaged in such undertakings. Penalties ranged from fines and confiscation of goods from those involved in illicit business to more brutal retribution. While the legal texts do not tell us exactly what punishments were meted out and whether there was widespread illicit business, they do indicate the range of perceived crimes relating to illicit business and the role of the state in protecting citizens and safeguarding its tax revenue. A few examples will illustrate the scope of the ancient laws and perhaps indicate which illicit business practices had come to the attention of the state and law scholars. The state apparently kept strict controls over weights and measures with officials marking or stamping them and apparently returning to check them after six months 'so there might be no diminution in them.' Forgery was regarded as a very serious crime with at least two of the legal texts recommending the death penalty for forging a royal edict. 'Elaborate rules' were established to foster trade and ensure the proper collection of state taxes such as customs duties. Commodities were not allowed to be sold at the place of production. 'Toll-houses' were erected near markets so that the state could more easily take its prescribed revenue from merchants. There was also official concern with undeclared goods and fines were prescribed if such goods were found. Violations of state monopolies such as salt – a royal licence was needed for that essential – were severe. Some imports such as 'weapons, mail armour, chariots, precious stones, grains and cattle' were banned while most prices were fixed by the state. As can be seen from the examples, the laws that relate to illicit business in ancient India covered a wide variety of activities. What is not so clear is how successful they were.

Source: Das Gupta (1930).

The challenges facing the ancient authorities with regard to counterfeit products have been documented by various civilizations. In ancient Greece (approx. 400 BCE), coins were frequently counterfeited by overlaying an inferior metal with a coating of precious metal (Finlay and Francis 2019). The relative ease with which counterfeit coins were introduced into markets in ancient Greece 'led to the rise of official coin testers, who were employed to weigh and cut coins to check the metal at the core' (Finlay and Francis 2019, 1). In Mesoamerica, the cacao bean become the most precious commodity and formed the basis of almost all trade throughout the region. According to Dreiss and Greenhill (2008, 5), because 'the cacao bean was the medium of exchange for every sort of commodity imaginable; as with any form of currency it was often counterfeited.' The method used to counterfeit cacao beans usually involved a process that allowed the quality of inferior-grade cacao to be masked and then passed off as a higher quality product (Gentle 2021).

In antiquity, other notable challenges to the commercial interests of authorities can be distinguished by three main activities. First, marauders attacked caravans carrying precious products such as silks and spices along important trade routes such as the Silk Road in areas where state authority was weak or non-existent (Shelley 2018). Second, pirates attacked merchant vessels that were laden with valuable commodities sourced from around the world. Third, smugglers sought to circumvent authorities seeking a monopoly of trade in specific goods (Liu 2010). While there are examples of state authorities such as those of the Han dynasty implementing coercive strategies to protects their commercial interests from the types of groups described above, it is important not to conclude that the state or authority only played the role of victim in the story of illicit business in the ancient world. In her research, Shelley (2018) makes the important point that many of these marauders and pirates were not operating in an autonomous fashion but were in fact acting on behalf of a rival state or with the permission thereof. Traditional lore on this topic has tended to favour the notion that danger to the movement of goods largely derived from tribes and nomads. However, Shelley (2018, 22) argues that 'the historical record reveals that the perpetrators of most identified raids in the pre-Islamic Middle East were governors.' She argues that the same principle applied to piracy because in reality most of it was state-sponsored (Shelley 2018). Moving forward in time, the next significant expansion of illicit business activity mirrored changes in the global economy as a result of the era of European exploration and the spread of imperialism and colonization across the world.

Illicit Business, Imperialism and Colonization

Until the 16th century, the European experience of illicit business activity tended to be limited to localized threats posed by banditry and piracy. However, the era of European exploration and colonization acted as the catalyst for the unprecedented expansion of global trade. Imperialism and colonization saw the introduction of new methods of natural resource exploitation and the cultivation of agricultural products in a more organized way that encouraged economies of scale as well as exponentially increasing contact between territories and peoples (Karras 2010). This presented great opportunities for illicit business to develop as a reflection of the rapid growth occurring in the formal global economy in which 'newly established legal frontiers began to be contested and transgressed' (Karras 2010, 54).

The extension of European control and the demarcation of the world through the establishment of colonial order in Latin America, Asia and Africa unintentionally incentivized illegal enterprises when the colonial authorities began to create legal structures to control and protect European commercial interests in the colonies. In Latin America the colonial economy was based on the understanding that 'economic activity should enhance the power and prestige of the state' (Skidmore et al. 2010, 19). Between the 16th and mid-17th centuries, Spanish and Dutch merchants overshadowed all other traders in the markets in Europe and further afield. For example, their monopolies of valuable trade commodities meant that they 'controlled imports of goods into England from the Levant, the Spanish and Portuguese empires, and the West Indies' (UK Parliament 2022). Imbalances in access to expanding economic opportunities led to the introduction of bans and prohibitions that proscribed a range of activities within the colonies which also immediately created new black markets for a vast range of goods and services. For example, smuggling became a prevalent feature in the British colonies due to the implementation of rigid policies such as the Navigation Act of 1651. This act was an attempt to wrest control of global trade from the Spanish and Dutch by prohibiting the movement of goods from British colonies on foreign vessels. In essence this meant that British goods could only be shipped from colonies to Britain on British-owned ships. Jones

(2001, 17) argues that following the British Crown's decision to implement constraints on foreign trade 'illicit trade flourished on the back of trading prohibitions, quasi-legal royal impositions, and rising taxes on both internal and external trade.' Smuggling is a prime example of an illicit business activity that developed in response to actions taken by the state. State regulations provided the incentive for entrepreneurs to operate illicit enterprises from which significant financial returns could be made, especially where alternative legal ways of earning a living might offer very meagre returns and poverty.

The causes of smuggling have largely remained the same since antiquity. Smuggling flourishes in circumstances where a state or proto-state tries to enforce a monopoly on production and/or trade in a particular item, bans trade with particular countries, bans the import or export of a particular item and/or exacts some form of tax on traders/commodities. This is why authors such as Harvey (2016, 2) have argued that 'smuggling has always been political – and, because of its extent and interconnectedness, geopolitical. In other words, it has always been a key factor in international relations, conflict, and globalization.' Box 2.2 provides a good example of the significance of geopolitics in providing the environment for the 'golden age of piracy' in the Mediterranean in the 17th century. But there must also be a demand for the item that provides a market for the smugglers and makes the business profitable. For example, in the 18th century, Britain's protectionist policies resulted in a switch from explicit taxes on wealth to ancillary taxes on consumable goods. During this period illegal imports were usually consumable items that were in high demand such as tea, tobacco and brandy (Farrell 2016, 272). Individuals or groups engaging in this type of illicit activity calculated the potential financial returns, made risk assessments and worked out modes of organizing to undertake the smuggling. For example, following the complete ban on importing silk to Britain, the smuggling of silk occurred concurrently through a highly organized and large-scale system that exploited the infrastructure and trade routes of the East India Company, and a smaller-scale haphazard method that utilized individual travellers to transport the illicit goods (Farrell 2016).

BOX 2.2 PIRACY IN THE MEDITERRANEAN IN THE 17TH CENTURY

Piracy in history generally invokes images of the Caribbean such as those generally promoted by Hollywood and other media over the years. However, less is known about piracy in the Mediterranean despite the fact that the 17th century was the inland sea's 'golden era of piracy.'

The Barbary Corsairs operated in the west, sailing from Tripoli, Tunis and Algiers on the north African coast primarily to capture slaves for the Arab market but also to exact tribute from merchants and even to take their cargoes. The Barbary Corsairs were greatly feared by the more adjacent European coastal populations in Spain and Italy but were also known to venture into the Atlantic to raid settlements in south-west England and as far afield as Iceland. It has been estimated that between 1580 and 1680 approximately 850,000 persons were enslaved by the pirates. They were known as Muslim pirates but they also attracted personnel from all over Europe.

In the east Mediterranean another group of pirates plied their fearsome trade. They were based in various ports in Italy and Spain but their major centre was Malta. Here, the Knights of Malta – the latest iteration of the Knights of the Hospitaller of Jerusalem from the Crusades – hoisted their flags (a white cross on a red background, not the Jolly Roger) and set out to attack merchant shipping in the eastern waters of the Mediterranean. These were the waters nominally controlled by the Muslim Ottoman Empire. The pirates were Christians whose legitimation narrative depicted their activities as a Catholic mission, another episode in the struggle between Muslim and Christian. However, their main prey was Greek shipping, owned and operated by adherents of the Greek Orthodox faith, as their ships were the major carriers of trade in the eastern Mediterranean.

This 'golden era of piracy' in the Mediterranean was aided and abetted by the prevailing geopolitical situation in the region in the 17th century. For most of the 16th century competing Spanish and Ottoman naval fleets had kept the Mediterranean relatively safe for commercial shipping. However, following the naval defeat of the Ottomans at the Battle of Lepanto in 1571 security on the sea began to decline. Both the powerful Hapsburg dynasty in Spain and the Ottoman rulers turned their energies to other matters instead of the expensive business of formal war with each other, the Hapsburgs to the New World and the Ottomans to their land borders. Furthermore, the counter-reformation aided a resurgence of Catholicism in Mediterranean lands to rekindle the idea of war against Islam. But if the massive apparatus of formal war had been dismantled by Hapsburgs and Ottomans what of those who had been involved? The men who had been 'the living materials of war ... were driven to a life of roving by the liquidation of international law.'-
Source: Greene (2010).

Not only are individuals and groups involved in smuggling, states themselves have also encouraged the smuggling of goods from territories outside of their control when they seek greater access to certain goods produced in those territories. This generally occurs because they perceive the market prices to be too high or want to break monopolies. For example, the British East India Company's state-sponsored scheme to smuggle opium from India into China was a direct response to a trade dispute between the British government and the Qing Dynasty in China (Harvey 2016). In the early 19th century, goods sourced from China such as tea, silk and porcelain were extremely profitable for British traders. However, China's steadfast refusal to participate in an exchange system that would have allowed British products to be sold in Chinese markets became the source of increasing tension and hostilities between the two nations. Britain was haemorrhaging large amounts of silver, the only form of payment accepted by the Chinese, in order to continue trade between the two nations.

As a counter-balance to the developing asymmetrical trading relationship with China and in an attempt to rebuild its dwindling silver reserves, Britain, through the auspices of the East India Company and independent British merchants, devised a scheme to smuggle Indian opium into China in exchange for silver (Miron and Feige 2005). The impact of this scheme fundamentally changed the social make-up of Chinese society. The influx of Indian opium created a contagion effect and millions of Chinese became reliant on opium. Initially, the Chinese authorities attempted to pressurize the British to cease their illegal trade. However, this was met with strong resistance from the British. What ensued was a series of conflicts between British and Chinese forces which resulted in the British capturing key Chinese ports and eventually acquiring Hong Kong as a British territory in 1841. The first Opium War ended on 17 August 1842 with the signing of the Treaty of Nanking (Hanes and Sanello 2002). The treaty outlined Britain's unrestricted trading rights in Chinese territories and compelled the Chinese to adhere to the principles of free trade, including the trade in opium. This example demonstrates the way that smuggling has been used as a tool by states to disrupt and transform unfavourable economic environments and to project national power in circumstances where states' economic interests are threatened.

Modern Developments in Illicit Business

At the beginning of the 19th century, vast changes were occurring across continental Europe. The defeat of Napoleon enabled Europe's great powers to establish long-term peace plans for the continent and this created the space and time for authorities to devote more resources to strengthening governance mechanisms in judicial systems and to address domestic problems such as those caused by criminal groups (Fijnaut 2019, 66). The establishment of new internal security organizations such as local and national police forces based on the model of the Napoleonic Gendarmarie became effective deterrents against the scourge of banditry and crime in Europe (Broers 2010). The impact of these changes was substantial and, by the mid-19th century, banditry had all but disappeared across most of Europe (Fijnaut 2019).

An exception to this trend was in Italy. During a period when European state authorities were stabilizing their control and establishing a clear monopoly of violence, Italy remained a largely decentralized society that provided the necessary environmental conditions for small, organized families to rapidly amass a great amount of power in the south of the country. Paoli (2019, 122) highlights that 'mafia' was originally a broad label that described groups of people in conflict with the state. However, in the late 19th century, the term 'mafia' had come to be used by the Italian government to characterize particular groups in Sicily that wielded significant influence over local populations through the use of violent and coercive measures (Paoli 2019) These groups were the antecedents to what is now referred to as the Italian mafia. The term is now used to describe other criminal groups that are organized along familial lines and located in other regions in the southern parts of Italy such as Calabria.

While there had been some attempts by the Italian authorities to address the influence of mafia groups in the late 19th century, it was not until fascism came to Italy that the Italian mafia faced a powerful and direct challenge from a ruling authority. However, it is important to point out here that when Benito Mussolini first came to power the fascist authorities and the mafia were not immediately in conflict. According to Reece (1973, 265),

> Above all else Mussolini was determined to destroy any possibility of effective land occupations and to suppress banditism. Since he had not yet in hand the police-state apparatus, which was to emerge only after 1924, he had during the first two years of his regime compelling reasons to enter into collaboration with influential mafiosi, men who were capable of enforcing law and order in the countryside.

This alliance proved to be transactional in nature and therefore short-lived. Buoyed by his electoral victory in 1924, Mussolini demonstrated an extraordinary pivot when he began a campaign to stamp out the mafia. Beginning in Sicily in May 1924, Mussolini famously analogized the power of the mafia in the city of Agrigento where he said 'the number of mafiosi was surpassed only by the number of their victims' (Reece 1973, 268). Mussolini described the mafia as an organization with specific and distinct structures and limitations, which was in stark contrast to the less structured portrayals of Sicilian life at that time (Coluccello 2016). Over the next few years, Mussolini implemented a decree throughout Italy that rejected the mafia as a parallel force to the state (Coluccello 2016, 122). Repression and violence were used by the state to systematically diminish the influence of the mafia in Sicily (Duggan 1989). The brutal tactics used during the siege of Gangi, that began on 1 January and ended on 10 January 1926, exemplifies the strategies used by the Italian authorities during their campaign against the mafia during the late 1920s. Although Mussolini's government claimed victory in its drive to eliminate the mafia, Castellano (2017, 404) contends that 'it could be said that Fascism did not defeat the mafia, but rather helped cement its place in the history books.'

In fact, the Italian mafia provides one of the most enduring examples of illicit business across time and space. While fascism may have tempered the influence of the mafia in Italy during the 1920s and 1930s, it certainly did not destroy it. Following World War II, the Italian mafia continued to expand both within and outside of Italy. During the 20th century, considerable attention was given to the impact of immigration to the United States in the post-war era and the subsequent establishment of Italian-American crime families in cities such as Chicago and New York. Cressey's (1969) work on the structures of organized crime groups (OCGs; in this case based on the Cosa Nostra in America) presented a novel although contested view of the organizational arrangements of mafia groups. His work conceptualized these groups as operating as a bureaucracy that was hierarchical in its structure with different actors assigned particular roles and levels of responsibility. Additionally, Gambetta (1993) characterizes the Italian mafia as an OCG in the business of manufacturing, sponsoring and retailing private protection to the citizenry. More recent contributions by Sergi (2021) have shone an important light on the activities of the mafia beyond the more familiar narrative of the American experience and advanced new knowledge on the mafia's operations in less-studied settings such as Australia.

Today, the Italian mafia is broadly divided into four main groups: the Cosa Nostra in Sicily, the 'Ndrangheta in Calabria, the Sacra Corona Unita in Puglia and the Camorra in Campania. Vander Beken (2015, 89) places considerable importance on the activities of these groups by depicting a southern criminal hub operating in Europe that 'is shaped around criminal groups based in Italy capable of developing important synergies with criminal groups based outside of the EU.' The nexus of this southern criminal hub includes black markets specializing in cocaine trafficking, human trafficking, smuggling and counterfeiting. However, the very nature of these illicit activities such as cocaine trafficking means that this nexus extends well beyond the borders of Europe. For example, the 'Ndrangheta has long-established connections in seemingly distant places such as Australia and is considered by some to have developed operations in over 25 countries around the world (Sergi 2021). Moreover, Den Held (2022) identifies members of the 'Ndrangheta operating as 'brokers' or 'middlemen' in Latin American countries including but not limited to Brazil, Colombia, Ecuador and Mexico. The evolution of OCGs that have morphed into transnational OCGs is one of the defining features of criminal developments in the 20th century.

These patterns can also be seen outside of the European examples. Japan has a long history of groups operating in conflict with authority. Gangs and bandits operating in the 17th century are considered to be predecessors of OCGs (yakuza) in modern-day Japan (Oxenbøll 2020). Initially, these groups offered members of Japanese society forms of gambling involving simple games of chance that eventually developed into more modern and sophisticated gambling ventures (Fijnaut 2019). Over time, these groups grew in size and influence through their ability to adapt to change and adopt new modes of illicit business. For example, during the industrialization era following the Restoration of the Meiji in 1968, many of these groups expanded their business portfolios into the construction industry by providing labour to large-scale development projects (Kaplan and Dubro 2003).

The yakuza also played an important role in the post-World War II reconstruction of Japan. Difficulties with the supply of goods allowed the yakuza to gain control of black markets that sprang up overnight to meet the demands of consumers (Dower 1999). The occupying forces were limited in their capacity to enforce law and order in post-war Japanese society but found a solution to their problems by granting informal policing powers to the yakuza (Baradel and Bortolussi 2021). These types of measures created a high-level of visibility for the yakuza as it straddled both licit and illicit sectors of Japanese economy and governance. Baradel and Bortolussi (2021, 215) argue that 'the yakuza came to be a visible feature of urban spaces across Japan through their connection with the semi-legal night-time economy, as well as their legal spaces (offices and yakuza-related companies).' Over the ensuing decades the yakuza incrementally expanded their business portfolios into ventures such as the entertainment industry, real estate and the stock market to increase their power and wealth.

It was not until the early 1990s that the Japanese government introduced a suite of legislation aimed to curtail the yakuza's activities and power through new regulations (Hill 2003). While these regulations have had some impact on limiting the yakuza's ease of access to formal markets, they also unintentionally acted as a push factor for the expansion of the group's role in a range of illicit business. These currently include drug trafficking, human trafficking, extortion, prostitution and gambling, to name but a few. Fijnaut (2019) points out that over the past few decades the yakuza have managed to evolve into a transnational conglomerate that operates and has connections in diverse places such as the Republic of Korea, Thailand, the Philippines, the Americas and Europe.

China also shares the historical experience of society-based groups morphing into sophisticated international criminal syndicates (triads) over time. In the 18th century, secret societies began to appear in the communities inhabiting the southern area of China (Kassab and Rosen 2019). These 'black societies' were originally groupings of subjugated immigrant workers in Shanghai and Hong Kong (Broadhurst 2015). These groups supported culturally vulnerable internal migrant populations by offering support in the form of social capital to disaffected individuals in exchange for *guanxi* or reciprocal obligation to the organization (Lo 2010). The authorities during the Qing Dynasty and later during the British colonial period perceived these societies as a danger to the political and economic interests of the authorities and acted against them. According to Broadhurst (2015, 158), 'the criminalization of membership of triad society led to their full transformation into the "black society," whose members often involved themselves in protection, mercenary violence and predatory crime.' The developing organizational arrangements of these groups enabled them to expand their presence in illicit markets and led to a transition into more sophisticated and large-scale activities such as drug trafficking. In 1949, the victory of the Chinese Communist Party over the Kuomintang-led Chinese government resulted in the establishment of the People's Republic of China and communist rule across the country. A cornerstone of this rule in the post-war era was a zero-tolerance policy towards criminality and deviant behaviour. While the omnipresence of the state and its capacity to actively enforce this policy appear to have subdued the influence of triad groups in much of mainland China it simultaneously concentrated triad power on the country's east coast (Fijnaut 2019). Following World War II, Hong Kong became the epicentre of triad power. In conjunction with changing geopolitical circumstances, the triads capitalized on weakened British governance and began to seek influence and control of growing labour markets, ports, gambling and prostitution (Broadhurst 2015). Moreover, following the death of Mao and the beginning of significant economic reform in China, triad groups began to reappear on the mainland to reclaim their place in Chinese society. Broadhurst (2015, 157) argues that 'the rapid change from a socialist command economy to a capitalist economy engendered a parallel increase in crime.'

Triad societies have demonstrated a gradual shift to criminal syndication. They have progressively advanced their business acumen and expanded their operations internationally over the past 40 years. Central to this rapid expansion has been the triads' ability to exploit the notion of social capital in the form of *guanxi* that works as a glue that binds membership to the organization, and to use the expanding Chinese diaspora to its own advantage (Lo 2010). This has allowed these groups to control elements of illicit markets in foreign settings such as the United Kingdom, the United States and Australia which host significant numbers of the Chinese expatriate population (Silverstone 2011). They have also made significant links with Latin American OCGs which has enabled Mexican cartels to easily source precursor chemicals to produce methamphetamine as well as new locations to launder the proceeds of their crimes (McCarthy-Jones et al. 2020). Large triads such as Sun Yee On and 14K have successfully redefined their business models to become more corporatized and encompass a wide range of legal and illegal activities that include venturing into copyright and internet-based businesses as well as drug trafficking and human trafficking and large-scale financial crime (Broadhurst 2015). Importantly, the expansion and transnationalization of groups such as the Japanese yakuza and the Chinese triads is a result of the significant changes brought about by the process of globalization in the second half of the 20th century.

Globalization and Illicit Business

Globalization, as noted in Chapter 1, is a process whereby economic and political barriers are broken down to create greater interconnectedness and interdependence. While the process commenced centuries ago, with trade and colonization it accelerated in the 20th century and became a defining feature of that century (Robertson and White 2007). The rapid advances in and the subsequent transnationalization of technology across the globe created the necessary conditions for the expansion of international business, trade and communication. Great attention has been paid to the many interconnected linkages among legal businesses that arose in the globalizing economy. However, less attention has been paid to the growth of illicit economic activities that have shadowed the changing patterns of formal and legal business. Across the world, illicit businesses have proved their ability to quickly adapt to changing environments and, in many cases, became early adopters of new technologies. They have demonstrated entrepreneurial talents that have enabled their illicit businesses to thrive. This is why at the beginning of the 21st century authors such as Findlay (1999, 23) observed that globalization 'creates new and favorable contexts for crime' and Shelley (1995, 463) warned that 'transnational organized crime could undermine the nation-state in the 21st century.'

As we stated at the beginning of the book transnational organized crime is big business with the United Nations Office on Drugs and Crime (UNODC) estimating its cost to the global economy to be between US $900 billion and US $1.1 trillion annually (UNODC 2011), while the Global Financial Integrity group estimates the value of transnational crime at between US $1.6 trillion and US $2.2 trillion annually (May 2017, xi). According to UNODC (2010),

> [o]rganized crime has diversified, gone global and reached macro-economic proportions: illicit goods may be sourced from one continent, trafficked across another, and marketed in a third. Transnational organized crime can permeate government agencies and institutions, fuelling corruption, infiltrating business and politics, and hindering economic and social development. And it is undermining governance and democracy by empowering those who operate outside the law.

Examples of illicit business activities that form an integral part of transnational organized crime in the 21st century include, but are not limited to, arms, drug and human trafficking; counterfeit tobacco production and distribution; automobile theft and sale; illegal trade in wildlife; financial and accounting services that support transnational crimes; illegal logging and timber smuggling; illegal movement and dumping of toxic and hazardous waste and nuclear materials; trade in stolen art, cultural artifacts and antiquities; illegal trade in body parts; manufacture and sale of counterfeit luxury goods; identity theft; and the production of fake documents and cybercrime such as online scams and the dissemination of ransomware. This growth in the scale and types of illicit activities has been described as a mirroring effect of expanding formal markets and has been seen as a symptom of the widening inequality within and between states. This process has been characterized as the 'the dark side of globalisation' (Haine and Thakur 2011).

The perennial problem of weak states and an absence of authority in many parts of the world makes these locations particularly susceptible to infiltration by OCGs, the privatization of violence, small arms trafficking, civil war, the spread of infectious diseases and environmental degradation. In these settings, the corruption and co-option of political elites, bureaucracies, members of law enforcement and the judiciary into criminal networks occur on a regular basis and seriously undermine governance mechanisms that are supposed to deal with the problems caused by illicit business. These places can also become hubs that host and/or facilitate the operations, transportation, financial administration and banking of transnational criminals. The deficiencies of government authority in weak states enable the cross-border movement of offenders and the cross-border networking of offenders, and the blending of illicit trade with licit cross-border traffic via land, sea and air.

> Increased opportunities to travel across countries and continents have not diminished economic inequalities but have resulted in the victimization and

exploitation of residents from the poorer South by organized crime groups in the North supported by their criminal counterparts in the South.

(Van Dijk 2007, 285)

Conclusion

The history of illicit business is long, complex and varied. However, as we have shown in this chapter, a constant theme throughout history has been the symbiotic relationship between state authority, or the lack of it, and illicit business. In many instances the actions of a state's leaders and its operating agencies have contributed greatly to creating the necessary conditions or environmental factors that enable illicit business to emerge. Beginning with examples from antiquity and then moving forward in time to the present day we have highlighted how this pattern has occurred across different times and spaces. The remainder of the book concerns contemporary examples of illicit business in the 21st century to demonstrate the scale, depth and diversity of illicit business practices, the problems they present to state and society, and the structures and processes that define their operations.

References

Baradel, M. and Bortolussi, J. (2021) 'Under a setting sun: The spatial displacement of the yakuza and their longing for visibility.' *Trends in Organized Crime* 24 (2) 209–226. Available at https://doi.org/10.1007/s12117-020-09398-4.

Bauman, R. (1996) *Crime and Punishment in Ancient Rome*. London: Routledge.

Broadhurst, R. (2015) 'Black societies and triad-like organized crime in China.' In F. Allum and S. Gilmour (eds) *The Routledge Handbook of Transnational Organized Crime*, pp. 157–170. London: Routledge.

Broers, M. (2010) *Napoleon's Other War: Bandits, Rebels and Their Pursuers in the Age of Revolutions*. Oxford: Peter Lang.

Castellano, C. (2017) 'The fascist anti-mafia operation in Campania, 1926–1927.' *Modern Italy* 22 (4) 403–417. Available at https://doi:10.1017/mit.2017.57.

Coluccello, R. (2016) *Challenging the Mafia Mystique: Cosa Nostra from Legitimisation to Denunciation*. London: Palgrave Macmillan. Available at https://doi.org/10.1057/9781137280503_8.

Cressey, D (1969) *Theft of a Nation: The Structure and Operations of Organized Crime in America*. New York: Harper and Row.

Das Gupta, R. (1930) *Crime and Punishment in Ancient India*. Calcutta: Book Company.

Den Held, D. (2022) 'The 'Ndrangheta: Versatile middlemen in the cocaine pipeline to Europe,' *InSight Crime*, 23 November. Available at https://insightcrime.org/investigations/ndrangheta-versatile-middlemen-cocaine-pipeline-to-europe.

Dower J. (1999) *Embracing Defeat: Japan in the Wake of World War II*. New York: W. W. Norton & Co.

Dreiss, M. and Greenhill, S. (2008) *Chocolate: Pathway to the Gods*. Tucson: University of Arizona Press.

Duggan, C. (1989) *Fascism and the Mafia*. New Haven, CT: Yale University Press.

Farrell, W. (2016) 'Smuggling silks into eighteenth-century Britain: Geography, perpetrators, and consumers.' *Journal of British Studies* 55 (2) 268–294.

Fijnaut, C. (2019) 'Searching for organized crime in history.' In L. Paoli (ed.) *The Oxford Handbook of Organized Crime*, online edition, pp. 53–95. New York: Oxford University Press.

Findlay, M. (1999) 'The globalisation of crime.' *AQ: Australian Quarterly* 71 (4) 23–27.

Finlay, R. and Francis, A. (2019) 'A brief history of currency counterfeiting.' The Reserve Bank of Australia. Available at https://www.rba.gov.au/publications/bulletin/2019/sep/a-brief-history-of-currency-counterfeiting.html#fn0.

Gambetta, D. (1993) *The Sicilian Mafia: The Business of Private Protection*. Cambridge, MA: Harvard University Press.

Gentle, P. (2021) 'Cocoa as an early form of money in the economic sense: Satisfying store of value, unit of account and medium of exchange requirements.' *SocioEconomic Challenges* 5 (4) 89–97.

Greene, M. (2010) *Catholic Pirates and Greek Merchants: A Maritime History of the Mediterranean*. Princeton, NJ: Princeton University Press.

Haine, J. and Thakur, R. (2011) *The Dark Side of Globalization*. Washington, DC: Brookings Institution Press.

Hanes, W. and Sanello, F. (2002) *The Opium Wars: The Addiction of One Empire and the Corruption of Another*. Naperville, IL: Source Books.

Harvey, S. (2016) *Smuggling: Seven Centuries of Contraband*. London: Reaktion Books.

Hill, P. (2003) *The Japanese Mafia: Yakuza, Law, and the State*. Oxford: Oxford University Press.

Jones, E.T. (2001) 'Illicit business: Accounting for smuggling in mid-sixteenth-century Bristol.' *Economic History Review* 54 (1) 17–38.

Kaplan, D. and Dubro, A. (2003) *Yakuza: Japan's Criminal Underworld*. Berkeley: University of California Press.

Karras, A. (2010) *Smuggling, Contraband and Corruption in World History*. Plymouth: Rowman and Littlefield.

Kassab, H.S. and Rosen, J.D. (2019) *Illicit Markets, Organized Crime, and Global Security*. Cham: Palgrave Macmillan.

Kehoe, D. (2011) 'Law and social formation in the Roman Empire.' In M. Peachin (ed.) *The Oxford Handbook of Social Relations in the Roman World*, pp. 144–163. Oxford: Oxford University Press.

Liu, X. (2010) *The Silk Road in World History*. Oxford: Oxford University Press.

Lo, T.W. (2010) 'Beyond social capital: Triad organized crime in Hong Kong and China.' *British Journal of Criminology* 50 (5) 851–872. Available at https://doi.org/10.1093/bjc/azq022.

May, C. (2017) *Transnational Crime and the Developing World*. Washington, DC: Global Financial Integrity.

McCarthy-Jones, A., Doyle, C. and Turner, M. (2020) 'From hierarchies to networks: The organizational evolution of international drug trade.' *International Journal of Crime, Law and Justice* 63 (December) 100436.

Miron, J. and Feige, C. (2005) 'The Opium Wars, opium legalization, and opium consumption in China.' NBER Working Paper No. 11355. Cambridge, MA: National Bureau of Economic Research. Available at https://www.nber.org/system/files/working_papers/w11355/w11355.pdf.

Oxenbøll, M. (2020) 'Bandits and peasants in medieval Japan.' In M. Gordon, R. Kaeuper and H. Zurndorfer (eds) *The Cambridge World History of Violence*. pp. 207–227. Cambridge: Cambridge University Press,. Available at https://doi:10.1017/9781316661291.011.

Paoli, L. (2019) 'The Italian Mafia.' In L. Paoli (ed.) *The Oxford Handbook of Organized Crime*, online edition, pp. 121–141. New York: Oxford University Press.

Reece, J. (1973) 'Fascism, the mafia, and the emergence of Sicilian separatism (1919–43).' *Journal of Modern History* 45 (2) 261–276.

Robertson, R. and White, K. (2007) 'What is globalization?' In G. Ritzer (ed) *The Blackwell Companion to Globalization*, pp. 54–66. Oxford: Blackwell.

Sergi, A. (2021) 'Stumbling upon places and cultures: An involuntary ethnography in researching the Australian 'Ndrangheta.' *Journal of Criminology* 54 (4) 448–465.

Shelley, L.I. (1995) 'Transnational organized crime: An imminent threat to the nation-state?' *Journal of International Affairs* 48 (2) 463–489. Available at http://www.jstor.org/stable/24357599.

Shelley, L. (2018) *Dark Commerce: How a New Illicit Economy is Threatening our Future*. Princeton, NJ: Princeton University Press.

Silverstone, D. (2011) 'From triads to snakeheads: Organised crime and illegal migration within Britain's Chinese community.' *Global Crime* 12 (2) 93–111. Available at https://doi10.1080/17440572.2011.

Skidmore, T., Smith, P. and Green, J. (2010) *Modern Latin America*. Oxford: Oxford University Press.

UK Parliament (2022) The Navigation Laws. Available at https://www.parliament.uk/about/living-heritage/transformingsociety/tradeindustry/importexport/overview/navigationlaws/.

United Nations Office on Drugs and Crime (UNODC) (2010) *The Globalization of Crime: A Transnational Organized Crime Threat Assessment*. Vienna: UNODC.

United Nations Office on Drugs and Crime (UNODC) (2011) *Estimating Illicit Financial Flows Resulting from Drug Trafficking and Other Transnational Organized Crimes. Research Report*. Available at www.unodc.org/documents/data-and-analysis/Studies/Illicit_financial_flows_2011_web.pdf.

Vander Beken, T. (2015) 'The many faces of organized crime in Europe, and its assessment.' In F. Allum and S. Gilmour (eds) *The Routledge Handbook of Transnational Organized Crime*, pp. 83–96. London: Routledge.

Van Dijk, J. (2007) *The World of Crime: Breaking the Silence on Problems of Security, Justice and Development Across the World*. New York: SAGE.

3

ILLICIT BUSINESS, INFORMAL SECTORS AND SHADOW ECONOMIES

Introduction

All the other chapters in this book deal with criminal activities. After all, the book is about illicit business. However, this chapter on the informal economy is different as many of the activities in the informal economy are widely considered to be legitimate by society or are tolerated by government authorities. They are not criminal although they often suffer from negative perceptions. So, why should we consider the informal economy in this book? There are three main reasons. First, informal sector economic activities largely take place outside of the state's tax, regulatory and social welfare systems. In the sense that informal business activities are not formally sanctioned by the state and operate outside of the state's rules and compliance systems, they could be construed as illicit. Second, many people operating in the informal economy are located in structures of deprivation, discrimination and poverty that make social mobility and the realization of their human capabilities to lead 'the kind of lives they value' distant dreams (Sen 1999, 18). They are subject to 'unfreedoms' such as poverty, tyranny and systematic social deprivation which may not be in breach of the law but may be considered morally wrong (Sen 1999, 3). Third, informal economic activities are carried out in all countries, rich and poor alike, and can account for a significant proportion of national incomes and employment, especially in developing countries. This all takes place away from the supervision of the state.

This chapter provides an introduction to informal economic activities across the world. It deals with the conceptualization of the informal economy, an area of academic writing that is characterized by contrasting views, definitions and terminology; delineation of what and who can be included in the informal economy, a tricky task given the conceptual confusion; the socioeconomic processes that govern non-formal economic activities; and the relationship of the

DOI: 10.4324/9781003293620-3

state and the formal sector to the informal sector. A distinction is drawn between high-income and developing countries with the emphasis on the latter as the informal economy is so important for the livelihood and survival of millions of people in these nations.

What Is the Informal Economy?

Babysitting, house cleaning and gardening for unrecorded cash payments, selling items online, and some 'off the books' cash transactions for transport services are examples of informal economic activities in wealthy countries. In the developing world, street vendors selling chewing gum, newspapers, clothes, food and drinks are engaged in informal work; likewise, small repair businesses that might fix your car, motorbike, watch, bag, clothes or shoes. The domestic worker who cleans and cooks for the more affluent is also likely to be informally employed as are many workers in construction. Peasant farmers and agricultural wage labourers are also off the official radar insofar as their incomes and terms of employment are concerned. The snapshot of the informal economy in India presented in Box 3.1 clearly illustrates the sector's extent in one developing country.

BOX 3.1 THE INFORMAL SECTOR IN INDIA

From 2010–2019, the Indian economy grew by 6%–7% per annum so that in the 2020s it has become the world's third largest economy when measured in purchasing power parity terms. During the period there had also been a halving of the numbers of people living in extreme poverty. Furthermore, a flourishing start-up and innovation culture has evolved to help to propel the country towards its goal of becoming a high-income economy by 2047.

Despite this economic success, the vast majority of workers and business establishments remain in the low productivity informal sector. It is estimated that 90.7% of employment lies in the informal sector with an even higher percentage of businesses operating informally. Workers struggle to find 'good jobs,' a situation exacerbated by the entry of another 12 million persons into the labour force each year. An estimated 79% of all jobs in urban India are in the informal sector spread between construction, manufacturing and services. There are 36 million street vendors. Many have no or limited access to social benefit schemes. There are five million domestic employees, 92% of whom are women, girls and children. Most live in and work up to 15 hours per day seven days per week. There are also 37.4 million home-based workers, especially in manufacturing. Jobs previously located in the formal sector are becoming increasingly precarious due to the increase in part-time, contract and non-union conditions. In rural areas, informal employment accounts for 96% of jobs with 82% of employed persons in agriculture having no written job contract. Poverty is the lot of 28.4% of agricultural labourers compared to 15% of all farmers. Women are slightly more likely than men to be in the informal sector in both urban and rural situations and frequently receive lower pay than men. Informal workers mostly find it impossible to get bank loans and must resort to informal, and frequently usurious, lenders to tide them over when work is short or emergencies occur. Investment in more productive technologies is beyond reach.

Source: World Bank (2023); OXFAM (2022); D'Costa (2023).

While the informal economy has existed for millennia since states in the ancient world tried to exercise control over economic activities, its conceptualization only really began in the 1950s when academics began to seek paths to socioeconomic development for newly independent countries in the emerging Third World. These countries were characterized as having dual economies that presented stark contrasts (Boeke 1953; Lewis 1954). On the one hand, the modern economy was modelled on Western capitalism. It was dynamic, possessed advanced technology and was efficient in its use of capital and labour for high levels of production. By contrast, the traditional economy was portrayed as being backward, inefficient and with low productivity. It also possessed untapped surplus labour which would eventually be absorbed into the growing formal economy as industrialization took its course. This was the thinking of modernization theory that predicted that traditional societies would make a rapid transformation to modern societies modelled along Western lines (Moore 1963). But these predictions were not fulfilled as the modern economy did not grow as planned, while informal economic employment did, both in rural and urban areas. This attracted more academic scrutiny of these enterprises and the workers who operated outside of the formal economy. Thus, in 1973, Keith Hart came up with the concept of the 'informal economy' to describe the market vendors and self-employed entrepreneurs in his study of Ghana (Hart 1973). This was a dynamic and vibrant economy which operated outside of the state's supervision unlike the somewhat disparaging 'backward' characterizations associated with the proponents of the dual economy. The term caught on and has been widely utilized in academic and policy circles ever since.

There has been considerable debate and changing ideas about how to define the informal economy. This has not been assisted by the profusion of related terms such as the hidden economy, shadow economy, parallel economy, black economy, alternative economy, and so on. Many of these terms carry negative connotations, something we argue is wise to avoid. We will not stray too far into the conceptual fog created by the competing and overlapping signifiers of economic activities occurring outside of the state's control. Instead, we will clearly delineate a useful and practical way to define the informal economy while describing its features, its extent, its operation and the policy issues associated with it.

The definition we are utilizing for the informal economy broadly delineates it as the 'market-based and legal production of goods and services that is hidden from public authorities for monetary, regulatory or institutional reasons' (Elgin et al. 2021, 49; Schneider et al. 2010). The term 'market-based' refers to prices being controlled by supply and demand rather than by government. The legality of informal economic production indicates that its enterprises and workers are not engaged in criminal activities. This means we are not including activities such as drug production and trafficking or human trafficking in our chosen definition of the informal economy. While informal activities in accordance with this book's use of the term are not formally authorized and monitored by the state they are generally approved of or are tolerated by the authorities, albeit often tacitly. The 'hidden' characteristic of informal economic activities that features in our definition is ascribed to monetary reasons, such as wishing to avoid taxes or social security payments; regulatory factors, such as the costs incurred in time and money spent dealing with the government's bureaucratic processes and regulatory requirements; and institutional considerations, such as corruption and weak rule of law.

One problem with utilizing a broad definition of the informal economy is that it runs the risk of obscuring its heterogeneity. As we have already seen, a multitude of different occupations can be classified as informal from an online salesperson to a scavenger on a rubbish tip. There is also variation in income among informal workers. While many are poor and vulnerable there are others who can make a decent living – take, for example, the very low-paid agricultural day labourer on the one hand, and the taxi driver on the other. There are major differences in the nature of employment in the informal economy (Chen 2012). Some persons are self-employed. They could be employers or own-account workers. They might be contributing family workers in both informal and formal enterprises. Informal workers may also be in wage employment as employees of informal enterprises or as casual and day labourers, temporary or part-time workers, paid domestic workers, contract workers, unregistered or undeclared workers, and industrial outworkers (home-based workers). The differentiation of employment types has implications for earnings, poverty and gender as shown in the Women in Informal Employment: Globalizing and Organizing (WIEGO) model of informal employment (Chen 2012, 9). It shows earnings to be higher for employers and regular informal workers, less for own-account operators and informal wage workers, and least for industrial outworkers and unpaid family workers. The highest paid categories of informal employment are predominantly male domains while the lower ones are predominantly occupied by women. As one would expect, the model shows the risk of poverty increases with the lower paid categories of employment.

A further aspect of differentiation concerns occupational health and safety (OHS) among informal sector workers. Jobs can vary considerably in terms of comfort and health risks. However, many jobs are injurious to health and low on comfort. For example, studies of informal sector OHS in Ghana provide a long list of hazardous conditions faced by workers. Although varying between industries there are psychosocial, physical and ergonomic dangers, poor sanitation, food poisoning, fire hazards and exposure to harmful chemicals (Adei et al. 2021). A particularly modern-day problem involves the recycling of e-waste, a business in which participants can suffer from cuts and crush injuries, exposure to various forms of toxicity from heavy metals, inorganic acids and dust (Asampong et al. 2015). Some workers experience chest pains, indigestion, weakness, gastritis, breathing problems, skin irritation, and muscle and lower back pain. Although Ghana's National Health Insurance Scheme is open to informal sector workers and provides free healthcare, a very low percentage of such workers are reportedly enrolled.

The motivations to enter the informal sector vary. One way of examining motivation is through the ideas of exit and exclusion. Thus, some workers and enterprises are 'excluded' from the formal economy due to entry regulations that they perceive as onerous and the lack of human capital (de Soto 1989; Perry et al. 2007). The enterprises see the state's requirements for registration in the formal economy as too expensive for the benefits on offer while the 'excluded' workers may not have the education and skills that are needed for employment in the formal economy. Those who are 'excluded' are often associated with low productivity, low pay and low-skilled employment (Elgin et al. 2021; La Porta and Schleifer 2014). The motivation of those who 'exit' the formal economy voluntarily is often because they perceive that the benefits from participating in the informal economy – flexibility, independence and lower regulatory compliance requirements – outweigh those that could be obtained in the formal economy (Elgin et al. 2021). Many persons may exit because they cannot afford to participate in the formal economy. Both modes of informality can and do co-exist in the same overall economy (Nordman et al. 2016).

Another way of analysing why firms and workers join the informal economy is to classify them in terms of evaders, avoiders and outsiders (Kanbur 2009). The evaders are businesses that are covered by regulations but do not comply. Presumably, the businesses determine that the risks of non-compliance are outweighed by the financial returns. The state may lack the capacity or interest to investigate non-compliance or its agents can be bought off at a lower cost than complying with regulations. Avoiders are businesses that shape their activities so that they are outside the scope of the state's regulations, while outsiders are businesses that are not covered by regulations.

Are the Informal and Formal Economies Linked?

A legacy of the dualist model and use of the exclusive labels of formal and informal might lead us to believe that the two types of economy operate as separate systems. But this is incorrect as there are multiple inter-relationships.

First, many informal enterprises engage with businesses from the formal economy either as suppliers of inputs and finished goods or services. These transactions can operate directly such as with agricultural labourers or via subcontracting such as finishing garments in the home.

Second, the relationship can also work in the other direction whereby persons in the informal sector purchase outputs produced by the formal sector to sell to consumers. In some cases the formal sector product may be modified before sale by the informal sector workers; for example, breaking up packets of soap powder and other grocery products into smaller, more affordable lots for poor purchasers or altering a vehicle so that it can accommodate more passengers or cargo.

Third, formal enterprises hire wage workers under informal arrangements. These workers could be employed on a temporary basis or part-time or even to work from home. There is also sub-contracting where the workers are employed on an informal basis.

Fourth, at the level of the household there can be persons in the same household working in both the formal and informal sectors; for example, a formally employed male factory worker and a female street vendor operating informally.

Finally, until recently there has been ambiguity in economic theory about whether a cyclical relationship exists between the formal and informal economies. But recent econometric work involving a study of 158 countries including 36 advanced economies found that 'informal-economy output movements are strongly positively correlated with formal-economy output movements' (Elgin et al. 2021, 95). By contrast, informal employment generally behaves 'acyclically.' The direction of causality is from the formal to the informal economy. In all these cases there appears to be linkage between the formal and informal economies.

While the dualist model depicted two separate economic systems subsequent theorists and empirical studies have revealed the presence of these multiple linkages between formal and informal sectors. 'Legalists,' so called because they focus on the 'rules of the game,' see capitalists from the formal sector colluding with the state to create the rules that discriminate against informal enterprises and workers by excluding them or pushing them to exit from the formal sector (de Soto 1989). This prevents the enormous entrepreneurial potential of the informal sector from being unlocked and unnecessarily keeps millions of people poor and disadvantaged. This position was enthusiastically adopted by international financial institutions such as the World Bank in the 1990s to support the rolling back of the state and allowing market forces much greater scope.

The 'structuralists,' so called because they are concerned with the nature and effects of structures in the global economy, argue that workers in the informal sector receive unfavourable treatment from the globalized capitalist system (Moser 1978; Castell and Portes 1989). They see the informal economy subordinated to the formal economy to produce cheap goods and services through structures of highly unequal power relations. Workers in the informal economy are paid low wages and do not receive the benefits and protection that the state should provide. They are marginalized and because of their location in structures of disadvantage they have very limited possibilities for improving their lot. Being outside of the state, informal workers must rely on their own resources, determination and innovation to earn a livelihood as the example in Box 3.2 demonstrates.

BOX 3.2 DETERMINATION AND INNOVATION IN FINANCE AMONG STREET VENDORS

A major problem encountered by people working in the informal sector in developing countries is the lack of access to formal channels of credit. Banks perceive them as having inadequate collateral. There have been schemes to provide microcredit for businesses to poor people that have followed the pioneering example of Bangladesh's Grameen Bank but many street vendors operate outside of such arrangements out of choice or necessity. In Baclaran, a district of Metro Manila famous for having numerous street vendors selling a wide variety of goods, the informal traders have had to devise their own methods of securing the credit that is so vital for their livelihoods and survival. The area is known for its cheap prices and easy access from different parts of the metropolis. According to social scientist Redento Recio, Baclaran's street traders have devised five options for obtaining credit informally. The first is to obtain loans from family members. The second is to take out a loan from the local vendors' cooperative but this possibility is only available to members and 'semi-fixed' stalls – and many of Baclaran's traders are non-members and lack the qualifying stalls or are ambulant. The third option is to utilize *hango* (harvest) which is a consignment agreement between hawker and supplier in which the hawker obtains the desired goods but only pays for them after a day of vending. The fourth credit mechanism is *paluwagan* (easing up). This is a mutual savings scheme which involves putting aside money during the peak season which runs from September to December, when shoppers flock to Baclaran to do their Christmas shopping. The money saved can then be used by the vendors 'to ease' their passage through the leaner months of trading. The final option for vendors is to use the services of loan sharks. At the time of Recio's research the loan sharks were charging a monthly interest of 20% with loans extended up to four months. These rates were higher than those charged by banks to which the vendors had no access. The vendors can get deeply into debt with multiple loans and then must sell or rent out their claimed vending spaces. In general, the vendors of Baclaran live precariously with government 'at best ambivalent' towards the recognition of street vending as legitimate. The traders need to devise their own ways of dealing with this precarity and have demonstrated determination and ingenuity to safeguard their livelihoods.

Source: Recio (2021).

Poverty and Vulnerability in the Informal Sector

As we have already observed, not everybody in the informal sector is poor. However, a large body of research consistently shows that workers in the informal sector face a higher risk of poverty than those in the formal economy (OECD-ILO 2019). Looking more closely at the statistics, we can find a negative association between the level of informal employment and gross domestic product (GDP), a country's score on the multidimensional Human Development Index (HDI) published by the United Nations Development Programme (UNDP) and labour productivity but a positive correlation with poverty (OECD-ILO 2019, 17). In countries for which data is available, 42% of informal workers including those in agriculture and 31% of workers excluding agriculture live in poverty. In short, poverty affects those working in informal sector activities much more than those working in the formal sector. But experience shows that remedying the situation may not simply take the form of introducing policies to increase the number and percentage of the labour force in formal employment. For example, in South Africa and Honduras reductions in the number of people informally employed was associated with increases in the incidence of poverty, while in Egypt and Pakistan the data show that the growth of informality was associated with declines in poverty. These examples demonstrate that it is necessary to look closely at specific cases of informality and poverty utilizing a 'poverty-in-context' approach; that is, the environments in which informality and poverty occur can differ, alerting us to the fact that there is no one-size-fits-all policy solution to address informality and poverty.

Despite the absence of a universally applicable policy formula, we can still identify informality's role in a cluster of factors that lead to and maintain poverty. To do this, it is necessary to move beyond the measurement of poverty in exclusively monetary terms. This is achieved by viewing poverty as a multidimensional phenomenon (World Bank 2023a; Alkire et al. 2015). Poverty can be seen as 'pronounced deprivation in wellbeing' (World Bank 2001). That wellbeing comprises various components. For example, the HDI, mentioned above, is a composite index that measures wellbeing not only in terms of per capita income but also incorporates life expectancy and education. The concept of multidimensional poverty provides insight into the mutually reinforcing problems facing low-income earners in the informal sector. It identifies deprivations such as in access to education and health services and the availability of infrastructure such as water and electricity. The World Bank's multidimensional poverty measure showing the different indicators and their weights is set out in Table 3.1. But there are additional factors that can be taken into account such as insecurity brought about by war or poor law and order, low

TABLE 3.1 The World Bank's Multidimensional Poverty Measure Indicators and Weights

Dimensions	Parameter	Weight
Monetary poverty	Daily consumption or income is less than US $1.90 per person	1/3
Education	At least one school-age child up to the age of grade 8 is not enrolled in school	1/6
	No adult in the household (age of grade 9 or above) has completed primary education	1/6
Access to basic infrastructure	The household lacks access to limited-standard drinking water	1/9
	The household lacks access to limited-standard sanitation	1/9
	The household has no access to electricity	1/9

Note: This table first appeared in World Bank (2020) 'Poverty and shared prosperity 2020: Reversals of fortune.' Washington, DC: World Bank, p. 69. doi: 10.1596/978-1-4648-1602-4. License: Creative Commons Attribution CC BY 3.0 IGO.

self-confidence, a sense of powerlessness and lack of human rights such as freedom of speech (Haughton and Khandker 2009; Sen 1999).

With these considerations in mind, we can clearly identify two major problems that threaten the wellbeing of low-income households getting their remuneration from informal activities. The first is that it is extremely difficult to experience upward social mobility. A set of restrictive and mutually reinforcing factors – Sen's (1999) 'unfreedoms' – work against household socio-economic improvement. How can the household better its standing when its income does not allow capital accumulation, its members' education and skill sets are insufficient for the formal sector and the family is subject to poor health because of inadequate nutrition and lack of basic infrastructure services? The second is that they are particularly vulnerable to changes in their environment (Abraham and Kumar 2008). Such changes might be at the individual level and include sickness, an accident at work or a death in the family, all of which need to be paid for. They could be broader environmental changes such as a downturn in the local labour market, a severe weather event that destroys people's houses or forced physical relocation away from the place of work. An example of such adverse changes in the environment can be seen with the recent COVID-19 pandemic's effect on informal workers.

The Extent of the Informal Economy

Businesses and workers in the formal economy are registered and monitored by a variety of state agencies. By contrast, there has always been difficulty measuring the extent of the informal economy because the businesses and workers in this sector go about their work mostly unrecorded and unrecognized by the state. However, recent improvements in research methodologies have resulted in more accurate and comprehensive data becoming available on a variety of measures relating to the informal economy. The International Labour Organization (ILO) and the World Bank have been the leaders of these advances in gathering and processing the relevant information (ILO 2018; Elgin et al. 2021). But agreement and standardization have not yet occurred among all parties that report on informal economy activities and therefore one can expect some minor variations in the data cited on what appear to be the same measures.

The ILO, from which the following statistics on informal economy employment are drawn, estimates that two billion of the world's employed population aged 15 years and over are engaged in the informal economy (ILO 2018). This accounts for 61.2% of total global employment. These are staggeringly large figures that emphatically indicate the vast extent of the informal economy and the reliance of a huge proportion of humanity on it for their livelihoods and survival. However, there is considerable variation between regions – from 25.1% in Europe and Central Asia to 85.8% in Africa. The level of countries' socio-economic development is positively correlated to formality in the economy. Thus, in emerging (middle-income countries as defined by the World Bank) and developing countries (defined as low-income countries by the World Bank) 69.6% of the working population are in informal employment, while in high-income economies the figure is 18.3%. Note that the global share of informal employment in total employment decreases to 50.5% when agriculture is excluded.

While the majority of countries have experienced a decrease in informal employment over the past 20 years, some have experienced upward trends (e.g. the Russian Federation and Serbia) while some others have maintained constant high levels of informal employment (e.g. Pakistan and Côte d'Ivoire). Worldwide, people living in rural areas are much more likely to be in informal employment (80.0%) than those residing in urban areas (43.7%). This is because agriculture is the economic sector with the highest level of informal employment (93.6%). In terms of gender, men are slightly more likely to be employed in the informal economy than women – 63.0% compared to 58.1%. However, the global figure hides regional variations, notably that in middle-income countries a larger proportion of women are in informal employment than men. In Africa, this reaches 89.7% for women compared to 82.7% for men, a figure which is still extraordinarily high.

In terms of output, the informal economy accounts for 32%–33% of global GDP (Elgin et al. 2021). This ranges from 19% of GDP in high-income economies to 36%–37% in middle- and low-income economies. The informal sector's share of GDP is greatest in sub-Saharan Africa and Latin America and the Caribbean. However, as with employment the trend in the informal sector's contribution to GDP has generally been downward. This may cease or even reverse when economic crises occur such as the Asian financial crisis 1997–1998 and the global financial crisis 2007–2009 when formal sector economic enterprises and workers were badly affected.

Policy and the Informal Sector

In most countries, governments want to reduce the size of the informal sector for a variety of reasons. In high-income countries, tax authorities see opportunities for considerable additional income for the state to invest in public goods. In low-income countries, there is frequently a desire to reduce the informal sector and expand the formal sector to promote poverty reduction, increased productivity, competitiveness, improvement in OHS and greater government revenue. As we have seen, success in socioeconomic development generally leads to a reduction in the size of the informal sector and an improvement in the population's socioeconomic welfare.

There is no shortage of policies and programmes that have attempted to deal with the informal sector but there is no magic bullet, no particular policy mix that will resolve all the issues relating to the informal sector (Ohnsorge and Yu 2021; OECD-ILO 2019). Situations are complex and, as has been demonstrated, there is great heterogeneity in the informal sector. However, it is possible to identify the key issues that need to be addressed using four broad goals in what is termed a 'comprehensive approach' (Chen 2012): create more jobs; register informal enterprises and regulate informal jobs; extend state protection to the informal workforce; and increase the productivity of informal enterprises and the incomes of the informal workforce.

The first goal – to create more jobs – has widespread support and can be seen as fundamental for improving the lot of millions of informal sector workers. But the new or redesigned jobs must supply a decent income and preferably they should be in the formal sector where remuneration is generally higher than in the informal sector. However, as experience has shown, it is seldom easy to create jobs. Governments cannot simply decree the creation of new jobs. They need to offer incentives that encourage the private sector to invest in growth and entrepreneurs to engage in new businesses. Furthermore, workers in the informal sector must believe that new formal sector opportunities offer better remuneration and security than their current pursuits in the informal sector.

The second goal – to register informal enterprises and regulate informal jobs – is a longstanding policy objective in many developing countries but an objective that has often remained unfulfilled. The approach requires the simplification of the bureaucratic procedures involved in business registration and education that convinces the target informal sector businesses that it is worthwhile to shift to the formal sector. The benefits must be perceived as outweighing the costs. The second aspect of this goal is to design regulations that will discourage employers from hiring workers informally and ensure that employment, health and other benefits are provided for all workers. Such objectives may be difficult to achieve. For example, in a study of the vigorous government promotion of small and medium-sized enterprises (SMEs) in upper-middle-income Thailand, 1997–2015, only 23.6% of the targeted SMEs transitioned from the informal to the formal sector, while the growth in productivity was modest (Turner et al. 2016).

The third goal is concerned with extending state protection to the informal workforce. Currently, many workers do not receive health and social security benefits or OHS safeguards. Action has been taken in many developing countries to provide such assistance. For example, there has been a global drive to provide conditional cash transfers to poor workers in the informal sector. The conditions of the cash transfers usually involve regular health check-ups for children and enrolling children in school (World Bank 2023b; Handa and Davis 2006). The rationale is that monetary poverty is reduced while simultaneously improving health and education in poor households. Almost all countries in Africa have social safety net programmes (Guven et al. 2021). For example, in Benin the Insurance for Building Human Capital (ARCH) programme provides a group of services to informal economy workers, namely universal health insurance, pensions, micro-credit and training. Improvements in OHS for informal workers has been a major aim of the ILO. One approach involves gathering reports of accidents and diseases that affect informal economy workers and identifying channels that can be used to bring these facts to the attention of policymakers and implementers (OECD-ILO

2019). Encouraging dialogue was central to improvements made in Accra's public markets in Ghana. The StreetNet Ghana Alliance representing traders worked with the city authority, Accra Metropolitan Assembly, to identify low-cost solutions to OHS problems such as fire hazards and poor sanitation.

The fourth goal is about increasing the productivity of informal enterprises that will lead to higher incomes for participants. This could be seen as a stage in the longstanding policy stance of many international organizations, such as the World Bank and the ILO, to work towards formalizing the informal economy. A critical component of any attempt to increase informal enterprises' productivity is to address the problem of lack of access to credit. Money is needed to invest in aspects of production such as technology, distribution and facilities on which productivity gains will be based. Another boost to productivity is training so that the informal workforce acquires more skills and knowledge to apply in the work-place. It is also necessary to take a broad view when looking for productivity gains. There needs to be a conducive organizational environment. Some of the items discussed in the first three goals mentioned above are elements of such an enabling environment. Also, government and private enterprises in the formal sector must create a favourable attitude to supporting and assisting the informal sector. Some of these changes would also benefit the formal sector such as reduced corruption, greater government accountability and more efficient and effective public adminis-tration. It is a complex policy mix that involves mutually reinforcing measures that remove the impediments to better incomes and improve welfare for those in the informal economy.

Conclusion

This chapter has shown that negative perceptions of the informal economy are misplaced. Its participants are generally not engaged in illegal enterprises. They work in legal businesses. They are not criminals like the other actors and businesses discussed in the remainder of the chapters in this book. But dis-paraging myths surrounding the informal economy need to be dispelled. There are over two billion people in the developing world whose legitimate livelihoods depend on informal enterprises and employment. Even in high-income econo-mies informal economic activities are carried out, although their scale is far below that which is found in developing countries. People in the informal economy are only a problem for governments insofar as too little has been done to address the poverty, deprivation and vulnerability that are evident among large numbers of informal economy participants. In fact, such workers perform important functions in the overall economy and for society more generally. They are connected to the formal sector in a variety of ways and act as cheap (and often exploited) labour. They are caught in structures of disadvantage but, despite their enormous numbers, they mostly lack a powerful voice in politics and policymaking. This is yet another difficulty they face in their struggle to survive and improve their incomes and welfare.

References

Abraham, R.A. and Kumar, K.S.K. (2008) 'Multidimensional poverty and vulnerability.' *Economic and Political Weekly* 43 (20) 77, 79–87.

Adei, D., Braimah, I., Mensah, J.V., Mensah, A.A. and Agyemang-Duah, W. (2021) 'Improving upon the working environment of informal sector workers in Ghana: The role of planning.' *Cogent Medicine* 8 (1). doi:doi:10.1080/2331205X.2021.1911441.

Alkire, S., Foster, J., Seth, S., Santos, M.E., Roche, J.M. and Ballon, P. (2015) *Multidimensional Poverty Measurement and Analysis*. Oxford: Oxford University Press.

Asampong, E., Dwuma-Badu, K., Stephens, J. Srigboh, R., Neitzel, R., Basu, N. and Fobil, J. (2015) 'Health seeking behaviours among electronic waste workers in Ghana.' *BMC Public Health* 15, 1065. Available at https://doi.org/10.1186/s12889-015-2376-z.

Boeke, J. (1953) *Economics and Economic Policy of Dual Societies as Exemplified by Indonesia*. New York: Institute of Pacific Relations.

Castell, M. and Portes, A. (1989) 'World underneath: The origins, dynamics, and effects of the informal economy.' In A. Portes, M. Castells and L.A. Benton (eds) *The Informal Economy: Studies in Advanced and Less Advanced Developed Countries*. Baltimore, MD: Johns Hopkins University Press.

Chen, M.A. (2012) 'The informal economy: Definitions, theories and policies.' Working Paper No. 1. Manchester: Women in Informal Employment: Globalizing and Organizing (WIEGO). Available at https://www.wiego.org/publications/informal-economy-definitions-theories-and-policies.

D'Costa, A.P. (2023) 'India's workforce woes.' *East Asia Forum*, 12 April. Available at https://www.eastasiaforum.org/2023/04/10/indias-workforce-woes/.

De Soto, H. (1989) *The Other Path: The Invisible Revolution in the Third World*. New York: Harper and Row.

Elgin, C., Kose, M.A., Ohnsorge, F. and Yu, S. (2021) 'Understanding the informal economy: Concepts and trends.' pp. 3–32 In F. Ohnsorge and S. Yu (eds) *The Long Shadow of Informality: Challenges and Policies*. Washington, DC: World Bank.

Guven, M., Jaint, H. and Joubert, C. (2021) *Social Protection for the Informal Economy: Operational Lessons from Countries in Africa and Beyond*. Washington, DC: World Bank.

Handa, S. and Davis, B. (2006) 'The experience of conditional cash transfers in Latin America and the Caribbean.' *Development Policy Review* 24 (5) 513–536.

Hart, K. (1973) 'Informal income opportunities and urban employment in Ghana.' *Journal of Modern African Studies* 11 (1) 61–89.

Haughton, J. and Khandker, S.R. (2009) *Handbook on Poverty and Inequality*. Washington, DC: World Bank.

International Labour Organization (ILO) (2018) *Women and Men in the Informal Economy: A Statistical Picture*, 3rd edition. Geneva: ILO.

Kanbur, R. (2009) 'Conceptualizing informality: Regulation and enforcement.' IZA Discussion Paper No. 4186. Bonn: Institute of Labor Economics.

La Porta, R. and Schleifer, A. (2014) 'Informality and development.' *Journal of Economic Perspectives* 28 (3) 109–126.

Lewis, W.A. (1954) 'Economic development with unlimited supplies of labour.' *The Manchester School* 22 (2) 139–191.

Moore, W. (1963) *Social Change*. Englewood Cliffs, NJ: Prentice Hall.

Moser, C.N. (1978) 'Informal sector or petty commodity producer: Dualism or independence in urban development.' *World Development* 6 (9–10) 1041–1064.

Nordman, C.J., Rakotomanana, F. and Roubad, F. (2016) 'Informal versus formal: A panel data analysis of earning gaps in Madagascar.' IZA Discussion Paper No. 9970. Bonn: Institute of Labor Economics.

Ohnsorge, F. and Yu, S. (eds) (2021) *The Long Shadow of Informality: Challenges and Policies.* Washington, DC: World Bank.

Organisation for Economic Co-operation and Development-International Labour Organization (OECD-ILO) (2019) *Tackling Vulnerability in the Informal Economy.* Paris: Development Studies Centre, OECD.

OXFAM (2022) 'OXFAM in India 2022: A glance at the informal sector in India.' OXFAM India. Available at https://www.oxfamindia.org/knowledgehub/factsheets/glance-informal-sector-india.

Perry, G., Maloney, W., Arias, O., Fajnzylber, P., Mason, A. and Saavedra-Chanduvi, J. (2007) *Informality: Exit and Exclusion.* Washington, DC: World Bank.

Recio, R.B. (2021) 'How can street routines inform state regulation? Learning from informal traders in Baclaran, Metro Manila.' *International Development Planning Review* 43 (1) 63–88.

Schneider, F., Buehn, A. and Montenegro, C.E. (2010) 'Shadow economies all over the world: New estimates for 162 countries from 1999 to 2007.' Policy Research Working Paper 5356. Washington, DC: World Bank.

Sen, A. (1999) *Development as Freedom.* Oxford: Oxford University Press.

Turner, M., Sermcheep, S., Anantasirijkiat, S. and Srisangnam, P. (2016) 'Small and medium-sized enterprises in Thailand: Government policy and economic development.' *Asia Pacific Journal of Public Administration* 38 (4) 251–269.

World Bank (2001) *World Development Report 2000/2001: Attacking Poverty.* New York: Oxford University Press.

World Bank (2020) *Poverty and Shared Prosperity 2020: Reversal of Fortune.* Washington, DC: World Bank.

World Bank (2022) 'The World Bank in India.' Washington, DC: World Bank. Available at https://www.worldbank.org/en/country/india/overview.

World Bank (2023a) 'Multidimensional poverty measures.' Washington, DC: World Bank. Available at https://www.worldbank.org/en/topic/poverty/brief/multidimensional-poverty-measure.

World Bank (2023b) 'Evaluations: Conditional cash transfers.' Washington, DC: World Bank. Available at https://www.worldbank.org/en/programs/sief-trust-fund/brief/evaluations-conditional-cash-transfers.

4
ILLICIT BUSINESS, MONEY LAUNDERING AND THE CRIME-TERROR NEXUS

Introduction

In the 21st century, money laundering has become a ubiquitous criminal service that is accessed by a spectrum of groups and individuals. These range from organized crime groups (OCGs) seeking to turn dirty money into clean cash to wealthy individuals seeking to avoid legitimately earned money being subjected to taxation in certain jurisdictions around the world. Indeed, the intentional act of disguising wealth from the authorities is not new. It can be seen throughout history, with examples of individuals hiding their personal wealth from royal authorities dating back 3,000 years in China (Tucker 2022).

During the early 20th century in the United States, the mafia's unique method of hiding its illicit proceeds from the US authorities led to the development of the term 'money laundering.' During the Prohibition era (1920–1933), the mafia developed novel methods to disguise its growing wealth accumulated from the sale of bootleg alcohol and prostitution. Most notably, this was achieved by investing its illegitimate wealth in legitimate laundromat businesses (Schneider and Windischbauer 2010). These businesses were chosen because their cash-based business models acted as the perfect medium to commingle the proceeds of crime with legitimately earned cash from the laundromat businesses. Hence, 'washing money' and 'money laundering' became the common terms used to describe the deliberate strategy and process undertaken by criminals to avoid taxation or confiscation of illicit proceeds by the state.

Today, money laundering takes place on a much larger scale than the simplistic scheme first set up by the mafia decades ago. In a global market, money laundering itself has become an essential service and a lucrative illicit business that offers diverse types of money laundering methodologies to accommodate the varied demands of the market (Tucker 2022). These offerings range from simple strategies

DOI: 10.4324/9781003293620-4

that target cash-intensive businesses to more complex approaches that exploit free trade zones and tax havens by using offshore assets such as shell companies. Different groups use different and often bespoke methodologies to launder money. However, all these methods rely to some degree on core principles. Levi (2014) argues that a standardised description of money laundering involves the presence of three key elements: *placement, layering* and *integration*. 'Placement' is the initial insertion of illicit proceeds into a financial system. This is usually followed by the act of 'layering' that requires illicit proceeds to be passed through a financial system or systems to further disguise the provenance of the money. This step usually requires the 'use of a variety of identities, shell companies and trusts in a number of countries to make the trail more difficult to follow' (Levi 2014, 421). The final step in the process is 'integration.' During the integration process, illicit proceeds are reintroduced into the financial system by using illicit funds to purchase legitimate items ranging from luxury goods to real estate.

The international inter-governmental Financial Action Task Force (FATF) similarly identifies three broad approaches used by organized crime and terrorist groups to transfer money, conceal its true origins, and reintegrate it into the formal economy:

1. The first involves the movement of value through the financial system using methods such as cheques and wire transfers.
2. The second involves the physical movement of banknotes using methods such as cash couriers and bulk cash smuggling.
3. The third involves the movement of value using methods such as the false documentation and declaration of traded goods and services (FATF 2016, 1).

Money Laundering Methods

From its modern inception by the US mafia, money laundering has become a global business that employs a variety of methods to convert income from illicit businesses into legal tender. Because the amounts of money have become so large and officials across the world have become more vigilant in trying to curtail it, the money launderers have been forced to innovate to find new ways of transforming profits from illegal enterprises into legitimate wealth. However, some old practices still operate and sit side by side with the modern ones. In this section, we identify the leading modes of money laundering and how they work to process billions of dollars in illicit income each year.

Cash-Intensive Businesses

A simple, longstanding and still much-used method of money laundering is to put illicitly acquired money through legitimate cash-intensive businesses. It is closely associated with the 'placement' phase of the money laundering process. Rather than having to rely solely on laundromats, individuals and groups now make use of other legitimate businesses such as tanning salons, nail salons, car washes, drycleaners, strip clubs, bars and hotels to provide the fronts to launder the proceeds of crime (Naím 2010). These businesses can either be used to commingle illicit funds with clean money made from the legitimate business activities, or the 'legitimate' business may only exist and operate as a cover rather than simultaneously functioning as a lawful profit-making venture. As Riccardi and Levi (2018, 145) have argued, using these types of businesses makes it easier to justify illicit proceeds as legitimate revenues. It thus becomes possible to deposit large volumes of cash in banks as regular earnings from the ostensibly legitimate companies' activities. This makes such businesses difficult to audit which is why they remain an attractive option for criminal groups. In these circumstances, the authorities are unable to easily determine the 'normal' income for cash-based businesses – thus making them ideal money laundering facilities. However, there are distinct limitations to this approach. The amount of money that can be laundered through each business without raising suspicion depends on the services offered that can be reasonably attributed to the business. This is why other methods are often employed in conjunction with or in place of money laundering through cash-intensive businesses.

Smurfing and Cuckoo Smurfing

Two different but closely related strategies known as 'smurfing' and 'cuckoo smurfing' have become increasingly popular methods to launder money. These methods are referred to as 'placement' or 'structuring' techniques (Maitland-Irwin et al. 2012). Smurfing involves using third parties to divide up large amounts of cash into smaller amounts that can then be deposited into financial institutions without generating transaction reports. By using this technique, criminals can easily launder large amounts of money in an inconspicuous manner. Importantly, 'smurfs' are aware of their role in the scheme which is vital for criminals seeking to obscure the provenance of the money being laundered.

Cuckoo smurfing differs from smurfing because it involves professional remitters who 'swap' the money of respective clients. In order for this method to work, remitters located in the corresponding locations of the criminal and innocent individual must be used (AUSTRAC 2023). This allows the remitters' clients to move the value of their money over vast distances without moving anything tangible across such distances. Criminals are then able to receive matched payments overseas without creating a money trail that can be traced back to them. Just like the behaviour of a cuckoo bird, the criminals have essentially taken over someone else's nest for the purposes of exploitation and profit.

Money or Value Transfer Services

Money or Value Transfer Services (MVTS) operate in a range of developing nations and most pre-date Western banking systems. Like cuckoo smurfing, this exchange system allows people to move cash outside of the standardized international banking system. It is important to note that these types of networks rely heavily on brokers to organize financial transactions. Examples of MVTS include Hawala in India and the Middle East, Hundi in Pakistan and Fei ch'ien in the People's Republic of China (McCusker 2017). The process used in Hawala relies heavily on trust because it is based on a ledger system between two brokers located in different countries (Shelley 2018). A client initially pays money to a broker in their home country. That broker then instructs another broker in a different country or area to pay the final recipient. The only movement of money in this system is localized and the transaction is only recorded in the ledgers of each broker. The closed nature of this system and its non-digital format makes it very difficult for the authorities to identify and interdict this activity, thus rendering it an attractive option for OCGs.

Trade-Based Money Laundering

Trade-Based Money Laundering, often referred to as TBML, is a method used to hide, transfer and change the proceeds of crime into what appear to be everyday goods and services. According to Zdanowicz (2009, 856), 'money laundering through the over- and under-invoicing of goods and services, is one of the oldest methods of transferring value across borders, and it remains a common practice today.' TBML schemes work by deliberately distorting the value of goods or services to facilitate the movement of money between importers and exporters. In 2006, the FAFT published a detailed account of the impact of TMBL in the global economy. It identified that the international trading system was particularly susceptible to manipulation by nefarious actors including OCGs and terrorist organizations (FATF 2016). TBML can involve a range of techniques. Tucker (2022, 54–55) categorized these techniques to include over- and under-invoicing, multiple invoicing, over- and under-shipping, phantom or ghost shipping and fraudulent shipping. The advantage of TBML is that it facilitates the use of illicit proceeds to acquire legal goods than can then be used for import or export purposes. The goods can then be shipped to and sold in a range of markets around the world, thus making this method of money laundering extremely challenging for law enforcement agencies to detect.

The economic rise of China and the implementation of its long-term projects such as the Belt and Road Initiative have provided fertile conditions for the expansion of TBML by criminals connected to the Chinese financial system (Kupatadze and Kumar 2022). Illicit proceeds are sent to bank accounts in China using a combination of wire transfer companies, casinos or other bank accounts. According to McCarthy-Jones et al. (2020), businesses associated with criminals in China, but located in a variety of locations around the world, provide money exchange and import and export services to legitimate companies that have a genuine reason to import specific goods from China. These money exchange businesses deliberately provide generous exchange rates as a 'carrot' to entice legitimate companies to use their businesses for the purposes of exchanging dollars into Chinese yuan. The illicit proceeds in the bank accounts in China are transferred to other businesses in China to complete the purchase of items such as white goods, furniture, children's toys, textiles or clothing. The legitimate company (the importer) pays the money exchange company using legitimate funds for the goods that have been acquired for export. Once this money is received, the exchange company transfers the legitimate money to the criminal group (Langdale 2021). Chinese American criminal Xizhi Li developed a novel money laundering operation that provided efficient services at discount prices and specifically integrated elements of TBML into his illegal schemes (Rotella and Berg 2022). Central to Li's business was its ability to synthesize sources of supply and demand from criminal clients in Mexico, who needed to covert dollars into Mexican pesos, and wealthy clients in China who wanted to exchange Chinese currency for US dollars to purchase assets such as real estate in the United States. While much of his scheme relied on the use of couriers and mirror transactions (the on-selling of illicit money to multiple clients), according to Rotella and Berg (2022, 1),

> [t]here were variations on the system. Li sometimes washed funds through companies owned by confederates in the United States and Latin America who sold seafood and other goods to China. Taking advantage of the $80 billion in trade between Mexico and China, launderers also sent goods from China to Mexican front companies connected to drug lords. Those companies would sell the products for pesos, creating a legitimate paper trail for money initially earned from the sale of drugs.

However, it is not just drug trafficking organizations that use this method. The Taliban in Afghanistan is also known to have utilized TBML. By using TBML 'they can covertly move their assets out of the countries in which they were derived and into the countries in which they plan to carry out their operations' (Tucker 2022, 56). More recently, a Chinese-Australian operation known as the Xin Money Laundering Network enabled the movement of approximately US $6.6 billion from Australia while concurrently creating a significant real estate portfolio in Australia's largest city, Sydney. A key part of the Xin network's methodology was to adopt a TBML strategy that leveraged *daigou* (overseas-based shoppers operating on behalf of consumers in China) to guarantee that no actual funds crossed international borders (AFP 2023).

Offshore Financial Centres, Tax Havens and Secrecy Jurisdictions

Another method of money laundering utilizes specific locations around the world that offer legitimate financial services to customers. But such services further enable financial crimes such as tax evasion and money laundering. These locations are known as offshore financial centres (OFCs), tax havens and secrecy jurisdictions. According to Zoromé (2007, 7), 'an OFC is a country or jurisdiction that provides financial services to non-residents on a scale that is incommensurate with the size and the financing of its domestic economy.' In this sense OFCs act as havens for illicit business (FATF 2010). They provide illicit businesses with the opportunity to manage their monetary assets outside of the normal regulatory authorities found in larger states. The OFCs are usually countries or locations that have minimal or zero corporate taxes. Such tax havens usually restrict public disclosure about companies and their owners, a service which gives a significant amount of protection to companies operating in these settings. This is why these places are sometimes referred to as secrecy jurisdictions (GFI 2023). The Cayman Islands, the Bahamas, Hong Kong, the British Virgin Islands, Luxembourg, the Netherlands and Panama are among the locations known to be used as tax havens or secrecy jurisdictions. Foreign businesses funnel payments, profits or investments through subsidiaries or shell companies operating in these offshore financial centres (Cobham et al. 2015). The combination of these factors creates ideal conditions for OCGs to utilize these offshore centres to manage their proceeds of crime.

Anti-Money Laundering and Counter-Terrorism Financing

The growth of money laundering during the latter half of the 20th century led to the development of several policy initiatives at the national and international level. In the United States, the Bank Secrecy Act (1970) is considered to be the first major piece of legislation to address the issue of money laundering. A defining feature of the Act was that it made it mandatory for financial institutions to report cash deposits over US $10,000 as well as introducing obligations on the part of financial institutions to conduct due diligence in relation to their customer base and to monitor and report suspicious activity (FinCEN 2023). This legislation was designed to minimize the amount of illicit money entering the US financial system.

These US measures became the benchmark for banking policy aimed at deterring the flow of illicit funds into national banking systems and as such have been transferred to most nations in the world. Since then, a range of anti-money laundering (AML) initiatives and policies have been developed at the national and international level. Beare (2015, 265) has described this as the 'establishment of bureaucratic engines' whose prime purpose is to counter money laundering activities. In 1989, the creation of the FATF by the Group of Seven (G7), an informal grouping of rich nations, sought to provide global leadership and guidance for the future development of AML policies and international cooperation. At a meeting in Brussels, Belgium, in 1995, an informal network of Financial Intelligence Units (FIUs) from 24 countries met for the first time to exchange ideas on AML. This led to the formal creation of the Egmont Group of FIUs. The Egmont Group is an international organization that supports continued cooperation and exchanges between FIUs from a range of countries. Since its inception in 1995, membership of the Egmont Group has grown to over 170 countries (Egmont Group 2023). Despite the rise in the number of international agreements and the expansion of AML activities the amount of money laundered has continued to increase. However, law enforcement agencies and banks now hold out great hopes for the application of new technologies to stem the tide of illicit funds moving between different jurisdictions (see Box 4.1)

BOX 4.1 NEW TECHNOLOGIES AND ANTI-MONEY LAUNDERING

Studies estimate that money laundering activity adds up to between 2% and 5% of global GDP – US $800 billion to US $2 trillion – annually and the amounts laundered continue to grow. This is despite financial organizations investing heavily in combating financial crime – valued at an estimated US $214 million in 2020. But there are now hopes that developments in artificial intelligence (AI) and machine learning (ML) can be harnessed for more effective, efficient AML initiatives and policies.

Advances in these and allied fields of new technologies are making it possible to process huge datasets instantly and to draw pertinent conclusions about the relationships between the transactions and the accounts that are being used. ML is crucial to AML advances because it learns from customer data continuously, and in real time immediately new data becomes available. This will enable a greater understanding of which customers, transaction types and locations should be considered high risk. ML builds on what has already been learned by recognizing new patterns in the data that point to money laundering. These advances will enable banks' AML teams to focus their attention on the truly suspicious accounts and transactions. However, in instances where there are inadequate data, it will not be possible to harness the 'forward-looking intelligence' that ML promises. In such cases the traditional rule- and scenario-based tools could be more effective. This points to the fact that the incremental deployment of ML must be undertaken in combination with 'human insight' in a new hybrid AML mode. With the establishment of the new modes that rely heavily on ML, it is important that new governance systems are introduced to build trust in new arrangements. They need to be unbiased, transparent and explainable with customers assured of the fair use of personal data and of the legal right to explanation.

Meanwhile, the money launderers will not sit idly by watching the installation of new technologies for AML. They will be hard at work seeking their own innovations.

Sources: Craig (2022); Doppalapudi (2022); Featurespace (2022).

The use of money laundering and illicit financing is not confined to criminal groups. Terrorist groups are increasingly utilizing these methods to assist with financing their violent political activities. This is why AML strategies were expanded to address the issue of terrorism financing known as counter-terrorism financing (CTF). The need to develop CTF was the result of a shift in the traditional modus operandi of terrorist organizations in the post-Cold War era. The adoption of criminal strategies by terrorist organizations blurred the lines that had previously established clear distinctions between OCGs and terrorist organizations. This phenomenon is known as the crime-terror nexus.

Crime-Terror Nexus

For much of the 20th century, conventional thinking separated terrorist organizations from OCGs due to the perception that differences between religious or ideological motivations and profit-driven motivations were so substantial that it was unlikely that either group would find compelling reasons to intermingle. However, the rapid changes that occurred in the international system following the collapse of the Soviet Union and the end of the Cold War provided the opportunity to re-examine these assumptions. While Fukuyama (1989) proclaimed liberalism's defeat of communism as the 'end of history,' writers such as Kaplan (1994, 46) warned of a 'coming anarchy ... in which environmental and societal stress creates and fosters a criminal anarchy – and it is this anarchy that presents a "strategic danger."' Kaplan (1994) concentrated on internal security threats caused by problems existing in the state such as disease, overpopulation, weak state borders, the privatization of armed forces, resource scarcity and increasing power of drug trafficking organizations.

In essence, key security concerns in the post-Cold War era had shifted to prioritize threats emanating from within, rather than outside, the state. Snow (1996, 46) argues that this was because of the new post-Cold War environment in which a 'reduced willingness and ability to control internal violence' had led to a rise in disorderly, or as Snow termed them, 'uncivil' wars. Further contributions from Collier and Hoeffler (2004) sought to understand the motivations of violent groups operating in this new security environment which led to a body of work known as the 'greed vs grievance' debates. In particular, Collier and Hoeffler (2004) identified the growing economic imperatives that underpinned many civil wars. Moreover, the deterioration in state sponsorship of armed non-state actors that occurred because of the ending of the Cold War worked as a push factor for these groups to seek new sources of funding (Makarenko 2015). Thus, the core activities of some terrorist groups expanded to include financing activities that involved either collaboration with OCGs and/or the direct engagement of terrorist organizations in criminal activities to generate revenue. This expansion of activities meant that the differences between some terrorist organizations and criminal groups could no longer be easily delineated.

Sanderson (2004, 53) highlights the 'blurring of lines' between these groups by identifying similarities between organized crime and terrorist groups.

1. Both are generally rational actors.
2. Both use extreme violence and the threat of reprisals.
3. Both use kidnappings, assassinations and extortion.
4. Both operate secretly, though at times publicly in friendly territory.
5. Both defy the state and the rule of law (except when there is state sponsorship).

6. For a member to leave either group is rare and often fatal.
7. Both present an asymmetrical threat to the United States and 'friendly' nations.
8. Both can have 'interchangeable' recruitment pools.
9. Both are highly adaptable, innovative and resilient.
10. Both have back-up leaders and foot soldiers.
11. Both have provided social services, though this is much more frequently seen with terrorist groups.

The importance of understanding the similarities and reasons behind the commingling of criminal groups and terrorist organizations was brought into focus following the events of September 11, 2001 when Islamic terrorists hijacked and deliberately crashed planes in the United States thereby causing over 3,000 civilian deaths (known as 9/11). This led to the emergence of an important a body of work based on the concept of the crime-terror nexus. According to Wang (2010, 11), 'the crime-terror nexus includes two independent, but related, components: First, it incorporates the straightforward involvement in criminal activities by terrorists as a source of funding, and second, it refers to the linkages between organized criminal organizations and terrorist groups.' It is important to examine the causes of these linkages. For example, Dishman (2005, 244–245) points to the process of decentralization in the organizational arrangements of these groups as being the catalyst for the commingling of terrorist and criminal groups.

By moving away from strictly hierarchical structures to hybrid models that accommodate hierarchy and network formations, the roles of lower- to mid-level players in both terrorist and criminal groups were fundamentally changed. Dishman (2005, 244–245) argues that this was 'because networks marginalize or eliminate the command cadre,' and therefore disperse responsibilities across the network's membership. Network formations afford mid-ranking actors greater autonomy which means that these types of actors are less likely to adopt a singular focus in relation to the objectives of the organization. In the absence of centralized leadership that enforces a strict adherence to a set of behaviours designed to solely benefit the organization's needs, lower-level players are more likely to engage in a decision-making process that melds their personal and professional pursuits. Dishman (2005, 246) further identifies that beyond changes in command and control, 'a decentralized network is unable to provide continuous financial assistance to its nodes.' This creates conditions in which collaboration between members of terrorist organizations and criminal groups is more likely because both will be motivated by personal and professional reasons for their survival.

Further considerations have examined whether the nexus produces short-term (or largely transactional) cooperative partnerships between terrorist organizations and OCGs, or whether the nexus provides scope for longer-term relationships that have a transformative impact on each group. The work of Tamara Makarenko has been particularly influential in the development and conceptualization of the crime-terror nexus. Makarenko's (2004, 130) early work presented the nexus as existing on a continuum that demonstrated how a terrorist organization or OCG could move up and down the continuum as result of environmental conditions that impact its mode of operations. Makarenko (2004, 131) categorized the continuum into four main groupings: alliances; operational motivations; convergence; and the 'black hole.' Although Makarenko (2015, 236) has since developed her work on the nexus to include 'illustrating a relationship that exists on a series of planes: one operational, one evolutionary and one conceptual,' the discussion in this chapter will focus on the original linear concept and the forms of the nexus that are identified on this continuum.

Stages of Makarenko's Nexus

In the *alliance* stage, relationships can be initiated by either group. Therefore, alliances occur at either end of Makarenko's continuum. Alliances usually emerge when there is a specific need of one group that can be provided by the other. Makarenko (2004, 131) highlights the Medellín cartel's use of the Ejército de Liberación Nacional (ELN – National Liberation Army) to undertake a series of car bombings in Colombia on its behalf as an example of the alliance stage. The Medellín cartel's knowledge deficit in this area of tactical operations meant that organizational objectives were unachievable without the help of the ELN which had considerable experience of using such methods. However, these interactions did not produce a long-term relationship between each group. Instead, this is an example of how transactional alliances can form between groups for a specific and limited time and purpose.

In the *operational motivations* stage, groups seek to develop capabilities similar to those of their alliance (current or previous) partners. According to (Makarenko, 2004, 133), 'criminal groups using terrorism as an operational tool, and terrorist groups taking part in criminal activities as an operational tool,' constitute the second component of the crime-terror continuum. This behaviour is a result of a group's attempt to minimize its dependency on outside organizations and to increase the stability and security of the organization. Indeed, criminal groups such as the mafia in Italy and the Comando Vermelho in Brazil have been known to use political violence as a means to pressure authorities to alter policies for the benefit the group's criminal enterprises (Phelan 2021a; Makarenko 2004). Conversely, terrorist organizations have a long history of involvement in the international drug trade and other illicit business activities. For example, the Provisional Irish Republican Army was involved in kidnapping for ransom, extortion, robbery and drug trafficking as a means to fund its political activities (Horgan and Taylor 1999). In Colombia, the Fuerzas Armadas Revolucionarias de Colombia (FARC – Revolutionary Armed Forces of Colombia) evolved from its inception as a Marxist guerilla insurgency in the 1960s to one of the largest groups involved in drug trafficking by the time the group 'demobilized' in 2016 (Phelan 2021b).

The final stage of the nexus is *convergence* and it is described as the fulcrum point of the nexus. In this stage, groups could adopt a hybrid form in which they possess attributes of both a terrorist and a criminal organization. Additionally, groups in this part of the continuum may also progress further along the continuum to an end point that sees a total transformation of the group. Essentially, a terrorist group could move along the continuum to such a degree that it would then be categorized as a criminal group and the same could be said of a criminal group that evolves into a terrorist organization. Makarenko (2004) specifically identifies a range of groups such as the Albanian mafia in Europe, the Abu Sayyaf in the Philippines, and the FARC in Colombia as being demonstrative of the convergence stage of the nexus. In their examination of the Abu Sayyaf, Ugarte and Turner (2011) emphasize that historical labels belie the current reality of the membership, motivations and operations of the organization, all of which are a result of changes that have occurred across the decentralized nodes of the Abu Sayyaf network. Ugarte and Turner (2011) conclude that in some instances labels are more important than reality and this is a particularly salient point in relation to the crime-terror nexus. In each case, the *raison d'être* of each group had fundamentally altered, resulting in a confluence of activities, organizational objectives and behaviour that are distinct from the label that the group continues to use.

An additional aspect of the convergence stage of the crime-terror nexus – the 'black hole' syndrome – specifically considers the role of states and their complicit, or in some cases unintentional, role in exacerbating and/or encouraging the convergence stage of the nexus. These states include 'weak states' (Migdal 1988) 'failed states' (Rotberg 2004) and more recently 'mafia states' (McCarthy-Jones and Turner 2022). Makarenko (2004, 138) argues that

> the 'black hole' syndrome encompasses two situations: first, where the primary motivations of groups engaged in a civil war evolves from a focus on political aims to a focus on criminal aims; second, it refers to the emergence of a 'black hole' state – a state successfully taken over by a hybrid group.

These states offer havens for illicit activity and therefore provide ideal locations for groups to expand their activities, skills sets and organizational experience.

A recent example of this phenomenon is the activities of the ELN in Venezuela. Originally a Colombian Marxist-Leninist terrorist group, the ELN has historically operated along the Colombia–Venezuela border to pursue its political goals. However, the demobilization of the FARC allowed the ELN to swiftly fill the vacuum left by the FARC. Specifically, this meant appropriating the FARC's criminal enterprises which allowed the ELN to extend its reach further into Venezuela. This expansion has also been of benefit to the Venezuelan government which has been besieged by economic, political and social crises for almost a decade. According to InSight Crime (2020, 1), the weak state capacity of the Venezuelan government means that it has actively 'sought alliances with groups like the ELN in the midst of such institutional chaos.' This demonstrates the way in which geographical locations of the crime-terror nexus can be closely linked to weak state capacity in certain parts of the world. The case study presented in Box 4.2 illustrates the crime-terror nexus in West Africa where terrorist groups have gained control of illicit economies in the context of the region's weak states.

BOX 4.2 THE CRIME-TERROR NEXUS IN WEST AFRICA

In the Sahel region of Africa, the al-Qaeda-affiliated Jama'at Nusrat al-Islam wal-Muslimin (JNIM) and its involvement in a range of illicit activities provides a contemporary example of the problems posed by the crime-terror nexus. In 2023, the United Nations described JNIM as 'Al-Qaeda's Sahelian branch.' JNIM is the product of the 2017 amalgamation of several militant groups that include Ansar Dine, al-Qaeda in the Islamic Maghreb, al-Murabitun and Katiba Macina. JNIM adopted an organizational structure that represents and supports an assortment of ethnic groups, most notably with the large Tuareg populations that straddle Algeria, Burkina Faso, Niger and much of northern Mali. JNIM's focus on a localized approach with ethnic communities has allowed it to develop quasi-governance capabilities in many parts of the Sahel region. This is because JNIM has established control over a range of illicit economies in the area, which local populations rely on for access to certain goods and services. JNIM's ability to wrest control of economically significant areas of the Sahel from various state authorities has allowed the organization to operate as a gatekeeper along many trading routes. Its connection to illicit economies (kidnap for ransom, arms trafficking, drug trafficking, mining, vehicles, fuel, medical supplies and general goods) is used as a means to finance its terrorist activities, compete with other non-armed state groups in the area, and establish commercial relationships with local populations. The impact of the crime-terror nexus is clear: as local populations become more reliant on illicit economies to access goods, the role of state authorities is eroded, thus creating a more amenable environment for the expansion of JNIM in the region.

Source: ACLED (2023).

In the Sahel region of Africa, difficult terrain, porous borders, ethnic and tribal conflicts, extreme poverty, high levels of corruption and weak state capacity have contributed to increasing instability. The 'Arab Spring' that began in the early 2010s and which saw the removal of longstanding leaders, such as Muammar Gaddafi in Libya, led to significant changes in the security environment across north African and the Sahel. Marshall (2022, 1) observed that:

> Since 2011, Libya's bloody civil war and subsequent fragmentation has flooded the Sahelian states to the south with cheap arms and munitions.

Foreign fighters recruited from Sahelian communities by all sides in Libya's multidimensional conflict led to an influx of hardened veterans across the impoverished region, with Tuareg nomads from Gaddafi's Islamic Legion triggering the 2012 Malian civil war, a separatist rebellion quickly hijacked by jihadist militants linked to al-Qaeda in the Islamic Maghreb.

Historic trade routes across countries such as Algeria, Libya, Mali and Mauritania have been infiltrated by a mixture of criminal groups, armed groups and terrorist groups. Criminal networks involved in human trafficking and arms trafficking have benefited from the ongoing conflicts in the region in which all these groups have a vested interest. Rizk (2021, 1) highlights that 'criminal networks and armed groups leverage opportunities created by conflict to generate profit and project power. They operate in convergent spaces benefitting from state fragility and shared social networks.' This shows that Makarenko's 'black hole' syndrome is not limited to a specific state, but rather can take hold in multiple states and provide regional havens for the crime-terror nexus to emerge.

Conclusion

The significant growth of illicit business means that for many individuals and groups operating in the illegal economy profits have never been better. While sudden or significant increases in profits are welcomed in any business, for an illicit business these types of windfalls create a pressing need to develop strategies that disguise illicit proceeds from the authorities and enable the use of 'dirty' money in the legal economy. As this chapter has demonstrated, there are a range of methodologies that can be employed to achieve these goals. The importance of money laundering to illicit businesses is so great that new bespoke illicit businesses exclusively offering money laundering as a service have emerged as important players in the criminal landscape. However, the need for money laundering is not limited to criminal organizations. Changes in the international security environment at the end of the 20th century meant that terrorist organizations were forced to move into criminal activities as a source of financing. As with criminal groups, money laundering capabilities and services became an integral part of the terrorists' organizational models. The crime-terror nexus demonstrates the way in which criminal organizations and terrorist groups share more commonality than in previous eras, which has encouraged many of these groups to form alliances and share intelligence and tactical capabilities. Thus, as this chapter has highlighted clear delineations between these groups may no longer be easily made. But what is clear is that regardless of a group's motivations, without the ability to launder money the continuation of each group would be severely threatened.

References

Australian Federal Police (AFP) (2023) 'Property and cash restrained as alleged money laundering group charged.' Media release, 2 February. Available at https://www.afp. gov.au/news-media/media-releases/property-and-cash-restrained-alleged-money-launder ing-group-charged.

Australian Transaction Reports and Analysis Centre (AUSTRAC) (2023) 'Cuckoo smurfing – factsheet.' Available at https://www.austrac.gov.au/sites/default/files/2021-06/ 21-1074%20Cuckoo%20Smurfing%20Factsheet_d04.pdf.

Beare, M.E. (2015) 'Responding to transnational organized crimes: "follow the money."' In F. Allum and S. Gilmour (eds) *The Routledge Handbook of Transnational Organized Crime*, pp. 263–278. London: Routledge.

Cobham, A., Janský, P. and Meinzer, M. (2015) 'The financial secrecy index: Shedding new light on the geography of secrecy.' *Economic Geography* 91 (3) 281–303.

Collier, P. and Hoeffler, A. (2004) 'Greed and grievance in civil war.' *Oxford Economic Papers* 56 (4) 563–595.

Craig, P. (2022) 'How to trust the machine: Using AI to combat money laundering.' EY, 31 August. Available at https://www.ey.com/en_au/trust/how-to-trust-the-machine–u sing-ai-to-combat-money-laundering.

Daugherty, A. (2015) 'Colombians charged in massive China-based money laundering scheme.' *InSight Crime*, 11 September. Available at https://www.insightcrime.org/ news/analysis/colombians-charged-china-drug-money-laundering-scheme/.

Dishman, C. (2005) 'The leaderless nexus: When crime and terror converge.' *Studies in Conflict and Terrorism* 28 (3) 237–252.

Doppalapudi, P., Kumar, P., Murphy, A., Werner, S., Rougeaux, C. and Stearns, R. (2022) 'The fight against money laundering: Machine learning is a game changer.' McKinsey & Company, 7 October. Available at https://www.mckinsey.com/capabili ties/risk-and-resilience/our-insights/the-fight-against-money-laundering-machine-lea rning-is-a-game-changer.

Drug Enforcement Administration (DEA) (2017) 'National drug threat assessment.' Available at https://www.dea.gov/documents/2017/2017-10/2017-10-01/2017-nationa l-drug-threat-assessment.

Egmont Group (2023) 'FAQs.' Available at https://egmontgroup.org/faqs/.

Featurespace (2022) 'AML technology and a new approach to fighting financial crime.' 26 May. Available at https://www.featurespace.com/newsroom/aml-technology-and-a -new-approach-to-fighting-financial-crime/.

Financial Action Taskforce (FATF) (2006) 'Trade-based money laundering.' Available at https://www.fatf-gafi.org/content/dam/fatf-gafi/reports/Trade%20Based%20Money% 20Laundering.pdf.coredownload.pdf.

Financial Action Taskforce (FATF) (2010) 'Money laundering vulnerabilities of free trade zones.' Available at https://www.fatf-gafi.org/content/dam/fatf-gafi/reports/ML %20vulnerabilities%20of%20Free%20Trade%20Zones.pdf.coredownload.pdf.

Financial Action Taskforce (FATF) (2016) 'Guidance for a risk-based approach for money or value transfer services.' Available at www.fatf-gafi.org/publications/fatfre commendations/documents/rba-money-or-value-transfer.html.

Financial Crimes Enforcement Network (FinCEN) (2023) 'BSA Timeline.' https://www. fincen.gov/resources/statutes-and-regulations/bank-secrecy-act/bsa-timeline.

Fukuyama, F. (1989) 'The end of history?' *The National Interest*, 16, 3–18.

Global Financial Integrity (GFI) (2023) 'Secrecy jurisdictions.' Available at https://gfin tegrity.org/issue/secrecy-jurisdictions/.

Horgan, J. and Taylor, M. (1999) 'Playing the "Green Card" – financing the provisional IRA: Part 1.' *Terrorism and Political Violence* 11 (2) 1–38.

Hübschle, A. (2011) 'From theory to practice: Exploring the organised crime-terror nexus in sub-Saharan Africa.' *Perspectives on Terrorism* 5 (3/4) 81–95.

InSight Crime (2020) 'ELN in Venezuela.' 28 January. Available at https://insightcrime. org/venezuela-organized-crime-news/eln-in-venezuela/.

Kaplan, R. (1994) 'The coming anarchy.' *The Atlantic*, February, 44–76. Available at https://www.theatlantic.com/magazine/archive/1994/02/the-coming-anarchy/304670/.

Kupatadze, A. and Kumar, L. (2022) 'Everything, everywhere all at once: Understanding the implications of the belt and road initiative on trade-based money laundering (TBML) and illicit supply chains.' Global Financial Integrity. Available at https://34n8bd.p3cdn1.secur eserver.net/wp-content/uploads/2022/11/EVERYTHING-EVERYWHERE-REPORT-07. 11.2022.pdf?time=1700075536.

Langdale, J. (2021) 'Chinese money laundering in North America.' *European Review of Organised Crime* 6 (1) 10–37.

Levi, M. (2014) 'Money laundering.' In L. Paoli (ed.) *Oxford Handbook of Organized Crime*, pp. 419–443. Oxford: Oxford University Press.

Makarenko, T. (2001) 'Transnational crime and its evolving links to terrorism and instability.' *Janes Intelligence Review* 13 (11) 22–24.

Makarenko, T. (2004) 'The crime-terror continuum: Tracing the interplay between transnational organised crime and terrorism.' *Global Crime* 6 (1) 129–145.

Makarenko, T. (2015) 'Foundations and evolution of the crime–terror nexus.' In F. Allum and S. Gilmour (eds) *Routledge Handbook of Transnational Organized Crime*, pp. 234–249. London: Routledge.

Maitland-Irwin, S.A., Choo, K.-K. R. and Liu, L. (2012) 'An analysis of money laundering and terrorism financing typologies.' *Journal of Money Laundering Control* 15 (1) 85–111.

Marshall, W. (2022) 'Africa's crime-terror nexus: Transnational organised crime, illicit economic networks and violent extremism in the Sahel.' *Global Risk Insights*, 16 February. Available at https://globalriskinsights.com/2022/02/africas-crime-terror-nexus-transnationa l-organised-crime-illicit-economic-networks-and-violent-extremism-in-the-sahel/.

McCarthy-Jones, A., Doyle, C. and Turner, M. (2020) 'From hierarchies to networks: The organizational evolution of the international drug trade.' *International Journal of Law, Crime and Justice* 63, 100436.

McCarthy-Jones, A. and Turner, M. (2022) 'What is a "Mafia State" and how is one created?' *Policy Studies* 43 (6) 1195–1215.

McCusker, R. (2017) 'Underground banking: Legitimate remittance network or money laundering system?' Australian Institute of Criminology. Available at https://www.aic. gov.au/publications/tandi/tandi300.

Migdal, J.S. (1988) *Strong Societies and Weak States: State-Society Relations and State Capabilities in the Third World*. Princeton, NJ: Princeton University Press.

Naím, M. (2010) *Illicit: How Smugglers, Traffickers and Copycats Are Hijacking the Global Economy*. New York: Random House.

Phelan, A. (2021a) 'Revisiting the terror-crime nexus in Latin America: Militant proto-state governance and challenges to state security.' In C. Close and D. Impiombato (eds) *Counterterrorism Yearbook 2021*. Canberra: Australian Strategic Policy Institute. Available at https://www.jstor.org/stable/pdf/resrep31258.16.pdf.

Phelan, A. (2021b) 'FARC's pursuit of "Taking Power": Insurgent social contracts, the drug trade and appeals to eudaemonic legitimation.' *Studies in Conflict and Terrorism* 44 (12) 971–993.

Riccardi, M. and Levi, M. (2018) 'Cash, crime and anti-money laundering.' In C. King, C. Walker and J. Gurulé (eds) *The Palgrave Handbook of Criminal and Terrorism Financing Law*, pp. 135–163. Cham: Palgrave Macmillan. Available at https://doi.org/10.1007/978-3-319-64498-1_7.

Rizk, J. (2021) 'Exploring the nexus between armed groups and the trafficking and smuggling of human beings in the central Sahel and Libya.' *Studies in Conflict and Terrorism*. Published online 21 November. doi:doi:10.1080/1057610X.2021.2002687.

Rotberg, R.I. (2004) *When States Fail: Causes and Consequences*. Princeton, NJ: Princeton University Press.

Rotella, S. and Berg, K. (2022) 'How a Chinese American gangster transformed money laundering for drug cartels.' *ProPublica*, 11 October. Available at https://www.propublica.org/article/china-cartels-xizhi-li-money-laundering.

Sanderson, T.M. (2004) 'Transnational terror and organized crime: Blurring the lines.' *SAIS Review of International Affairs* 24 (1) 49–61.

Schneider, F. and Windischbauer, U. (2010) 'Money laundering: Some facts.' Economics of Security Working Paper, No. 25. Berlin: Deutsches Institut für Wirtschaftsforschung. Available at https://www.econstor.eu/bitstream/10419/119350/1/diw_econsec0025.pdf.

Shelley, L. (2018) *Dark Commerce: How a New Illicit Economy Is Threatening Our Future*. Princeton, NJ: Princeton University Press.

Snow, D.M. (1996) *Uncivil Wars: International Security and the New Internal Conflicts*. Boulder, CO: Lynne Rienner Publishers.

The Armed Conflict Location and Event Data Project (ACLED) (2023) 'Actor profile: Jama'at Nusrat al-Islam wal-Muslimin (JNIM).' ACLED, 13 November. Available at https://acleddata.com/2023/11/13/actor-profile-jamaat-nusrat-al-islam-wal-muslimin-jnim/.

Tucker, O.M. (2022) *The Flow of Illicit Funds: A Case Study Approach to Anti-money Laundering Compliance*. Washington, DC: Georgetown University Press.

Ugarte, E.F. and Turner, M.M. (2011) 'What is the "Abu Sayyaf"? How labels shape reality.' *Pacific Review* 24 (4) 397–420.

Wang, P. (2010) 'The crime-terror nexus: Transformation, alliance, convergence.' *Asian Social Science* 6 (6) 11–20.

Zdanowicz, J.S. (2009) 'Trade-based money laundering and terrorist financing.' *Review of Law and Economics* 5 (2) 855–878.

Zoromé, A. (2007) 'Concept of offshore financial centers: In search of an operational definition.' IMF Working Paper 07/87. Available at http://www.imf.org/external/pubs/ft/wp/2007/wp0787.pdf.

5

THE DRUG TRAFFICKING BUSINESS

Introduction

Drug trafficking is one of the most lucrative forms of illicit business and its activities pose significant challenges to global security. According to the United Nations Office on Drugs and Crime (UNODC 2022a, 60), 'in 2020 an estimated 284 million people or 5.6 per cent of the global population had used a drug in the past 12 months.' This highlights the global scale of the demand that is driving the supply of illicit drugs. To facilitate this enormous illicit business requires organization on a massive multinational scale. An almost indeterminant number of actors operating in diverse geographical locations are increasingly opting to cooperate rather than compete. This shift has enabled huge quantities of illicit drugs to be transported from source countries to markets in affluent parts of the world where consumers continue to drive the demand for these substances.

International governance organizations such as UNODC typically gather data and statistics on illicit drug use and production under four broad categories: cannabis, cocaine, amphetamine-type stimulants (ATS) and opioids (UNODC 2016). These categories represent the illicit substances that are most widely consumed by the global population and as a result demand the greatest level of state intervention. This chapter provides an overview of the types of illicit business activities and organized crime groups (OCGs) that are associated with the production and distribution of cannabis, cocaine, ATS and opioids for the global market in illicit drugs.

Cannabis

Cannabis is known to have existed almost 12,000 years ago in parts of Central Asia, close the Altai Mountains where modern-day People's Republic of China, Kazakhstan, Mongolia and the Russian Federation converge (Pisanti and

DOI: 10.4324/9781003293620-5

Bilfulco 2019). The plant's migration from its home in Central Asia was a result of nomadic communities incrementally expanding their movement across Asia and into parts of the European continent (Crocq 2020). It then travelled to the Americas and Africa as a result of European colonization beginning in the 15th century. In numerous cultures around the world, the cannabis plant has shown to be a versatile resource that has been utilized in the production of 'food, oil, and fibre, as well as for medicinal, recreational, and religious purposes' (de Souza et al. 2022, 1). However, Bonini et al. (2018) argue that the value of the cannabis plant and its many uses became only became more widely recognized in Europe as a result of the British colonization of India in the 19th century. Since then, the production and consumption of the plant and its derivatives have been prolific. A key reason for this is that, unlike other drugs such as heroin and cocaine that are produced in discrete parts of the world and then exported, cannabis is largely produced domestically. According to the UN *World Drug Report* (UNODC 2022b) an estimated 209 million people consumed cannabis in 2020 making it the most used drug in the world. However, in contrast to other illicit drugs that will be examined later in this chapter, the use of cannabis and its perceived impact on society has significantly changed.

For much of the 20th century cannabis remained illegal in most countries; however, the past few decades have seen a trend towards many states regulating the medicinal use of cannabis and some have even experimented with decriminalizing and legalizing the recreational use of cannabis in certain settings. A large number of countries around the world have chosen to legalize medical marijuana. In Europe, this includes countries such as Austria, Croatia, Finland, France, Germany, Greece, Italy, North Macedonia, Poland, Romania, Slovenia and the United Kingdom.

There has also been substantial policy development by a range of states in relation to the recreational and or personal use of cannabis. In 2012, Washington and Colorado became the first two US states to allow the legal sale and use of cannabis to individuals over the age of 21. At the time of writing, this number had risen to 21 states in the United States (Montgomery and Allen 2023) In Europe, Spain and the Netherlands have adopted a policy of tolerance in relation the personal use of cannabis, while the Czech Republic and Portugal have officially decriminalized practices associated with the personal use of cannabis.

Significant policy changes have also been occurring at the international level. Following longstanding advice from the World Health Organization (WHO), in 2020 the UN removed cannabis from Schedule IV of the Single Convention on Narcotic Drugs, 1961. Schedule IV is used to categorize drugs that are not considered to have any credible therapeutic use, such as heroin (INCB 2023). However, cannabis does remain listed as a Schedule I substance which means that it is considered to be a substance with addictive properties and consequently poses a high risk of abuse.

More recently, in 2021, Malta became the first European nation to legalize the recreational use and cultivation of cannabis for people over the age of 18, and, in 2022, Thailand became the first country in Southeast Asia to decriminalize cannabis (Walden and Ford 2022). The Thai government stated that the decriminalization policy aims to support the development of agricultural and tourism industries across the country, with the government offering to give away one million cannabis plants to Thai citizens interested in developing new commercial ventures for the new domestic market (Burgess 2023). Since then, Thailand has experienced an explosion of new businesses selling cannabis products to locals and tourists.

This wave of new states adopting progressive policy approaches to the production and use of cannabis within their borders has changed the structure of illicit activity associated with the cannabis industry. The legalization of cannabis in specific areas of the United States has had a significant impact on the relationship between organized crime and the traditional illegal trade in cannabis. The price of illegal cannabis coming from Mexico into the United States began to decrease in line with the advancement of US legalization policies. The Drug Enforcement Administration (DEA 2020) noted that the legalization of cannabis in many parts of the United States has almost replaced the market for illicit cannabis from Mexico.

The above-mentioned changes in the United States have affected the business models of OCGs such as the Mexican cartels, which previously were the dominant producers and suppliers of cannabis to the US market. As Mexican cartels have increasingly moved into the production of ATS, the rural landscape of parts of Mexico that had been traditional cannabis growing regions have experienced significant upheaval. For example, the area where the states of Chihuahua, Durango and Sinaloa meet is known as Mexico's Golden Triangle and represents the traditional epicentre of Mexican drug production. However, recent research by Dudley et al. (2022, 12) suggests that farmers in the Golden Triangle are abandoning marijuana and opium poppy production in significant numbers and are instead investing in the production of 'cash crops such as tomatoes and chilis, among other fruits and vegetables.'

Despite these developments, it is important to emphasize that these changes do not mean that the industry is free from criminality. Illicit businesses are still finding opportunities in settings where legalization efforts have been strongly supported. For example, in 2021, a group of individuals in Colorado were indicted for their involvement in a marijuana cultivation and money laundering scheme (Tabachnik 2021). The group were allegedly part of a substantial operation that produced significant amounts of illicit marijuana in the city of Denver. The proceeds were directed to China through social media apps that offered access to digital wallets and QR codes to be used as part of the money laundering scheme.

Similar problems are evident in Europe, where the link between cannabis and organized crime remains of crucial concern to law enforcement across the continent. According to Europol (2023), '[e]ach year about 22 million users of cannabis spend an estimate EUR 9 billion on the drug, thus making the illicit market for it the largest of its kind in the EU.' The demand in Europe is a driving factor for illicit businesses to adopt novel inventions that aim to support the increase in the strength, quality and production of cannabis across the

European Union. These factors explain why domestically produced plants are beginning to displace imported resin in many European countries. Europol (2023) has also cited concerning links between OCGs engaged in illicit cannabis production and their increasing involvement in human trafficking. The actors responsible for these links are predominantly Albanian organized crime groups. According to the Organized Crime Index (2023), Albania has been one of the primary producers of cannabis in Europe for at least a decade and is also a hub for human trafficking in Europe.

Despite substantial changes in the way many states approach the production and use of cannabis the relationship between OCGs and cannabis industries around the world has remained intact. While state intervention through processes of decriminalization and legalization may have been a catalyst for change in certain traditional illicit markets, these policies have not managed to completely dismantle the links between the cannabis industry and illicit business. Furthermore, in many countries laws and sometimes harsh penalties remain for those producing and selling cannabis products.

Cocaine

Similar to cannabis, the coca leaf, which is the main ingredient used to produce cocaine, has a long and diverse history in South America. Its use by indigenous populations in the Andean region of South America dates back to 700 BCE (Calatayud and González 2003). However, its cultural significance was not acknowledged until much later during the era of the Incan empire. According to Peterson (1977, 18), during this period 'the plant was carefully cultivated on its own plantations, had central religious significance and became identified with the politically powerful as one of the prerogatives of rank.' When the Spanish conquistadors arrived in Latin America the use of coca was initially prohibited. However, the conquistadors soon saw the great utility of the coca leaf due to its capacity act as an effective stimulant that alleviated feelings of hunger, thirst and altitude sickness. These properties were seen as essential to maximizing the local population's capacity to work continuously in the silver and gold mines. As a result, the Spanish legalized the use of the leaf to encourage its use among the working indigenous population (Goldstein et al. 2009). The coca leaf eventually made its way to Europe, but its value to European populations did not increase until the middle of the 19th century when a German researcher developed an effective process for the extraction of the cocaine alkaloid from the coca leaf. These developments led to a surge in its popularity due to its newly acquired medicinal value as an anaesthetic. Coca's use further expanded so much so that in the late 19th and early 20th centuries it was used as an active ingredient in medicinal tonics sold in pharmacies in Europe and the United States, the most famous being early iterations of Coca-Cola®.

In the first half of the 20th century, the popularity and use of cocaine declined both medically and recreationally. Emerging research on the health impact of cocaine use overwhelmingly identified its addictive properties and potential for physical and social harm as a result of long-term use (Peterson 1977). By the early 1960s, the problems associated with a range of narcotics were seen as an international concern and global governance institutions such as the UN were formulating policies that aimed to achieve an international consensus on the management of these issues by states. This culminated in 1961 when the UN passed the Single Convention on Narcotic Drugs. The Convention acts as an international governance mechanism to control activities associated with the cultivation, production and distribution of narcotic drugs. Thereafter, cocaine and the activities of Latin American OCGs became one of the key targets of the United States' 'War on Drugs' that began in the 1970s and is still evolving today (Bagley 1988).

Latin American Organized Crime Groups

OCGs have operated in parts of Latin America since the continent gained independence from Spanish colonial rule in the 19th century. Post-independence, fledgling nations such as Colombia struggled to develop and enforce state control over significant parts of their territories which provided the opportunity for criminal groups to begin smuggling a range of items including precious stones, flora and fauna (Stone 2016). The long history of smuggling in Colombia meant that OCGs built extensive knowledge and capability in trafficking contraband from the region to external markets. This enabled such criminal groups to easily switch the base of their business models from smuggling to drug trafficking. This transition primarily occurred during the late 1960s and 1970s when the international demand for recreational drugs soared.

During the 1970s and 1980s, the production of cocaine flourished in the Andean region, and Colombia became the world's largest supplier (Cárdenas 2007). During this time, two cartels emerged as the main groups competing for control of the Colombian drug trade: Medellín and Calí. The most notable figure to emerge during this period was Pablo Escobar, the leader of the Medellín cartel. At its height during the 1980s, the Medellín cartel was the most powerful drug trafficking organization in the world. Escobar's successful business model was based on simple principles. According to Bowden (2001) the Medellín cartel adopted a strategy based on *plata o plomo* ('silver or lead'; in other words a bullet). To facilitate the cartel's activities, bribes would be offered to people in positions of power whose political, economic or societal resources were required by the cartel. While the preference was for bribes to be offered and readily accepted, the group also regularly threatened and used the 'lead' option to achieve their organizational goals (Bowden 2001). The 1989 assassination of presidential candidate Luis Carlos Galán, a liberal politician who openly opposed Escobar and the activities of drug cartels in Colombia is considered to be one of the most potent examples of the *plata o plomo* policy.

Following Galán's assassination, and in response to the growing power of Escobar and his Medellín cartel, the Colombian government established an elite organization from within the Colombian National Police, known as the Bloque de Búsqueda (Search Bloc). The Search Bloc spearheaded the Colombian government's kingpin strategy with an ultimate goal of removing Escobar from power and permanently dismantling cartel leadership (Hylton 2008). Over the course of several years, and with the assistance of members of the DEA, the Search Bloc attempted to track down and locate Escobar and other key members of the Medellín cartel. Curiously, at the same time another drug producing group was formed comprised of former associates of Escobar. It sought to weaken the cartel by targeting key members of the organization. This group was known as 'Los Pepes,' a Spanish acronym for 'the People Persecuted by Pablo Escobar.' Los Pepes worked to systematically abolish the infrastructure of Escobar's organization by targeting its remaining network of criminal associates, assassins, businesses partners and legal business interests while simultaneously funnelling actionable intelligence to the Search Bloc (Hylton 2008, 40). The confluence of these two factors played an important role in unravelling the hierarchical leadership structure of the cartel. Without its key leaders in place, the cartel's operations were significantly disrupted and the group's power severely diminished. On December 2, 1993, the Search Bloc located and killed Pablo Escobar on a rooftop in a middle-class neighbourhood of Medellín (Bowden 2001). Despite the removal of Escobar and the collapse of the Medellín cartel in the 1990s, Colombia remained the epicentre of cocaine production.

In the late 1990s, the international community determined that the Colombian state required assistance to combat the continuing impact of the cocaine illegal trade. This led to the development of Plan Colombia, a counternarcotics strategy between the United States and Colombia (Sweig 2002). Plan Colombia aimed to apply pressure on the drugs trade through a number of strategies. First, the aid package provided US training to the Colombian military, and a large portion of the funds were spent upgrading Colombian military equipment (Mejía 2016). It provided assistance to increase the Colombian military's presence in remote parts of Colombia where levels of coca production had increased. The use of aerial spraying of coca crops was introduced and local farmers were encouraged to participate in crop substitution programmes (Reyes 2014). However, these strategies did not always produce the intended outcomes. For example, criticisms emerged early on in relation to the ineffective and dangerous use of aerial spraying. While coca crops were destroyed during the aerial spraying, so too were legal crops cultivated in close proximity to the coca plantations (Veillette 2005). These problems adversely impacted local farming populations and a lack of investment in alternative development policies, such as viable crop substitution programmes, did not provide incentives to coca farmers to cease cultivation of the valuable crop (Beittel and Rosen 2019; Ramirez et al. 2004). These problems were amplified because of the nature of the cocaine supply chain.

The cocaine supply chain begins in the Andean region of South America and from there it weaves its way to every corner of the globe. It is a complex system that utilizes a range of actors to produce and transport vast quantities of the product from its home in some of the poorest parts of Latin America to some of the most affluent markets in the world. However, as with so many complex supply chains, the profits are not shared equally among all actors. For example, peasant farmers in rural parts of South America are the primary growers of raw coca leaf which is the base ingredient for the production of cocaine. However, actors operating at this end of the supply chain find themselves in a precarious position due to the monopsony in which they are trapped. The creation of monopsony, whereby there is one main buyer in a market, enables the buyer to dictate terms and strategically force price increases along the rest of the supply chain (Wainwright 2016, 17). This means that vulnerable coca farmers at the bottom of the supply chain are forced to absorb the increasing cost of doing business. Wainwright (2016, 17) explains that 'in the same way a monopolist can dictate prices to its consumers, who have no one else to buy from, a monopsonist can dictate prices to its suppliers, who have no one else to sell to.'

The absence of normal market conditions that enable acute exploitation at the bottom of the supply chain do not entirely explain why the cocaine industry has continued to expand. The role of state intervention and the unintended consequences that these interventions create must also be considered. For example, the pressure applied by the Colombian government has worked as a push factor for organized crime groups to invest in significant innovations, specifically in relation to their processing methods (Mallette et al. 2018). This has led organized crime groups to develop new methods to process coca leaves that facilitates the production of a greater amount of cocaine salts using fewer coca leaves (McDonald 2013). These types of business innovations demonstrate the way that illicit business can adapt and streamline processes that improve, in some cases substantially, their modes of production which ultimately increase their profit margins and market share of illicit industries. Such changes have led to increases in coca production, with UNODC reporting that coca cultivation grew by 35% from 2020–2021 (UNODC 2023a).

Colombian organized crime groups have also increasingly focused on supply chain management and greater efficiency in their business models rather than previous approaches that favoured territorial control and dominance over supply routes (McCarthy-Jones et al. 2020). These business decisions have significantly changed the criminal landscape in Colombia. At the height of the 'cartel' era, Colombia was consistently experiencing some of the highest homicide rates in the word (Maclean 2014). However, there has been a significant reduction in homicide rates which in part has been attributed to the shift in business acumen and the resulting strategies utilized by criminal groups (Doyle 2016). The leaders of key organizations have also changed. A phenomenon known as the 'invisibles' describes a new breed of drug boss that sits in stark contrast to the well-known images of drug kingpins such as Pablo Escobar. These individuals are owners of successful legitimate businesses in Colombia and Latin America (McDermott 2018). They are highly educated individuals, many whom have attended some of the leading tertiary education institutions in the United States. They favour collaboration over competition and have developed business models that are not founded on the use of violence (McDermott 2018). Thus, Zaitch and Antonopoulos (2019, 142) have observed that 'these trends and changes are mainly the result of the remarkable capability of criminal networks, particularly those involved in illegal drug trafficking, to learn, adapt, innovate and rebel.' In 2023, UNODC Executive Director Ghada Waly warned that significant growth in the global cocaine supply means that the 'potential for the cocaine market to expand in Africa and Asia is a dangerous reality' (UNODC 2023a).

Amphetamine-Type Stimulants

The development of ATS began during the late 19th century as an attempt to mimic the medicinal properties of Ephedra, a plant that had been a key component of Chinese medicine dating back thousands of years (Vearrier et al. 2012). The isolation of the alkaloid ephedrine in 1885 provided the impetus for the expansion a range of synthetic substitutes for Ephedra such as amphetamine and methamphetamine (Lee 2011). During the first half of the 20th century, ATS became popularized therapeutically due to their ability to treat a range of ailments including, but not limited to, respiratory problems, fatigue, obesity, hypertension, depression, colic, Parkinson's disease and epilepsy (Vearrier et al. 2012). During this early period, 'amphetamines and their analogs were being presumptively promoted as effective and safe without risk of addiction' (Vearrier et al. 2012, 40). Indeed, allied forces during World War II (most notably the British and US militaries) dispensed ATS to soldiers. At the time the mood-altering properties of ATS were considered a valuable tool to enhance the productivity, wellbeing and morale of soldiers deployed to battlefields across Europe (Rasmussen 2011). ATS were also used by the United States during the Korean War and the Vietnam War.

During the 1950s and 1960s, medical research started to investigate the individual and social harm associated with regular use of ATS. In the 1960s, the recreational use of ATS began to increase prompting policymakers, particularly in the United States, to consider the need for tighter controls. In 1971, the establishment of the UN Convention on Psychotropic Substances created the first international control system for psychotropic substances including ATS (UNODC 2023c). The Convention provided a global governance framework to augment states' attempts to prevent problems from occurring because of rapid broadening and growth of synthetic drug use (UNODC 2023c). In this climate, ATS were no longer considered a therapeutic panacea. National and international regulatory regimes swiftly became more rigorous and restrictive, causing a reduction in the legal production and distribution of ATS. However, as Cherney et al. (2005, 6) point out, 'despite a decline in licit pharmaceutical manufacture of ATS, clandestine production became the major source of global supply for ATS.'

Unlike cannabis, cocaine or heroin, the manufacture of ATS is relatively uncomplicated. It requires less resources than plant-based drugs, is lighter in weight and can be trafficked in larger quantities. Production of ATS is not geographically constrained to certain parts of the world. With the right ingredients and equipment, ATS can be manufactured anywhere. This is one of the reasons why the illicit production of ATS such as methamphetamine began with domestic production servicing domestic demand. For example, in the 1960s and 1970s, US, Canadian and Australian outlaw motorcycle gangs such as the Hell's Angels became the first OCGs to move into the illicit production of methamphetamines (Vearrier et al. 2012; Cherney et al. 2005). They constructed small-scale 'backyard' labs to produce the illicit methamphetamine that was then distributed through localized networks.

By the 1990s, increasing demand from the US, East Asian and Southeast Asian markets instigated changes in relation to the production of ATS (Broadhurst and Farrelly 2014). Established OCGs in Asia, Latin America and the Middle East began to diversify their business models that had been based on traditional illicit drugs such as heroin and cocaine. These changes began in the Golden Triangle in Southeast Asia, an area that incorporates the border areas where Myanmar, Laos, Thailand and China converge. The region has a long history of criminal activity, specifically related to smuggling and drug trafficking that can be traced back to the introduction of poppy cultivation by British colonizers in the late 19th century (Luong 2019). During the second half of the 20th century, the Golden Triangle was a key source for heroin and opium production. However, in the 1990s, significant counter-narcotics strategies reduced the poppy crops in the Golden Triangle. Criminal groups looked for other opportunities in illicit drugs and the production of ATS exploded (Broadhurst and Farrelly 2014). While ATS are produced by all the countries in the Golden Triangle, currently Myanmar is the largest single source of ATS production and trafficking (UNODC 2022a). In late 2022, the heads of National Drug Law Enforcement Agencies of Asia and the Pacific identified complex criminal networks operating in the Golden Triangle, as well as the vast expansion of methamphetamine production in Myanmar as pressing problems for policymakers and law enforcement agencies across the region (UNODC 2022a).

In 2023, UNODC's *Global Drug Report* revealed that global seizures of ATS, particularly amphetamine and methamphetamine, had dramatically increased in recent years (UNODC 2023b). However, the surge in production emanating from the Golden Triangle does not explain the dramatic increases on a global scale. Previously, UNODC identified that the synthetic drug market in East, Southeast Asia and Oceania 'is not a separate and self-contained entity, but part of a larger complex global network with interconnected channels for supply and demand' (UNODC 2015, 4). To appreciate the scope and complexity of the ATS supply chain, we must look to other productions hubs.

Over the last 20 years, Mexican OCGs have developed large-scale manufacturing capabilities to support their move into the production of ATS. This has led to the Mexican supply of ATS outpacing the demand from the US market (McCarthy-Jones 2018). The changed market conditions have also led to Mexican cartels seeking new distribution opportunities for their products as far away as Europe and the Asia-Pacific (McCarthy-Jones and Baldino 2016). However, Mexican drug trafficking organizations would not have been able to accomplish this global business expansion without assistance from other OCGs. Increasing cooperation between criminal groups operating in Latin America and Asia is key to understanding these recent developments and foremost among these actors are members of Chinese OCGs (Rotella and Berg 2022).

As Flannery and Felbab-Brown (2022, 1) explain,

> in drug trafficking, Chinese brokers are the dominant suppliers of scheduled and non-scheduled, unregulated precursor chemicals for the production of methamphetamine, fentanyl and other synthetic opioids and previously also of finished fentanyl and its analogs. Mexican drug cartels then sell fentanyl and methamphetamine throughout North America and increasingly beyond. Chinese actors also launder money for Mexican drug trafficking cartels.

Another essential element that supports these business connections is the control of, or access to, maritime resources and infrastructure. For example, the Cártel de Jalisco Nueva Generación has infiltrated Mexico's largest port Lázaro Cárdenas in Michoacán which enables it to receive precursor chemicals from China and to ship large quantities of ATS and other illicit drugs across the Pacific and onwards to markets around the world (Knobloch 2020). For example, in January 2019, the Australian, US and Mexican authorities interdicted a mega-shipment bound for Melbourne of 1.7 metric tons of crystal methamphetamine in California (ABC 2019). McCarthy-Jones (2018, 5) argues that 'the symbiotic relationship between Chinese and Mexican OCGs needs to be understood as an illicit network that enables seemingly autonomous groups to pool resources based on common interests and purpose.'

In the Middle East, another type of ATS known as Captagon has been spreading across the region in recent years. In the 1960s, Captagon was dispensed in the form of pill that could treat conditions such as attention deficit disorder and narcolepsy (Nader 2023). Captagon contains fenethylline, which has not been produced by legal pharmaceutical companies since the mid-1980s because of its inclusion in Schedule II of the UN Convention on Psychotropic Substances. Large markets for counterfeit Captagon are located in countries such as Jordan, Saudi Arabia, Kuwait and the United Arab Emirates (UAE). In 2020, the Italian authorities seized over 14 tons of Captagon that were concealed in machinery at the port of Salerno (Walsh 2020). Since then, authorities in Europe and the Middle East have continued to seize large-scale shipments of the pills. In September 2023, the UAE interdicted Captagon pills valued at over US $1 billion (Bubalo 2023). Recent reports have pointed to the role of the Syrian Arab Republic in driving the massive production of Captagon (Nader 2023; Bubalo 2023; Schwaller 2023). Alliances between Syria, members of Hezbollah and organized crime syndicates in the Middle East have developed an extensive production and distribution network that enables commercial quantities of counterfeit Captagon to be manufactured (Nader 2023). Syria's involvement in the trade in Captagon is a result of extreme economic volatility and crippling international sanctions that have been in place since the beginning of the Syrian Civil War in 2011 (Walsh 2020). In times of economic decline, the co-option of illegal industries such as drug trafficking is not new. McCarthy-Jones and Turner (2022) observed similar circumstances in Venezuela following the sharp decline in oil prices in 2014. Similarly to Syria, the Venezuelan state was motivated to move into the drug trafficking industry as a means to 'generate significant revenue for the finance-starved regime' (McCarthy-Jones and Turner 2022, 13). For now, only appears to be established in markets across the Middle East. However, the combination of state-led support for the continued large-scale production of this type of ATS means that supply may soon outstrip demand from the Middle East. As we have seen from the experiences of Mexico and North America, under these conditions criminal actors begin to look for market expansion further afield in order to keep demand for the product at pace with growing supply.

Opioids

The history of opium can be traced back to the practices of the ancient Sumerians circa late 3000 BCE (Brownstein 1993). In ancient times, opium was used in religious ceremonies to induce a state of euphoria and eventually it came to be used for medicinal purposes such as sedation and pain relief. According to Brownstein (1993), from the 10th century, opium was gradually introduced to populations in India and China by itinerant Arab merchants. During the 17th century in China, opium use, in the form of smoking, increased rapidly as a result of the prohibition of tobacco smoking. During this period, opium dens spread across China, further popularizing the recreational use of opium (Niewijk 2017). Access to this large domestic market was central for British commerce at the time. As Shelley (2018, 45) points out, '[i]llicit trade in opium became an important revenue generator for the Crown in the 19th century because it was a key export of India, Britain's most important colony.' As previously discussed in Chapter 2 in this volume, during the 19th century, the Chinese authorities' attempts to prohibit the use of opium by banning all imports thereof led to a series of trade disputes between China and Britain that ultimately culminated in the First and Second Opium Wars.

Similarly to the historical development of cocaine and ATS, during the late 19th century, chemists were able to begin isolating active ingredients from opium which led to the development of new drugs used in pharmacology such as morphine and eventually heroin. While heroin was initially hailed as an alternative to morphine for its perceived medicinal benefits, its highly addictive properties were identified shorty after its commercialization by the pharmaceutical company Bayer (UNODC 1953). In the early 20th century, the problem of heroin addiction was seen most notably in the United States and concerns over its 'street use' led to the passing of the 1914 Harrison Narcotic Act (Jones et al. 2018) The Act was intended to regulate the production and distribution of opiates and cocaine in the United States. It also proscribed doctors from dispensing opiates to patients identified as suffering from opiate addiction. At the international level, the League of Nations and subsequently the UN developed a series of policy frameworks to assist countries in controlling illicit narcotics. Since the establishment of the UN Single Convention on Narcotic Drugs in 1961, heroin has been included in Schedule IV of the Convention which categorizes drugs that are not considered to have any valid therapeutic use (INCB 2023). In the 20th century, synthetic alternatives to morphine and heroin such as methadone were created and began to be used as treatment for addiction to heroin. However, these new alternatives did not stop the illicit demand and supply of heroin.

Throughout the 20th century, the illicit cultivation of opium to produce drugs such as heroin continued to grow. Epicentres of production include Afghanistan, Southeast Asia (the majority are produced in Myanmar) and Latin America (the main production sites are in Mexico and Colombia) (ACIC 2019). Opiates originating from Afghanistan supply the overwhelming majority of global users and Afghanistan remains the largest producer of illegal opium estimated to be approximately 80% of global production (UNODC 2023b, 22). According to the UN, 'income from opiates in Afghanistan amounted to some $1.8–$2.7 billion in 2021' (UNODC 2021, 3). However, following the withdrawal of western forces and the Taliban's rapid return to power in 2021, the future of the illicit opium production in Afghanistan remains unclear. In a move that echoed its stance in the 1990s, the Taliban has again banned the production and use of opium. While this could lead to a significant reduction in opium production, thus drastically reducing the global supply, there are other issues that may emerge as a result of this prohibition. For example, over the past two decades, the Afghan economy has become increasingly reliant on revenue from the illicit production and trade of opium, something that is particularly salient to populations in rural parts of the country. Indeed, UNODC identified that 'in 2019, for example, opium poppy was cultivated in about a third of rural villages in Afghanistan and created the equivalent of roughly 190,700 full-time jobs (UNODC 2021, 10). Moreover, new reports point to the Taliban's increasing involvement in the production of methamphetamine. This shift is attributed to the highly profitable and significantly less labour-intensive production of methamphetamine when compared to the plant-based substances opium and heroin (O'Donnell 2023). These considerations continue to be driving factors in the current surge in both supply and demand for synthetic illicit drugs.

Since the development of synthetic alternatives to plant-based opiates, in the 21st century 'opioid' has become an umbrella term used in relation to natural and synthetic products. Opioids include products created with natural materials (codeine, heroin, morphine) and synthetic-based and semi-synthetic-based products such as fentanyl, methadone and oxycodone. The development of synthetic opioids and the commercial production thereof during the latter half of the 20th century led to a significant increase in opioid use. According to UNODC's *World Drug Report* (2023, 22), '[a]n estimated 60 million people used opioids in 2021, representing 1.2 per cent of the global adult population. Half of those were in South Asia or South-West Asia.'

However, in the 1990s, the misuse, overuse and abuse of opioids increased rapidly in affluent countries in North America. One of the main causes of this problem did not relate to illicit business, but instead to the relentless marketing of opioids by multinational pharmaceutical companies that encouraged the overprescription of opioid medication by doctors (LRHA 2023). Others have also pointed to systemic problems in the structure of the health system in USA that allows health insurers to favour pain relief such as oxycodone over other types of treatment as being contributing factors to the crisis. This is why oxycodone (marketed as OxyContin in North America) became the drug and brand most associated with opioid abuse (Campbell 2021). Mounting evidence of severe problems arising from addiction to oxycodone led to the introduction by Purdue Pharma (the company that manufactured and marketed OxyContin) of abuse-deterrent varieties of the opioid which were designed to make the pill more difficult to convert into powder form (Cicero and Ellis 2015). This period has been described as the first opioid epidemic or opioid crisis. The United States and Canada have implemented significant policies and programmes to address the overwhelming economic and social problems caused by the first opioid epidemic. Stronger regulations and guidelines for the medicinal use of opioids as pain relief have reduced the availability of these legal products, but this has not significantly reduced the number of users. According to Campbell (2021, 1), one of the unintended consequences of the introduction of abuse deterrents was that 'many people who were addicted to OxyContin turned to heroin, which was cheaper and easier to get. This spurred a surge in heroin-related fatal overdoses, which is often termed the second wave of the overdose crisis.' The emergence of a second opioid crisis, that began with a shift in demand to heroin, also provided an opportunity for synthetic drugs that mimic the effects of heroin to be offered on the market. However, the source of the supply that is currently meeting demand is markedly different from that which dominated the first wave.

Over the past decade the illicit production of opioids by OCGs, especially in relation to fentanyl, has surged. The United States is currently experiencing its worst opioid epidemic to date (UNODC 2023b). The majority of overdoses are linked to the use of fentanyl, which now kills around 200 Americans per day (Felbab-Brown 2023). All illicit fentanyl reaching the United State has been manufactured abroad. The vast majority of illicit fentanyl entering the United States is the result of actors operating in diverse locations such as East Asia and Latin America, particularly China and Mexico. Similar to the innovations identified in processing techniques in the cocaine industry, UNODC (2023b, 14) has recently pointed to the impact of improved synthesis routes for synthetic drugs. There is evidence that Mexican OCGs have developed substitute methods for the synthesis process used in the production of fentanyl. These methods are 'operationally easier or utilize non-controlled chemicals' (UNODC 2023b, 14).

The cooperation between Chinese and Mexican actors is central to explaining the rapid rise of the illicit supply of fentanyl. However, Felbab-Brown (2023) has identified that while this cooperation includes linkages between traditional OCGs, the network also relies heavily on individuals operating in legitimate arenas such as chemical and pharmaceutical businesses. Legal businesses, mostly located in China, manufacture precursor chemicals which are then sold to Chinese and Mexican OCGs. These groups use the precursors to create fentanyl that will be trafficked to large markets in North America and further abroad. Beyond the movement of precursors from legitimate businesses to OCGs for the purposes of illicit drug production and trafficking, the symbiotic relationship between Chinese and Mexican OCGs is based on a quid pro quo system (McCarthy-Jones 2018). This system has seen the exchange of precursor chemicals for money laundering services, shipments of cocaine and, more recently, desirable black market products such as natural timber and endangered wildlife (Felbab-Brown 2023; McCarthy-Jones 2018; South China Morning Post 2015). While the illicit production and sale of fentanyl for these groups is extremely lucrative, this represents but one part of their business models. It is well documented that traditional drug trafficking groups have expanded their activities into areas such as mining, agriculture, fisheries and transport (Cota 2023; Salvador Herrera and Martinez-Alvarez 2022; Mistler-Ferguson 2022). The diverse business portfolios of drug trafficking organizations are not just profitable for these groups. They act as a layer of protection against pressure from law enforcement agencies that still favour traditional methods that solely focus on drug interdiction. As Felbab-Brown (2023, 1) succinctly argues, the '[a]uthorities need to take aim at the traffickers' entire business empires and try to cut off their revenue streams wholesale, whether that means going after poaching and wildlife trafficking, illegal fishing, or other illicit activities.'

Conclusion

Drug trafficking remains one of the most profitable forms of illicit business. It is a global industry that impacts populations on every inhabited continent. As this chapter has demonstrated, the main types of drugs that fuel this illicit trade can be divided into four categories: cannabis, cocaine, ATS and opioids (including opiates). Apart from the recent development of synthetic-based drugs in the 20th and 21st centuries, the cultivation and use of plant-based illicit drugs in a diverse range of cultures can be traced back hundreds and even thousands of years in some cases. However, the 20th century witnessed a rapid rise in recreational drug use, especially in affluent populations around the world. Increasing demand has fuelled the supply of these substances which has precipitated the formation of a range of drug trafficking organizations in different parts of the world. While differences exist between these organizations, they all share an ability to leverage, to their best advantage, the absence of normal market conditions. Individual operators and small- to large-scale groups account for the majority of actors involved. But, as this chapter has shown, the profits to be made from the illicit manufacture of drugs is so great that even state actors will at times participate in the industry. The development and security problems caused by this industry pose significant challenges to policymakers and members of law enforcement agencies. The evolution of traditional drug trafficking organizations and the diversification of their illicit business models will continue to exacerbate these problems in the future.

References

Australian Broadcasting Corporation (ABC) (2019) 'Police allege $1.29bn "tsunami of ice" seizure shows Mexican cartels are targeting Australians.' 8 February. Available at https://www.abc.net.au/news/2019-02-08/methylamphetamine-destined-for-australia-seized-in-united-states/10792618.

Australian Criminal Intelligence Commission (ACIC) (2019) 'Illicit drug data report 2018–2019.' Available at https://www.acic.gov.au/sites/default/files/2020-09/Illicit%20Drug%20Data%20Report%202018-19_Internals_V10_Heroin%20CH.pdf.

Bagley, B.M. (1988) 'The new Hundred Years War? US national security and the War on Drugs in Latin America.' *Journal of Interamerican Studies and World Affairs* 30 (1) 161–182. doi: https://doi.org/10.2307/165793.

Beittel, J.S. and Rosen, L.W. (2019) 'Colombia's changing approach to drug policy.' *Current Politics and Economics of South and Central America* 12 (3) 413–449. Available at https://www.proquest.com/docview/2273676501?pqorigsite=gscholar&fromopenview=true.

Bonini, S.A, Premoli, M., Tambaro, S., Kumar, A., Maccarinelli, G., Memo, M. and Mastinu, A. (2018) 'Cannabis sativa: A comprehensive ethnopharmacological review of a medicinal plant with a long history.' *Journal of Ethnopharmacology* 227, 300–315. doi:doi:10.1016/j.jep.2018.09.004.

Bowden, M. (2001) *Killing Pablo*. London: Atlantic Books.

Broadhurst, R., and Farrelly, N. (2014) 'Organized crime "control" in Asia: Experiences from India, China, and the Golden Triangle.' In L. Paoli (ed.) *Oxford Handbook of Organized Crime*, pp. 634–654. Oxford: Oxford University Press.

Brownstein, M. (1993) 'A brief history of opiates, opioid peptides, and opioid receptors.' *Proceedings of the National Academy of Science USA*, 90, 5391–5393.

Bubalo, M. (2023) 'Captagon: UAE seizes billion dollar amphetamine haul.' BBC, 14 September. Available at https://www.bbc.com/news/world-middle-east-66810832.amp.

Burgess, A. (2023) 'What can Australia learn from Thailand a year after cannabis was decriminalised?' ABC News, 9 July. Available at https://www.abc.net.au/news/2023-07-09/thailand-cannabis-decriminalisation-weed-industry-australia-laws/102562846.

Calatayud, J. and González, A. (2003) 'History of the development and evolution of local anesthesia since the coca leaf,' Special Article. *Anesthesiology* 98, 1503–1508.

Campbell, E. (2021) 'OxyContin created the opioid crisis, but stigma and prohibition have fueled it.' *The Conversation*, 16 September. Available at https://theconversation.com/oxycontin-created-the-opioid-crisis-but-stigma-and-prohibition-have-fueled-it-167100.

Cárdenas, M. (2007) 'Economic growth in Colombia: A reversal of fortune?' *Ensayos Sobre Política Económica* 25 (53) 220–259.

Cherney, A., O'Reilly, J. and Grabosky, P. (2005) 'The Governance of Illicit Synthetic Drugs. NDLERF Monograph No. 9. Canberra: Australian Institute of Criminology. Available at https://www.aic.gov.au/sites/default/files/2020-05/monograph9.pdf.

Cicero, T.J. and Ellis, M.S. (2015) 'Abuse-deterrent formulations and the prescription opioid abuse epidemic in the United States: Lessons learned from OxyContin.' *JAMA Psychiatry* 72 (5) 424–430. doi:doi:10.1001/jamapsychiatry.2014.3043.

Cota, I. (2023) 'From chickens to cabs: Drug cartels expand across the Mexican economy.' *El País*, 21 September. Available at https://english.elpais.com/economy-and-business/2023-09-21/from-lemons-to-cabs-drug-cartels-expand-across-the-mexican-economy.html.

Crocq, M.A. (2020) 'History of cannabis and the endocannabinoid system.' *Dialogues in Clinical Neuroscience* 22 (3) 223–228. doi:doi:10.31887/DCNS.2020.22.3/mcrocq.

De Souza, M.R., Henriques, A.T. and Limberger, R.P. (2022) 'Medical cannabis regulation: An overview of models around the world with emphasis on the Brazilian scenario.' *Journal of Cannabis Research* 4 (33) 1–15. Available at https://doi.org/10.1186/s42238-022-00142-z.

Doyle, C. (2016) 'Explaining patterns of urban violence in Medellin, Colombia.' *Laws* 5 (1) 3–20.

Drug Enforcement Administration (DEA) (2020) '2020 National Drug Threat Assessment.' Available at https://www.dea.gov/sites/default/files/2021-02/DIR-008 21% 202020%20National%20Drug%20Threat%20Assessment_WEB.pdf.

Dudley, S., Asmann, P. and Dittmar, V. (2022) 'The end of (illegal) marijuana: What it means for criminal dynamics in Mexico.' *InSight Crime*, December. Available at https://insightcrime.org/wp-content/uploads/2022/12/The-End-of-Illegal-Marijuana-InSight-Crime-Dec-2022-2.pdf.

Europol (2023) 'Cannabis.' Available at https://www.europol.europa.eu/crime-areas-and-statistics/crime-areas/drug-trafficking/cannabis.

Felbab-Brown, V. (2023) 'Why America is struggling to stop the fentanyl epidemic: The new geopolitics of synthetic opioids.' *Foreign Affairs*, 19 May. Available at https://www.foreignaffairs.com/mexico/why-america-struggling-stop-fentanyl-epidemic.

Flannery, N.P. and Felbab-Brown, V. (2022) 'How is China involved in organized crime in Mexico?' Brookings Institute, 23 February. Available at https://www.brookings.edu/articles/how-is-china-involved-in-organized-crime-in-mexico/.

Global Initiative Against Transnational Organized Crime (GI-TOC) (2023) *Global Organized Crime Index 2023 – Albania*. Available at https://ocindex.net/assets/downloads/2023/english/ocindex_profile_albania_2023.pdf.

Goldstein R.A, DesLauriers C. and Burda, A.M. (2009) 'Cocaine: History, social implications, and toxicity – a review.' *Disease-a-Month* 55 (1) 6–38. doi:doi:10.1016/j.disamonth.2008.10.002.

Hylton, F. (2008) 'Medellín: The peace of the pacifiers.' *NACLA Report on the Americas* 41 (1) 35–42. doi:doi:10.1080/10714839.2008.11725394.

International Narcotics Control Board (INCB) (2023) 'Yellow drugs list.' Available at https://www.incb.org/incb/en/narcotic-drugs/Yellowlist/yellow-list.html.

Jones, M.R., Viswanath, O., Peck, J., Kaye, A.D., Gill, J.S. and Simopoulos, T.T. (2018) 'A brief history of the opioid epidemic and strategies for pain medicine.' *Pain Therapy* 1, 13–21. doi:doi:10.1007/s40122-018-0097-6..

Knobloch, A. (2020) 'Mexico's military to control ports in war against cartels.' *Deutsche Welle*, 10 July. Available at https://www.dw.com/en/mexicos-military-to-take-control-of-ports-in-the-war-against-cartels/a-55169773.

Lee, M.R. (2011) 'The history of ephedra (ma-huang).' *Journal of the Royal College of Physicians Edinburgh* 41 (1) 78–84. doi:doi:10.4997/JRCPE.2011.116. PMID: 21365072.

Luong, H. (2019) 'Drug production, consumption, and trafficking in the Greater Mekong Sub-Region.' *Asian Survey* 59 (4) 717–737.

Maclean, K. (2014) 'The "Medellin Miracle": The politics of crisis, elites and coalitions.' *Development Leadership Program.* Available at http://publications.dlprog.org/The% 20Medellin%20Miracle.pdf.

Mallette, J.R., Casale, J.F., Colley, V.L., Morello, D.R. and Jordan, J. (2018) 'Changes in illicit cocaine hydrochloride processing identified and revealed through multivariate analysis of cocaine signature data.' *Science and Justice* 58 (2) 90–97. doi:doi:10.1016/j.scijus.2017.12.003.

McCarthy-Jones, A. (2018) 'Brokering transnational networks: Emerging connections between organised crime groups in the Pacific and Indian Oceans.' *Journal of the Indian Ocean Region* 14 (3) 343–353.

McCarthy-Jones, A. and Baldino, D. (2016) 'Mexican drug cartels and their Australian connections: Tracking and disrupting dark networks.' *Journal of the Australian Institute of Professional Intelligence Officers* 24 (1) 19–33.

McCarthy-Jones, A., Doyle, C. and Turner, M. (2020) 'From hierarchies to networks: The organizational evolution of the international drug trade.' *International Journal of Law, Crime and Justice* 63, 100436.

McCarthy-Jones, A. and Turner, M. (2022) 'What is a "Mafia State" and how is one created?' *Policy Studies*, 43 (6) 1195–1215. Available at https://doi.org/10.1080/ 01442872.2021.2012141.

McDermott, J. (2018) 'The "Invisibles": Colombia's new generation of drug traffickers.' *InSight Crime*, 15 March. Available at https://insightcrime.org/investigations/invisi bles-colombias-new-generation-of-drug-traffickers/.

McDonald, D. (2013) 'Less coca in Colombia means nothing for your supply.' *VICE News*, 28 August. Available at https://www.vice.com/en/article/znwbqw/the-news-a bout-colombian-coca-growing-is-all-kinds-of-misleading.

Mejía, D. (2016) 'Plan Colombia: An analysis of effectiveness and costs.' *Foreign Policy at Brookings.* Available at https://www.brookings.edu/wp-content/uploads/2016/07/ Mejia-Colombia-final-2.pdf.

Mistler-Ferguson, S. (2022) 'Mexico's cartels corner the Chinese market for illegal wild-life.' *InSight Crime*, 14 April. Available at https://insightcrime.org/news/mexico-ca rtels-corner-chinese-market-for-illegal-wildlife/.

Moncada, E. (2021) 'The politics of crime in Latin America: New insights, future chal-lenges.' *Latin American Politics and Society* 63 (1) 165–173. doi:doi:10.1017/lap.2020.37.

Montgomery, B.W. and Allen, J. (2023) 'Cannabis policy in the 21st century: Mandating an equitable future and shedding the racist past.' *Clinical Therapeutics* 45 (6) 541–550.

Nader, E. (2023) 'Syria: New captagon drug trade link to top officials found.' BBC, 27 June. Available at https://www.bbc.com/news/world-middle-east-66002450.

Niewijk, G. (2017) 'Ancient analgesics: A brief history of opioids.' *Yale Scientific*, 20 January. Available at https://www.yalescientific.org/2017/01/ancient-analge sics-a-brief-history-of-opioids/.

O'Donnell, L. (2023) 'The Taliban have a new drug of choice after cornering the market on heroin, they've pivoted to a quicker and more profitable alternative.' *Foreign Policy*, 13 September. Available at https://foreignpolicy.com/2023/09/13/taliban-afgha nistan-drugs-ban-economy-opium-poppy-meth-heroin-trade/.

Peterson, R. (1977) 'The history of cocaine.' In R.C. Petersen and R.C. Stillman (eds) *Cocaine: 1977.* Monograph #13, pp. 17–34. Rockville, MD: National Institute of Drug Abuse Research. Available at https://archives.nida.nih.gov/sites/default/files/m onograph13.pdf#page=26.

Pisanti, S. and Bifulco, M. (2019) 'Medical cannabis: A plurimillenial history of an evergreen.' *Journal of Cellular Physiology* 234, 8342–8351.

Ramirez Lemus, M.C., Stanton, K. and Walsh, J. (2004) 'Colombia: A vicious circle of drugs and war.' in C. Youngers and E. Rosin (eds) *Drugs and Democracy in Latin America: The Impact of U.S. Policy.* pp. 99–142. Boulder, CO: Lynne Rienner Publishers.

Rasmussen, N. (2011) 'Medical science and the military: The Allies' use of amphetamine during World War II.' *Journal of Interdisciplinary History* 42 (2) 205–233. doi: doi:10.1162/jinh_a_00212.

Reyes, L.C. (2014) 'Estimating the causal effect of forced eradication on coca cultivation in Colombian municipalities.' *World Development* 61 (1) 70–84.

Rotella, S. and Berg, K. (2022) 'How a Chinese American gangster transformed money laundering for drug cartels.' *ProPublica*, 11 October. Available at https://www.prop ublica.org/article/china-cartels-xizhi-li-money-laundering.

Salvador Herrera, J. and Martinez-Alvarez, C. (2022) 'Diversifying violence: Mining, export-agriculture, and criminal governance in Mexico.' *World Development* 151, 105769.

Schwaller, F. (2023) 'Captagon: The little white pill fuelling Syria's drug trade.' *Deutscher Welle*, 19 September. Available at https://www.dw.com/en/captagon-the-little-white-pill-fueling-syrias-drug-trade/a-66814328.

Shelley, L. (2018) *Dark Commerce: How a New Illicit Economy is Threatening our Future.* Princeton, NJ: Princeton University Press.

South China Morning Post (2015) 'How Mexican drug cartels have infiltrated Hong Kong.' 8 April . Available at http://www.scmp.com/news/hong-kong/article/1759760/how-mexican-drug-cartels-are-moving-hong-kong.

Stone, H. (2016) 'Organized crime and elites in Colombia: An InSight Crime report.' *InSight Crime*, 18 August. Available at https://www.opendemocracy.net/en/democra ciaabierta/organized-crime-and-elites-in-colombia-insightcrime-report/.

Sweig, J.E. (2002) 'What kind of war for Colombia?' *Foreign Affairs* 81 (5) 122–141.

Tabachnik, S. (2021) '21 indicted in Colorado in connection with international black market marijuana and money laundering scheme.' *Denver Post*, 10 June. Available at https://www. denverpost.com/2021/06/10/black-market-marijuana-money-laundering-indictment/.

The Lancet Regional Heath – Americas (LRHA) (2023) 'Opioid crisis: Addiction, over-prescription, and insufficient primary prevention .' Editorial (23) 100557. Available at https://www.sciencedirect.com/science/article/pii/S2667193X2300131X?via%3Dihub.

United Nations Office of Drugs and Crime (UNODC) (1953) 'History of heroin.' Available at https://www.unodc.org/unodc/en/data-and-analysis/bulletin/bulletin_1953-01-01_2_pa ge004.html#s0002.

United Nations Office of Drugs and Crime (UNODC) (2015) *The Challenge of Synthetic Drugs in East and South-East Asia and Oceania.* Vienna: UNODC. Available at http:// www.unodc.org/documents/southeastasiaandpacific/Publications/2015/drugs/ATS_2015_ Report_web.pdf.

United Nations Office of Drugs and Crime (UNODC) (2016) *Terminology and Information on Drugs*, 3rd edition. New York: United Nations Publications. Available at https:// www.unodc.org/documents/scientific/Terminology_and_Information_on_Drugs-E_3rd_ edition.pdf.

United Nations Office of Drugs and Crime (UNODC) (2021) 'Drug situation in Afghanistan in 2021: Latest findings and emerging threats.' November. Available at https://www. unodc.org/documents/data-and-analysis/Afghanistan/Afghanistan_brief_Nov_2021.pdf.

United Nations Office of Drugs and Crime (UNODC) (2022a) 'Asia Pacific drug law enforcement agencies review the drug situation and discuss strategies to respond.' UNODC Regional Office for Southeast Asia and the Pacific, 22 October. Available at https://www.unodc.org/roseap/2022/11/honlea/story.html.

United Nations Office of Drugs and Crime (UNODC) (2022b) *UN World Drug Report 2022*. Available at https://www.unodc.org/unodc/data-and-analysis/world-drug-report-2022.html.

United Nations Office of Drugs and Crime (UNODC) (2023a) 'Cocaine trafficking diversifying through new hubs and groups, with global supply at record levels, says new report from the United Nations Office on Drugs and Crime.' 16 March. Available at https://www.unodc.org/unodc/frontpage/2023/March/cocaine-traffick ing-diversifying-through-new-hubs-and-groups–with-global-supply-at-record-levels–sa ys-new-report-from-the-united-nations-office-on-drugs-and-crime.html.

United Nations Office of Drugs and Crime (UNODC) (2023b) 'Global drug report: Special points of interest.' Available at https://www.unodc.org/res/WDR-2023/Special_ Points_WDR2023_web_DP.pdf.

United Nations Office of Drugs and Crime (UNODC) (2023c) 'Convention on psychotropic substances 1971.' Available at https://www.unodc.org/unodc/en/treaties/psychotropics.html.

UN News (2020) 'UN commission reclassifies cannabis, yet still considered harmful.' 2 December. Available at https://news.un.org/en/story/2020/12/1079132.

Vearrier, D., Greenberg, M.I., Miller, S.N., Okaneku, J.T. and Haggerty, D.A. (2012) 'Methamphetamine: History, pathophysiology, adverse health effects, current trends, and hazards associated with the clandestine manufacture of methamphetamine.' *Disease-a-Month* 58 (2) 38–89. Available at https://fyi.org.nz/request/7967/response/25733/a ttach/8/Vearrier%20et%20al%202012.pdf.

Veillette, C. (2005) 'Plan Colombia: A progress report.' Library of Congress, Congressional Information Service, 17 February. Available at https://apps.dtic.mil/sti/pdfs/ ADA573962.pdf.

Wainwright, T. (2016) *Narconomics: How to Run a Drug Cartel*. London: Ebury Press.

Walden, M. and Ford, M. (2022) 'Thailand removes cannabis from narcotics list, decriminalises growing plants at home.' ABC News, 9 June. Available at https://www.abc.net. au/news/2022-06-09/thailand-cannabis-reform-one-million-marijuana-plants/101132734.

Walsh, M. (2020) 'What is the drug captagon and how is it linked to the Islamic State Group and a drug bust in Italy?' ABC News, 2 July. Available at https://www.abc.net.au/news/ 2020-07-02/italy-drug-bust-captagon-how-is-it-linked-to-islamic-state/12414804.

Zaitch, D. and Antonopoulos, G.A. (2019) 'Organised crime in Latin America: An introduction to the special issue.' *Trends in Organized Crime* 22 (2) 141–147.

6

THE ARMS TRAFFICKING BUSINESS

Introduction

Arms trafficking is a broad term that encompasses a range of activities associated with the illegal acquisition, sale, purchase, transport (import/export) and distribution of weaponry. Arms trafficking usually describes the illegal sale of small arms and light weapons. The illicit trade in arms is not considered to be one of the most profitable forms of illicit business when compared to other global industries such as human trafficking or drug trafficking. However, this specific illicit business produces a cascading effect that threatens state capacity in some of the most fragile parts of the world. This is because arms trafficking is used by individuals, groups and sometimes states as a means to challenge, change and/or claim power over populations and territories. Its effects distort the fundamental building blocks of peace and stability by weakening rule of law and threatening internal security arrangements that act as safeguards for democratic processes. Further complicating matters is that arms trafficking intersects with a range of other illicit industries. According to Mackenzie (2020, 90),

> the use of guns is ancillary to many illegal trades … Arms are present throughout drug trafficking and trade, in human trafficking, in the conflict that generates conflict diamonds, in the poaching stage of the wildlife trade and in a few cases, although it is not the norm, in antiquities looting such as the recent depredations in Iraq and Syria by ISIS [Islamic State of Iraq and the Levant].

Arms trafficking involves a 'multifaceted web of sellers, brokers, intermediaries, financiers and shipping companies' (Rothe and Ross 2015, 392). Foremost among these actors and central to the success of many arms trafficking schemes

DOI: 10.4324/9781003293620-6

are individuals known as arms dealers or brokers. These individuals are the bridges that link buyers to sellers located in disparate parts of the world. They facilitate and/or are responsible for sourcing arms and munitions, transporting the contraband across vast, challenging geographical distances and ensuring the quality and condition of the goods upon delivery to their destination.

In this chapter, we will present a brief history of arms trafficking before examining the proliferation of arms trafficking from the 20th century to the present day. Specifically, this chapter will analyse the illicit business activities of Viktor Bout, a prolific arms trafficker during the 1990s and early 2000s, and the impact that his business had on fuelling instability and conflict in Africa and other parts of the world. He has been a pivotal figure in the development of arms trafficking. The chapter then considers more contemporary examples of arms trafficking in diverse locations such as Mexico and Ukraine.

A Brief History of Arms Trafficking

The history of arms trafficking can be traced back to the 16th century when European merchants trafficked arms to buyers in the African, American and Asian continents (Grant 2015). The spread of arms and ammunitions across the world can also be attributed to the impact of European colonization in the proceeding centuries. Since these early beginnings, arms trafficking has continued to grow, experiencing significant expansion during the Industrial Revolution, the Cold War and the post-Cold War era. This expansion created a pressing need for states to develop regulatory frameworks to control the production and flows of arms, both legal and illegal, in all corners of the world. So, at the beginning of the 21st century a suite of treaties, protocols and conventions were drawn up including the Arms Trade Treaty, the Firearms Protocol, the Programme of Action on the Illicit Trade in Small Arms and the United Nations (UN) Register of Conventional Arms (UN 2023a).

Despite significant steps to control and monitor licit and illicit flows, the trade and trafficking of arms in the 21st century remains an opaque industry. This is because much of the trade and trafficking occurs in 'shadow worlds' that house 'black and grey markets' (Feinstein and Holden 2014, 446). While black markets describe profit-driven commerce controlled by criminals that occurs outside of the state's control and therefore is considered illegal in its entirety, grey markets encompass sales and purchases that involve representatives of a government, or, in other words, state-sponsored forms of arms trafficking (Arsovska and Kostakos 2008; Feinstein and Holden 2014). Legal transactions for arms involve the use of a document called an end-user certificate which identifies the buyer (Schmidle 2014). The grey market takes over when weapons are transferred from a legitimate buyer to countries or militant groups that have been placed under sanctions. This often involves forging end-user certificates.

During the Cold War, the practice of arms trafficking via grey markets became public knowledge because of the Iran–Contra Affair in the 1980s when senior officials from the United States used grey markets to broker a clandestine 'weapons for cash' deal with Iran. At the time the United States was attempting to negotiate the release of US hostages and it was thought that the deal might assist the United States's bargaining position. However, during this period, Iran was the subject of an arms embargo (established by the United States), thereby making it illegal for US officials to engage in such trade (Parry and Kornbluh 1988). Once the agreement with Iran was made, US officials doubled down when they diverted a significant portion of the money from the deal to support an armed group known as the Contras whose members were fighting an internal war against the left-wing Sandinista government in Nicaragua. The monetary support for the Contras was illegal and politically disastrous for the Reagan Administration because the US Congress, through the introduction of the Boland Amendments, had explicitly proscribed US government funding for the Contras (Fisher 1989). The Iran–Contra Affair exposed the way in which states may choose to involve themselves in shady or illegal arms deals when it suits their own broader interests, thus demonstrating some of the inherent problems that underpin attempts at arms control.

In the late 1980s, the sudden and unexpected end of the Cold War unleashed further challenges for global arms control. The collapse of the Soviet Union in 1991 created a vacuum in many former satellite countries whereby 'vast numbers of light weapons were released from controls and entered the international arms market' (Grant 2015, 87). The decades-long military competition between the Soviet Union and the United States created a surplus of arms because both nations had adopted policies that favoured stockpiling weapons and munitions during the conflict. The dissolution of the Soviet Union afforded unparalleled opportunities for individuals and groups operating in black and grey markets seeking to expand their interests in arms trafficking (Mackenzie 2020). In the early 1990s, stockpiles of light arms from the Soviet Union, particularly AK-47 rifles, became the main source of a new wave of trafficking that aimed to meet demand emanating from new conflicts emerging in the post-Cold War era. This situation provided an entrepreneurial individual named Viktor Bout with the opportunity to became one of the most prolific arms traffickers and 'shadow facilitators' in the 1990s and early 2000s (Farah 2013). His illicit business enabled thousands of arms to be trafficked to the African continent to be used in localized conflicts.

Post-Cold War Arms Trafficking and Viktor Bout

To this day, Viktor Bout remains an elusive individual due to the multiple legends that have sprung up about him and mask his true origins and identity. While various claims have been made about Bout's birthplace that cite countries including Ukraine and Turkmenistan, the most popular narrative is that he was born between 1963–1967 in Dushanbe, Tajikistan, which at the time was part of the Soviet Union (Feinstein and Holden 2014; Farah and Braun 2006). While studying at the Soviet Union's Military Institute for Foreign Languages Bout became an accomplished linguist who was fluent in multiple languages (Farah and Braun 2006). His advanced language skills were integral to the way in which he was able to develop a foothold in key illicit markets across multiple countries in the African, Asian, European and American continents.

According to Verloy (2002), Bout's network operated in places as varied as Afghanistan, Angola, Cameroon, the Central African Republic, Congo, Equatorial Guinea, Kenya, Liberia, Libya, Congo-Brazzaville, Pakistan, the Philippines, Rwanda, Sierra Leone, South Africa, Sudan, Swaziland, the United Arab Emirates and Uganda. Indeed, when he was finally captured in 2008 during a US-led covert operation in Thailand, Bout was attempting to close a deal with a group of individuals he thought were Colombian guerillas from the Revolutionary Armed Forces of Colombia (Fuerzas Armadas Revolucionarias de Colombia – FARC) (BBC 2012). The US Department of Justice (DOJ 2011, 1) stated that during the discussions 'Bout agreed to sell to the FARC millions of dollars' worth of weapons – including 800 surface-to-air missiles (SAMs), 30,000 AK-47 firearms, 10 million rounds of ammunition, five tons of C-4 plastic explosives, "ultralight" airplanes outfitted with grenade launchers and unmanned aerial vehicles,' which made this one of the largest deals ever attempted by Bout. So, how did this particular individual build up an arms trafficking empire that was so prolific and damaging that he became known as 'the Merchant of Death'?

Early on, Bout demonstrated a cunning business acumen and an uncanny ability to identify business opportunities in volatile environments. In the aftermath of the collapse of the Soviet Union, Bout obtained a collection of heavily discounted large transport planes from former Soviet military officials that enabled him to launch an international air freight business (Feinstein and Holden 2014). He used his air freight business as a legal cover and logistical support for his burgeoning arms trafficking business. According to Farah and Braun (2006, 55),

> Bout's initial stock in trade was the supply of guns and ammunition abandoned in arsenals around the former Soviet bloc. Many had airstrips built inside their compounds, making loading easy. Guards were often unpaid and their commanders were willing to sell the weapons for a fraction of the market value. This availability of weapons was married to an instant clientele of former Soviet clients, unstable governments, dictators, warlords, and guerilla armies clamoring for steady supplies across Africa, Asia, and Latin America.

By the mid-1990s, Bout had expanded his business dealings to the African continent. Here he carved out a large part of the African market for illegal weapons and set about supplying both state and non-state actors in the region. To achieve this, Bout invested heavily in creating important scaffolding to support his illicit business such as the sophisticated use of 'front companies' and localized complex aircraft registries to disguise his arms trafficking operations (Feinstein and Holden 2014). Moreover, his business model was largely built upon close relations with people in positions of power in fragile or weak states. These relationships enabled Bout to easily obtain formal government documentation from a range of countries which were used to give the appearance that Bout's activities were legitimate. For example, Bout successfully developed personal and professional relationships with a range of African leaders which included rebel leader Jonas Savimbi of the União Nacional para a Independência Total de Angola (UNITA – National Union for the Total Independence of Angola), President Charles Taylor of Liberia, President Mobutu of Zaire, President Muammar Gaddafi of Libya and leader of the Mouvement de Libération du Congo (Congolese Liberation Front) Jean-Pierre Bemba (Verloy 2002).

Farah (2013) has described Bout as a 'shadow facilitator' who worked in conjunction with networks of 'super fixers' and more localized 'fixers' in weak states. As a facilitator, Bout regularly used his connections in Russia and former Soviet states to source the majority of arms for his deals. For example, due to a large stockpile of arms, Ukraine became a primary target for the large-scale diversion of legal arms to the black market, as did Bulgaria which at the time was described as an 'Aladdin's cave' for arms dealers (Phythian 2000, 31). It is therefore unsurprising that these locations became key points for the expansion of post-Cold War arms trafficking networks (Feinstein and Holden 2014).

Aside from complex legal structures that protected his international freight business, Bout proved to be very adept at cultivating strong relationships that could provide him with a high level of protection from international law enforcement agencies. For example, from the outset, Bout maintained strong relationships with members of Russia's intelligence agencies which is thought to be one of the reasons why he was able to evade capture for so long (Farah 2013). However, another factor that provided a significant layer of protection to Bout and his businesses was the simple fact that, operating parallel to his arms trafficking business, Bout had created an almost unrivalled international transport and delivery service for legitimate goods that operated across multiple continents.

The logistics and infrastructure of Bout's network of companies were considered so effective that on occasion it was used by the UN to transport peace-keepers in Africa as well as by the United States during the early phase of the invasion of Iraq (Farah 2013). His adoption of network forms of organization also provided a high level of flexibility and moveability for the base of his business empire. For example, Bout's initial base was in Belgium. But, when the authorities there began to investigate his flights into war-torn African countries, Bout simply moved to the United Arab Emirates, then to South Africa and ultimately to Moscow, Russian Federation (Keefe 2013). He continued to evade the authorities until his arrest in Thailand in 2008. He was eventually extradited to the United States and, in 2011, he was convicted of conspiring to kill

Americans and to provide material support to terrorists (DOJ 2011). Bout served his jail sentence in the United States until 2022 when he was unexpectedly released as part of a prisoner swap between the United States and Russia.

During the 1990s and early 2000s, Bout developed a novel illicit business model that relied on a complex network of 'protectors and collaborators' that enabled Bout and his associates to generate large profits based on the exploitation of vulnerable populations in the developing world (Feinstein and Holden 2014, 452). The cascading effect of Bout's activities in Africa is best demonstrated by the intersections between arms trafficking and the illicit trade in conflict diamonds that emerged during this time.

Diamonds and Conflict

The discovery of large quantities of diamonds in South Africa in the late 19th century created the possibility that the market for precious stones could become awash with diamonds. Initially, competition between the owners of the newly discovered mines in the Kimberly region of South Africa increased the supply of diamonds which in turn led to a decrease in the value of the precious stone. To mitigate this problem, Cecil Rhodes and Barney Barnato, the owners of the two largest diamond operations decided to consolidate their companies in 1888 (De Beers 2024). The consolidation of the companies enabled the launch of a South African cartel named De Beers Consolidated Mines Limited – commonly known as De Beers. This business strategy set the course for the company's control over all facets of the diamond trade in the ensuing decades, so much so that by the end of the 20th century the De Beers cartel controlled 75% of the rough diamond trade (Bergenstock and Maskulka 2001, 38). De Beers' main goal was to control supply in the diamond trade so that the company could increase demand for its product despite the excess of supply. To achieve this De Beers developed a business strategy based on the idea that diamonds should be promoted as being scarce and therefore inherently valuable (Bergenstock and Maskulka 2001).

In the late 1940s, De Beers engaged N.W. Ayer & Son to devise an advertising campaign for its diamonds. The company developed the slogan that De Beers has used ever since: 'A Diamond Is Forever' (Rarick and Angriawan 2017). This campaign was so successful that it fundamentally changed consumer behaviour in large markets such as the United States and most major economies in the world and cemented the diamond as overwhelmingly the stone of choice to be used in an engagement ring (Friedman 2015). The success of De Beers' marketing campaign which led to the general increase in demand for diamonds during the latter half of the 20th century had unforeseen and far-reaching consequences in the developing world, and was most acutely felt on the African continent. Towards the end of the 20th century, the use of diamonds by various armed groups to drive conflict in parts of Africa became a key concern for the international community. These types of diamonds became known as 'conflict' or 'blood' diamonds.

According to Resolution 55/66 (UN General Assembly 2001, 1) 'conflict diamonds are rough diamonds used by rebel movements or their allies to finance conflict aimed at undermining legitimate governments.' Conflict or blood diamonds have become synonymous with the exploitation of the diamond industry to fund insurgencies and civil conflicts in Africa. At its peak, the illicit trade in conflict diamonds occurred most notably in Angola, Liberia and Sierra Leone. According to Olsson (2007, 268), 'fighting over diamond deposits is believed to have been an important reason for the initiation, maintenance and prolonging of civil unrest in Angola, Sierra Leone and Liberia.'

Between 1989 and 2003, Liberia experienced protracted conflict in the form of two civil wars. During this period, Charles Taylor, leader of the National Patriotic Front of Liberia (1989–1996) during the first war and President of Liberia (1997–2003) during the second war, emerged as a key actor in both conflicts (Bøås 2005). Despite sanctions and bans on weapons sales to Liberia, Taylor was able to ameliorate the impact of these sanctions through his association with Viktor Bout. Through his business relationship with Bout, Taylor secured unfettered access to a regular supply of arms in exchange for diamonds (Stohl and Yousif 2022). Under Taylor's leadership, the trade in conflict diamonds exploded and Liberia became a 'major centre for diamond-related criminal activity' (Smillie 2000, 26). Moreover, Taylor's consolidation of power in Liberia caused a spillover effect in the region whereby he used his position to support the activities of armed groups engaged in conflict outside of Liberia such as the Revolutionary United Front (RUF) in Sierra Leone.

In Sierra Leone, the RUF waged a decade-long war that killed an estimated 75,000 people (Smillie 2000, 24). During the conflict, the RUF established almost total control of Sierra Leone's diamond mines. It has been estimated that during the conflict the RUF raised approximately US $120 million each year from the sale of conflict diamonds (Davidson 2016, 44). Importantly, the support the RUF received from Liberia was crucial to its ability to wage war. Charles Taylor used his position as President of Liberia to provide the RUF with a range of arms and munitions, tactical support, intelligence and ongoing access to a black market where the RUF could use conflict diamonds as a currency for exchange (Davidson 2016). Taylor's influence and support was instrumental to the RUF's ability to maintain control of the diamond mines in Sierra Leone and perpetrate large-scale human rights violations against its citizenry, including the use of child soldiers in the conflict (see Box 6.1). In many cases, shipments of arms from Viktor Bout that were delivered to Charles Taylor in Liberia and then sold on to the RUF usually preceded the worst atrocities committed by the RUF against the civilian population in Sierra Leone (Solash 2010). As Smillie (2000, 26) points out, Taylor's interests in Sierra Leone were complex and varied because he 'acted as banker, trainer and mentor to the RUF' until he fell from power in 2003. In 2012, Taylor was convicted of war crimes and crimes against humanity owing to his support of the RUF and involvement in the conflict in Sierra Leone. However, these two nations were not the only examples of Bout's African clientele.

BOX 6.1 CHILD SOLDIERS

The term child soldier refers to the recruitment and deployment of children in armed conflicts around the world. The use of child soldiers has been documented in diverse locations including, but not limited to, Afghanistan, Myanmar, Chad, Colombia, the Democratic Republic of the Congo, the Philippines, Somalia, Sudan and Yemen. Not only are child soldiers used on the battlefield, they are sometimes used as scouts for intelligence gathering activities and reconnaissance. However, they also perform vital day-to-day activities such as meal preparation, transportation of baggage and equipment and delivering communications between the battlefield and protected positions. They are also subjected to ongoing sexual abuse and exploitation. The recruitment of child soldiers can be explained by push and pull factors. Push factors include instances of forced abduction, threats, coercion or manipulation by armed actors. Push factors refer to issues such as unstable or abusive home environments, extreme poverty, the expectation that a child should provide an income for their family and/or community, or even act as a protector of their community by enlisting. Despite the range of differing circumstances and specific motivations that may cause a child to become a soldier in conflict, the fact remains that any recruitment or use of children in conflict is an extreme violation of the rights of a child and is in contravention of international humanitarian law.

Source: UNICEF (2024).

In the 1990s, Bout brokered lucrative contracts to supply arms to the Angolan government which was engaged in a civil war with the rebel grouping known as UNITA. However, as the conflict progressed, Bout made the unusual decision to also supply arms to UNITA. So, how did UNITA convince the supplier of arms to its enemy, the Angolan government, to also supply their rebel group? This is the story of how one group's unique illicit business model made diamonds the currency of conflict during the Angolan civil war.

Between 1975 and 2002, Angola experienced over two decades of almost continuous conflict that was punctuated with short periods of fragile peace. The initial conflict began when Angola gained independence from Portugal in 1975. The main actors in the conflict were the communist aligned Movimento Popular de Libertação de Angola (MPLA – People's Movement for the Liberation of Angola), which eventually went on to form a government in Angola, and the anti-communist UNITA. By the early 1990s, the international community was taking an active role in attempting to broker peace in the nation. In 1994, the Lusaka Protocol was signed by the Angolan government and representatives of UNITA. The protocol included a ceasefire between both sides and a requirement for UNITA members to disarm and reintegrate back into Angolan society (Howard 2016). Importantly, the protocol also prohibited both sides from purchasing and importing foreign arms into

Angola. Despite this, both sides continued to acquire arms from diverse locations such as Bulgaria, the Czech Republic, India, Kazakhstan, Slovakia and
Ukraine (Phythian 2000). In 1997, the UN imposed sanctions on the sale of
arms to UNITA, and, in 1998, UNITA recommenced hostilities which led to
the resumption of the civil war.

In a bid to quell the violence, the UN Security Council swiftly passed a series
of resolutions and imposed further sanctions on UNITA. A key development in
the sanction regime was the introduction of government certificates to be supplied as a requirement for any transaction involving Angolan diamonds (Bone
2004). This was intended to prevent UNITA from using diamonds as a source
of funding. Despite these measures, it became evident that UNITA had developed a strategy to bypass UN sanctions. The UN sent a team led by Canada's
permanent representative Robert Fowler to investigate. The 2000 Fowler Report
uncovered what amounted to a blueprint of an illicit business. The report
demonstrated how conflict diamonds interfaced with arms trafficking to
empower specific groups engaged in conflict in the region using collaborators,
facilitators and representatives from specific companies and governments in
Africa (Power 2001).

During the Cold War, UNITA's anti-communist stance had led to substantial
funding from countries such as the United States, but, by the late 1990s, international sources of funding for UNITA had all but disappeared (Hoekstra
2018). This is why diamonds became the backbone of UNITA's political and
military economy. Beyond the sale of rough diamonds for cash and exchanging
rough diamonds for weapons and supplies for its army of soldiers, diamonds
were an important component of UNITA's strategy for acquiring friends and
maintaining external support (Pearce 2004). Stores of rough diamonds rather
than cash or bank deposits constituted the preferred means of stockpiling
wealth for UNITA. This approach protected the organization from problems
such as asset confiscation which at the time formed part of the sanctions
imposed by the international community (Power 2001).

For UNITA diamonds were an exceptionally valuable commodity because of
their durability, small weight and size, extremely high value and large global
demand. Furthermore, the portability and convertibility of diamonds meant that
arms dealers such as Viktor Bout were more than happy to accept diamonds as
payment for large shipments of arms. For example, in exchange for diamonds,
Bout and his associates supplied UNITA with a range of items including rocket-
propelled grenades and launchers, small arms (predominately AK-47s), mortars
and armoured transport vehicles (Schmidle 2014). As Sherman (2000, 700) points
out, 'profiting from illicit trade, organizations such as UNITA navigate their way
around sanctions, customs and other barriers in the incessant pursuit of weapons
and material. The end result is the prolongation of violence.'

The Fowler Report's focus on UNITA and conflict in Angola outlined in
detail the way in which diamonds had become the currency of conflict in Africa.
It demonstrated the way the trinity of arms, diamonds and conflict had formed

in parts of the African continent with devastating consequences for civilian populations. Importantly, the report named and shamed countries, groups and key individuals involved in the trade. At the time, a combination of the issues identified in the Fowler Report and the ongoing conflicts in Angola, Liberia and Sierra Leone prompted the international community to devise a plan to combat the flow and sale of rough diamonds from conflict zones. This became known as the Kimberley Process (see Box 6.2).

BOX 6.2 THE KIMBERLY PROCESS

The Kimberley Process is a multilateral control process that seeks to prevent conflict diamonds from entering the international market for rough diamonds. The central component of the Kimberly Process has been the establishment and implementation of the Kimberley Process Certification Scheme (KPCS). The scheme requires states to adhere to a system of internal controls that support the confirmation and certification that shipments of rough diamonds for export or import are considered as 'conflict free.' Legal shipments of conflict-free diamonds will be accompanied by a Kimberly Process Certificate that distinguishes a shipment of rough diamonds as meeting the requirements of the certification scheme. Since its inception in 2003, the KPCS has prevented 99.8% of the tide in conflict diamonds.

Source: Kimberly Process (2024).

Arms Trafficking in the 21st Century

In the 21st century, arms trafficking remains a pervasive problem. 'In many parts of the globe, small arms, and not nuclear, biological or chemical weapons, are today the principal source of threat to governments and their peoples' (Banerjee and Muggah 2002, 5). This is why the UN has warned that arms trafficking continues to undermine peace and security in many parts of the world (UN 2021). Lax regulations, inconsistent monitoring and enforcement, porous borders and a multitude of profit-driven actors combine to create permissive conditions than enable the supply of arms to some of the most unstable and insecure locations on the planet. The UN Office on Drugs and Crime (UNODC 2023, 4) highlights that contemporary

> [f]irearms trafficking does not happen in a vacuum but is driven by supply and demand. On the supply side, illicit firearms, their parts and components and ammunition have a price-tag. For criminals and trafficking networks involved in their distribution, they are lucrative trafficking commodities. In contrast, those that purchase illicit firearms need them as tools to perpetrate power and undermine the rule of law and local government as well as facilitators of violent crime and terrorism. As such illicit

firearms are intrinsically linked to the activities of petty criminals, organized criminal groups and terrorists.

Illicit arms trafficking disproportionately augments the power of non-state actors, which leads to increases in conflict that cause the displacement of vulnerable populations and ultimately reduces human security in a nation. This cascading effect is most evident in the case of Mexico. Since 2010, over 2.5 million weapons have been illegally trafficked into Mexico (Medina 2020, 13). Many of the weapons and ammunition that are smuggled into Mexico are transported by individuals hidden among the significant movement of people that occurs daily at crossings on the US–Mexico border. Many of these weapons 'mules' are individuals who travel to the United States from Mexico to purchase everyday items such as white goods that can be used to conceal arms on the return journey to Mexico. In other cases, the weapons are transported by individuals who have legitimate reasons to cross the border frequently due to employment on infrastructure projects in border areas (Grillo cited in NPR 2022).

There is also a symbiotic relationship between the problem of illegal drugs moving north from Mexico into the United States and the large flow of illegal arms moving south from the United States into Mexico. Experts on cartel violence in Mexico have argued that 'the same criminal networks that are moving huge amounts of drugs into the United States are also taking these guns south' (Grillo cited in NPR 2022, 1). In many cases the cartels employ the use of 'straw men' or 'straw purchases' to acquire weapons. A straw man is someone who legally purchases arms from gun shows or private sellers on behalf of another person or organization and is therefore complicit in the diversion of legally purchased firearms (Hureau and Braga 2018). In the same vein, straw purchases can be viewed as a tactic whereby

> [an] individual with a clean criminal record buys a firearm from a licensed outlet, quite possibly without violating any laws in so doing, precisely with the intention of selling it either on the black market (in the same country or not) or to a pre-determined buyer who would otherwise not be eligible to own such a firearm.
>
> *(UNODC 2020, 2)*

To ensure that straw purchases made on behalf of criminal organizations reach their intended destination in Mexico, specific strategies have been developed to take advantage of the geographical proximity to the largest arms market in the world, namely the United States. These patterns of trafficking across the US–Mexico border, have been described by the UNODC (2020, 11) as 'strategic "ant trafficking," whereby many people transport weapons in small consignments to meet large-scale demand and reduce the risk of disruption by law enforcement' (UNODC 2020, 11). The impact of arms trafficking into Mexico is significant. Mexico continues to have one the highest homicide rates in the world, hovering at around 30,000 homicides per year since 2017 (InSight Crime 2024), and according to Medina (2020) homicides in Latin America and the Caribbean are overwhelmingly – approximately 70% – the result of the use of firearms. The reinforcing nature of the relationship between drug trafficking and arms trafficking means that as drug trafficking organizations seek to expand their share of the drug market, they simultaneously create a greater need to acquire arms to protect their product, supply routes and market share. This presents a conundrum in that it is difficult to see how this cycle can be broken when one of the largest drug-producing countries in the world is the neighbour of the largest arms producer in the world.

In the 21st century, the causal links between conflict zones and increases in illicit arms trafficking to specific parts of the world remain. This phenomenon can be seen through the example of the Russian invasion of Ukraine in early 2022. The Russian Federation's decision to invade Ukraine reignited conflict between both countries which had previously erupted in 2014 when Russia annexed Crimea and supported pro-Russian separatists in the eastern and southern parts of Ukraine. These events placed Ukraine as a new hotspot for illegal arms trafficking (Kehoe Down 2018).

Unlike Ukraine's experience in the aftermath the Cold War, when large amounts of arms flowed out of the country destined for use in conflicts abroad, the ongoing conflict between Russia and Ukraine has reversed the flow of arms back into the country. For example, in 2024, the Stockholm International Peace Research Institute confirmed that during the period 2019–2023, Ukraine became the largest importer of arms in Europe and the fourth largest in the world owing to military contributions from allied states since February 2022. Beyond the supply of lethal weapons, the United States and the European Union has been active in their support of Ukraine to establish monitoring systems to assist with the security and accountability of the unprecedented number of arms arriving in the Ukraine (GI-TOC 2023; Mills 2024). Despite this, the diversion of small weapons and light arms as a result of the current conflict in Ukraine is a problem that could reoccur in the future. In 2023, the Global Initiative on Transnational Organized Crime (GI-TOC 2023, 272) warned that:

> Collectively, the rise in untracked, misappropriated, and found weapons will play into the hands of criminals assembling illicit stockpiles for exploitation at a later date when the fighting is not so intense and the ambit for arms trafficking expands, as occurred when the fighting in 2014 settled into a stalemate.

Russia's isolation from large parts of the international community has also impacted its traditional sources of weapons supply, creating opportunities to seek out weaponry from pariah states such as the Democratic People's Republic of Korea (North Korea) and Iran. Russia's flagrant disregard for the rules and conventions established by global bodies to which it claims membership demonstrates the continuing difficulties in maintaining a high level of integrity in efforts to control global arms flows. These complexities were on show during a meeting of the UN Security Council in April 2023 when the United States accused Russia of being in contravention of the Security Council's own resolution on arms (UN 2023b). This was supported by the United Kingdom, which declared that the 'Russian Federation has taken up the Council's presidency while it fails to meet the most basic obligations of a United Nations Member State. Moscow is violating the very sanctions it helped to draft as it sources weapons for its war' (UN 2023b, 1). Despite these problems, much of the international community is committed to confronting the pervasive impact of arms trafficking and the myriad of crimes that this illicit industry supports. Recently, UNODC launched its Global Strategy on Illicit Firearms and Interconnected Threats (2023–2030) which aims to thwart the use of illicit firearms as a 'critical crime and violence enabler, asset and connecting link to multiple crimes including organized crime and terrorism' (UNODC 2023, 2). Rather than treating arms trafficking as a discrete illicit business, new initiatives that identify the importance of arms traffickers and the practice of arms trafficking in the commission of other forms of transnational organized crime demonstrate the potential to bring about significant change across numerous criminal networks.

Conclusion

Arms trafficking exploits the complexities of illicit supply chains. It fuels conflict, contributes to global instability and insecurity and acts as the ultimate enabler of a range of crimes. In this chapter we explored the difficulties associated with the global control of arms by looking at examples of how arms deals can be conducted through legal settings, as well as the use of grey and black markets. The case of Viktor Bout demonstrated the cascading effect of small arms trafficking and its devastating impact on vulnerable populations in Africa, many of which to this day are still dealing with the legacy of conflict caused by arms trafficking. The example of arms trafficking to Mexico highlighted the potential for symbiotic relationships to be established between arms traffickers and members of other organized crime groups such as drug cartels. However, these overlapping relationships and interdependence create opportunities for policymakers and law enforcement officials. The interconnected nature of arms trafficking means that any progress at the local, national or international level will undoubtedly lead to future successes against a range of illicit business that possess an operational and business dependency on the supply of illicit arms.

References

Arsovska, J., and Kostakos, P.A. (2008) 'Illicit arms trafficking and the limits of rational choice theory: The case of the Balkans.' *Trends in Organized Crime* 11 (4) 352–378.

Banerjee, D. and Muggah, R. (2002) 'Small arms and human insecurity.' Colombo: Regional Centre for Strategic Studies. Available at https://smallarmssurvey.org/sites/default/files/resources/SASRCSS%202002%20human%20insecurity.pdf.

Bergenstock, D.J. and Maskulka, J.M. (2001) 'The De Beers story: Are diamonds forever?' *Business Horizons* 44 (3) 37–44.

Bone, A. (2004) 'Conflict diamonds: The De Beers Group and the Kimberley process.' In J.K. Alyson and I. Frommelt (eds) *Business and Security: Public-Private Sector Relationships in a New Security Environment.* pp. 129–147. Oxford: Oxford University Press.

Bøås, M. (2005) 'The Liberian civil war: New war/old war?' *Global Society* 19 (1) 73–88. Available at https://doi:10.1080/1360082042000316059.

British Broadcasting Corporation (BBC) (2012) 'Merchant of death: Viktor Bout sentenced to 25 years.' BBC News, 6 April. Available at https://www.bbc.com/news/world-us-canada-17634050.

Davidson, N. (2016) 'Are conflict diamonds forever?: background to the problem.' In *The Lion that Didn't Roar: Can the Kimberley Process Stop the Blood Diamonds Trade?* pp. 21–72. Canberra: ANU Press.

De Beers Group (2024) 'Our Story.' Available at https://www.debeersgroup.com/about-us/our-history.

Farah, D. (2013) 'Fixers, super fixers and shadow facilitators: How networks connect.' In M. Miklaucic and J. Brewer (eds) *Convergence: Illicit Networks and Security in the Age of Globalization,* pp. 75–95. Washington, DC: National Defense University Press.

Farah D. and Braun, S. (2006) 'The merchant of death.' *Foreign Policy* 157 (Nov.–Dec.) 52–61.

Feinstein, A. and Holden, P. (2014) 'Arms trafficking.' In L. Paoli (ed.) *The Oxford Handbook of Organized Crime,* pp. 444–459. Oxford: Oxford University Press.

Fisher, L. (1989) 'How tightly can congress draw the purse strings?' *American Journal of International Law* 83 (4) 758–766. Available at https://doi:10.2307/2203364.

Friedman, U. (2015) 'How an ad campaign invented the diamond engagement ring.' *The Atlantic,* 13 February. Available at https://www.theatlantic.com/international/archive/2015/02/how-an-ad-campaign-invented-the-diamond-engagement-ring/385376/.

Global Initiative Against Transnational Organized Crime (GI-TOC) (2023) 'Ukraine's criminal ecosystem and the war: Ukrainian organized crime in 2022.' In B. Madlovics and B. Magyar (eds) *Ukraine's Patronal Democracy and the Russian Invasion: The Russia-Ukraine War,* vol. 1, pp. 263–294. Budapest: Central European University Press. Available at https://doi.org/10.7829/jj.3985461.13.

Grant, J. (2015) 'The arms traffic in world history.' In G. Bruinsma (ed.) *Histories of Transnational Crime,* pp. 71–90. New York: Springer. Available at https://doi.org/10.1007/978-1-4939-2471-4_4.

Hoekstra, Q. (2018) 'The effect of foreign state support to UNITA during the Angolan War (1975–1991).' *Small Wars and Insurgencies* 29 (5–6) 981–1005. Available at https://doi.org/10.1080/09592318.2018.1519312.

Howard, A. (2016) 'Blood diamonds: The successes and failures of the Kimberley process certification scheme in Angola, Sierra Leone and Zimbabwe.' *Washington University Global Studies Law Review* 15, 137–159.

Hureau, D. and Braga, A. (2018) 'The trade in tools: The market for illicit guns in high-risk networks.' *Criminology* 56 (3) 510–545. Available at https://doi.org/10.1111/1745-9125.12187.

InSight Crime (2024) 'InSight Crime's 2023 homicide round-up.' 21 February. Available at https://insightcrime.org/news/insight-crime-2023-homicide-round-up/#mexico-1.

Keefe, P.R. (2013) 'The geography of badness: Mapping the hubs of the illicit global economy.' In M. Miklaucic and J. Brewer (eds) *Convergence: Illicit Networks and National Security in the Age of Globalization*, pp. 97–110. Washington, DC: National Defense University Press.

Kehoe Down, A. (2018) 'Ukraine sees jump in illegal weapons sales.' Organized Crime and Corruption Reporting Project, 23 October. Available at https://www.occrp.org/en/daily/8785-ukraine-sees-jump-in-illegal-weapons-sales.

Kimberly Process (2024) 'What is the Kimberly Process?' Available at https://www.kimberleyprocess.com/en/what-kp.

Mackenzie, S. (2020) 'Arms trafficking.' In *Transnational Criminology: Trafficking and Global Criminal Markets*, pp. 89–104. Bristol: Bristol University Press.

Marsh, N. and Pinson, L. (2021) 'Arms trafficking.' In M. Gallien and F. Weigand (eds) *The Routledge Handbook of Smuggling*, pp. 213–227. London: Routledge.

Medina, F. (2020) 'Mexico and the United States: A snapshot of illicit arms trafficking in Mexico.' *Revista Mexicana de Política Exterior*, special issue (July), 11–22. Available at https://revistadigital.sre.gob.mx/images/stories/numeros/ne2020/medinasnapshotrmpe2020.pdf.

Mills, C. (2024) 'Military assistance to Ukraine since the Russian invasion.' UK Parliament – House of Commons Library, 22 February. Available at https://researchbriefings.files.parliament.uk/documents/CBP-9477/CBP-9477.pdf.

National Public Radio (NPR) (2022) 'Much of firearms traffic from the U.S. to Mexico happens illegally.' NPR Morning Edition, 7 June. Available at https://www.npr.org/2022/06/07/1103445425/much-of-firearms-traffic-from-the-u-s-to-mexico-happens-illegally.

Olsson, O. (2007) 'Conflict diamonds.' Journal of Development Economics 82 (2) 267–286.

Parry, R. and Kornbluh, P. (1988) *'Iran-Contra's untold story.'* Foreign Policy 72, 3–30.

Pearce, J. (2004) 'War, peace and diamonds in Angola: Popular perceptions of the diamond industry in the Lundas.' *African Security Studies* 13 (2) 51–64.

Phythian, M. (2000) 'The illicit arms trade: Cold war and post-cold war.' *Crime, Law and Social Change* 33, 1–52. Available at https://doi.org/10.1023/A:1008321001956.

Power, M. (2001) 'Patrimonialism and petro-diamond capitalism: Peace, geopolitics and the economics of war in Angola.' *Review of African Political Economy* 90, 489–502.

Rarick, C.A. and Angriawan, A. (2017) 'Innovative disruption: The case of the diamond industry.' *Journal of Strategic Innovation and Sustainability* 12 (2) 91–96.

Rothe, D. L. and Ross, J.I. (2015) 'The state and transnational organized crime: The case of small arms trafficking.' In F. Allum and S. Gilmour (eds) *Routledge Book of Transnational Organized Crime*, pp. 391–402. London: Routledge.

Schmidle, N. (2014) 'Disarming Viktor Bout.' *New Yorker*, 27 August. Available at https://www.newyorker.com/magazine/2012/03/05/disarming-viktor-bout.

Sherman, J.H. (2000) 'Profit vs. peace: The clandestine diamond economy of Angola.' *Journal of International Affairs* 53 (2) 699–719.

Smillie, I. (2000) 'Getting to the heart of the matter: Sierra Leone, diamonds, and human security.' *Social Justice* 27 (4) 24–31.

Solash, R. (2010) 'Interview: Merchant of Death author Douglas Farah discusses Viktor Bout.' Radio Free Europe, 25 August. Available at https://www.rferl.org/a/Interview_Merchant_Of_Death_Author_Douglas_Farah_Discusses_Viktor_Bout/2137614.html.

Stockholm International Peace Research Institute (SIPRI) (2024) 'European arms imports nearly double, US and French exports rise, and Russian exports fall sharply.' 11 March. Available at https://www.sipri.org/media/press-release/2024/european-arms-imports-nearly-double-us-and-french-exports-rise-and-russian-exports-fall-sharply.

Stohl, R. and Yousif, E. (2022) 'The notorious Viktor Bout is back.' Stimson Centre, August 4. Available at https://www.stimson.org/2022/the-notorious-viktor-bout-is-back/.

Tan, A.T. (2023) 'Global arms trade.' In P. Williams and M. McDonald (eds) *Security Studies: An Introduction*, pp. 535–551. London: Routledge.

United Nations (UN) (2021) 'Arms trafficking, a "defining factor" in undermining peace.' UN News, 22 November. Available at https://news.un.org/en/story/2021/11/1106282.

United Nations (UN) (2023a) 'Small arms and light weapons.' Office for Disarmament Affairs. Available at https://disarmament.unoda.org/convarms/salw/.

United Nations (UN) (2023b) 'Security Council examines risks of illicit weapons exports, hears international instruments are paramount, in debate on arms control.' United Nations Meetings Coverage SC/15252, 10 April. Available at https://press.un.org/en/2023/sc15252.doc.htm.

United Nations General Assembly (2001) 'The role of diamonds in fuelling conflict: breaking the link between the illicit transaction of rough diamonds and armed conflict as a contribution to prevention and settlement of conflicts.' Resolutions 55/56, 55th session, Agenda item 175, 29 January. Available at https://documents.un.org/doc/undoc/gen/n00/562/75/pdf/n0056275.pdf?token=MZqpreMBORAWwIRiel&fe=true.

United Nations Children's Fund (UNICEF) (2024) 'Children recruited by armed forces or armed groups.' Available at https://www.unicef.org/protection/children-recruited-by-armed-forces.

United Nations Office on Drugs and Crime (UNODC) (2020) 'Global study on firearms trafficking.' Available at https://www.unodc.org/documents/data-and-analysis/Firearms/2020_REPORT_Global_Study_on_Firearms_Trafficking_2020_web.pdf.

United Nations Office on Drugs and Crime (UNODC) (2023) 'UNODC global strategy on illicit firearms and interconnected threats 2023–2030 - factsheet.' Available at https://www.unodc.org/documents/firearmsprotocol/2023/Strategy_FACT_SHEET_2023_Final.pdf.

United States Department of Justice (2011) 'International arms dealer Viktor Bout convicted in New York of terrorism crimes.' 2 November. Available at https://www.justice.gov/opa/pr/international-arms-dealer-viktor-bout-convicted-new-york-terrorism-crimes.

Verloy, A. (2002) 'The merchant of death.' *International Consortium of Investigative Journals*, 20 November. Available at https://www.icij.org/investigations/making-killing/merchant-death/.

7

KIDNAPPING AND HUMAN TRAFFICKING

Introduction

Kidnapping and people trafficking are universally regarded as serious crimes and attract long sentences for their perpetrators if caught. Both crimes have long histories but they are still very much evident today and have become criminal ventures that can be highly lucrative for the gangs and individuals involved. They bring misery and harm to those affected – victims, families, communities and even countries – but potentially rich pickings for criminals. Kidnapping and trafficking overlap but there are differences between them. They can both be viewed as illicit businesses and can be closely linked. Kidnapping is often found in trafficking. People are kidnapped before being trafficked. But kidnapping may be an end in itself where the object of the crime is to collect a ransom for the release of the victim or to apply pressure on others to take actions which will benefit the kidnappers. Also, the entire kidnap episode from abduction to release usually occurs within a country's borders. By contrast, trafficking is characteristically transnational with persons from one country ending up in another where they are exploited for their labour.

In this chapter, we will deal with kidnapping and trafficking separately but always remembering that they can be inter-connected. The first section of the chapter explores kidnapping by first identifying different types of kidnapping before moving on to cases that reveal the diversity of kidnapping enterprises and the involvement of different criminal actors. Attention is then given to steps that law enforcement agencies have used to combat this crime. The section on human trafficking highlights important aspects of this trade from a voluminous literature. These include locating human trafficking and slavery historically, defining human trafficking and differentiating it from people

DOI: 10.4324/9781003293620-7

smuggling, examining the extent of human trafficking today and setting out a variety of business models of human trafficking that have been created by criminal gangs in different places.

Kidnapping

Kidnapping has a long history stretching back to ancient times (Clutterbuck 1978; Bles and Low 1987). It frequently appears in Greek myths while there are mentions of the ransoming of hostages during China's Xia dynasty which ruled from 2070 BCE to 1600 BCE. According to the Roman historian Plutarch, Julius Caesar was seized by pirates and ransomed although he allegedly returned to avenge his captors. The Bible condemns kidnapping and recommends the death sentence for those who commit it. Richard I of England was captured and handed over to the Holy Roman Emperor who demanded a huge ransom. The term 'kidnapping' originated in 17th-century England to refer to the practice of children being abducted and transported to the American colonies to work as slaves – 'kids' (children) were 'napped' (snatched) (Schiller 1985). Furthermore, it is a crime that can affect persons from all social classes. It is not an act that exclusively targets the wealthy although they are particularly attractive targets for criminals because they command the highest prices.

There is some disagreement about which acts constitute kidnapping. For example, is a passenger plane hijack a kidnapping? Also, formal legal definitions can vary between different jurisdictions (Finkelhor et al. 1992). Thus, for the purposes of this book we have adopted a broad definition of kidnapping that acts as an umbrella under which different types of kidnapping can be accommodated. Kidnapping is the unlawful seizing and/or taking away of another person against their will. It can be undertaken by an individual or a criminal group. Its duration can vary from a few hours to several years and it occurs all over the world with some countries and regions experiencing higher incidences of the crime. For example, the Australian government in its overseas travel advice warns citizens of 'areas of particular concern' for kidnapping and provides a list of geographical locations that encompasses large areas of the world – West and East Africa, the Sahel, Afghanistan, Pakistan, parts of the Middle East, South America and Southeast Asia (Smartraveller 2023).

While it is possible to identify areas with higher incidences of kidnapping, it is notoriously difficult to gather accurate statistics. For example, in the United Kingdom, because different police forces vary in the ways they handle the crime, it is 'all but impossible' to obtain reliable figures (Heard 2019, 25). Another reason for the lack of accurate statistics on the incidence of kidnapping is that many cases are not reported either because of warnings and threats from the kidnappers to the victims' families or because affected families do not trust the law enforcement agencies. They see them as either incompetent or corrupt – or both. For example, in 2012, the official figure for the total number of kidnappings in Venezuela was 583 but the police estimated that at least 80% of cases went unreported while the Venezuelan Violence Observatory, a non-governmental organization (NGO), claimed that there were between 9,000 and 16,000 cases (Heard 2019, 11).

Types of Kidnapping

To distinguish between the different types of kidnapping a simple classificatory tool based on motivation can be utilized (Turner 1998). Two dimensions of motivation are employed – political and material. The political dimension runs from the 'non-political' to the 'highly political,' while the material dimension extends from 'no material gain' to 'maximum material gain.' When the two dimensions are put together they produce a matrix which identifies four distinctive types of kidnapping (see Table 7.1).

Cell 1 incorporates the classic criminal kidnap for ransom in which there are only material motivations. The kidnappers simply want to make money and have no political motivations. Cell 2 identifies kidnapping that has neither political nor material motivations, yet it is numerically the most common form of kidnapping. This is because it includes situations where there are custody battles over children. The parent who does not have custody or other family member lures or forcibly removes the child from the parent who has been awarded that custody. This type of kidnapping can involve the transfer of the child across international borders. In many countries parental abduction is a criminal offence but it is committed for affective reasons and does not usually involve criminal gangs. Cell 3 refers to kidnapping cases in which political and material motivations are combined. The kidnappers are often engaged in conflict with the state and use abductions to raise both their political profile and finance. In some cases, the material motivation can become dominant over time as devotion to the political cause weakens. Finally, Cell 4 describes kidnappings that are undertaken purely for political purposes. If demands are made by the abductors, they are not for money but for such things as the release of imprisoned colleagues or to apply pressure to the state for political change, often of a radical nature.

For our purposes, two of the types of kidnapping identified above can be overlooked. These are the varieties that don't have material motivation, Cell 2 – no

TABLE 7.1 A Typology of Kidnapping According to the Motivations of the Kidnappers

	Political	
	Non-political	Highly political
Maximum material gain Material No material gain	Cell 1 Money but no politics	Cell 3 Money and politics
	Cell 2 No money, no politics	Cell 4 Politics but no money

Note: This table first appeared in Turner, M. (1998) 'Kidnapping and politics.' *International Journal of the Sociology of Law* 26 (2) 145–160. Copyright Elsevier (1998).

money, no politics – and Cell 4 – politics but no money. This is because we are concerned with kidnapping as an illicit business practice. Thus, in the rest of this section we will make a closer examination of Cell 1 – money but no politics – and Cell 3 – money and politics. While all kidnappings may be formally classified as crimes, Cells 1 and 3 refer to those that are conducted as illicit business ventures. To explore these broad categories of kidnapping, we will examine the diversity of practices in two countries, Nigeria and the Philippines, where there have been numerous examples of both types.

Kidnapping in Nigeria

During the 2000s, kidnapping in Nigeria, Africa's most populous country with 225 million inhabitants, has increased so rapidly as to become a 'pervasive security threat and fast-paced and multifaceted criminal enterprise' (Assanvo and Okereke 2019). By 2012, the African Reinsurance Forum reported that Nigeria had become 'the global headquarters of kidnap for ransom,' accounting for 34% of the world's kidnap for ransom cases. In the first half of 2021, over 3,000 people were reported as having been kidnapped in Nigeria (Okoli 2022). A diverse group of actors have embraced this enterprise as a way to obtain material rewards and advance political agendas, the latter increasingly for profit. It has taken place in an environment characterized by poverty, inequality, unemployment, lack of opportunity, frustration and poor governance (Chinwokwu and Michael 2019). These factors have encouraged young men to join groups that engage in kidnapping as a means to address their marginal socioeconomic situation.

The genesis of Nigeria's contemporary kidnapping epidemic is often traced back to the early 2000s with Niger Delta militants abducting foreign oil workers to draw attention to the environmental damage caused by oil companies and the underdevelopment of communities in the region. Initially, the militants also engaged in sabotaging oil installations which, according to a 2007 senate committee, had lost the Nigerian government US $58.3 million in income over the previous nine years (Chinwokwu and Michael 2019). But kidnapping provided income for the perpetrators, whereas sabotage did not. Thus, kidnapping for ransom became the dominant pursuit of the 'militants' and its incidence increased. As this change occurred so did the list of potential targets with the addition of politicians, businessperson and their families. It even spread offshore into the Gulf of Guinea as criminal groups began to abduct seaborne victims.

From these early beginnings in the Niger Delta, kidnapping for ransom and political purposes spread across the country and diversified in form. According to one classification, there are six types of kidnapping: routine, invasion, highway, insider, seduction and feigned (Onuoha and Akogwu 2022) (see Figure 7.1). Routine kidnapping is regarded as the most common type empirically and in the popular imagination. It involves identifying a target, observing the target's movements and then abducting and holding the kidnappee. Ransom demands and

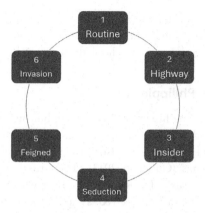

FIGURE 7.1 Types of Kidnapping

threats are then made and negotiations take place until the kidnappers accept the amount offered for release. Preferred targets are those whose kidnapping promises to secure substantial ransoms – expatriates, businesspeople, politicians, traditional leaders and their families. Highway kidnapping generally involves gangs stopping vehicles on a road and abducting persons from their vehicles. It is opportunistic as it is highly unlikely the kidnappers know in advance which vehicles they will stop and which persons they will remove. Insider kidnapping occurs when somebody who is closely associated with the victim initiates and/or facilitates the kidnapping. The insider could be a servant, a work colleague or a relative. The seduction type of kidnapping utilizes an attractive male or female to lure somebody into a relationship as a prelude to abduction. Feigned kidnapping refers to cases in which individuals pretend to have been kidnapped in order to extort money from others such as family members.

The final category of kidnap for ransom in Nigeria, invasion, features a mix of politics and money and involves the mass abduction of children from schools in the country's northern states. The first incident, in 2014, involved the abduction of 276 girls from Chibok secondary school by Boko Haram, a militant Islamist group known for its brutality and violent attacks on soft targets in northeast Nigeria (Pérouse de Montclos 2014; Onuoha and Akogwu 2022). Others mass kidnapping incidents followed, and by 2021 there had been 11 such incidents with 1,548 children abducted. Furthermore, the practice then spread into the adjoining northern regions but did not necessarily involve groups with political motivations. Bandit groups recognized the financial opportunities offered by mass kidnapping in regions where the rule of law was tenuous at best, and the state was weak and corrupt. Even when special response groups were formed in the military and police their success was very limited. The families of the kidnappees seem generally to have paid ransoms after negotiations that were often conducted by third parties, including the Red Cross, a cattle breeders association and a popular Islamic cleric (Onuoha and Akogwu

2022). As a result of the kidnappings and other terrorist attacks on schools, education has suffered through the closure of schools in the north of the country where 60% of Nigeria's out of school children are located.

Kidnapping in the Philippines

The Philippines has a long history of kidnapping but our analysis of it begins in the mid-1980s, a time of political turmoil associated with the ousting of the dictator Ferdinand Marcos. It was also a time when there was a surge in the numbers of kidnappings (Gutierrez 2013). The situation became so serious it was described as a 'crisis' (Turner 1995a). This was because the increasing incidence of kidnapping was perceived as a threat to investment, a graphic expression of declining public confidence in law enforcement, a challenge to the political legitimacy of the newly elected president and a matter of grave concern to the most affected community, the 1.8% of the population identified as Filipino-Chinese. It is impossible to provide accurate figures for the number of kidnappings then and now. For example, in early 1993, law enforcement officials counted 60 people abducted in the previous eight months while unofficial figures from a well-informed NGO reported 142 cases for 1992 (Turner 1995a). More recently, on 5 September 2022, the Philippine Chinese Chamber of Commerce and Industry pointed to a 'new spate of kidnappings' in the capital, Manila, and the rest of the island of Luzon and stated that there had been 56 cases in the previous ten days (The Star 2022). The police disputed the claim, initially saying that there had been only four kidnappings during the year, although later the number was increased to 27, still well below the unofficial tally. It is likely that the latter is nearer the mark than the police count as official data-gathering on the crime leaves much to be desired and victims' families often do not report kidnappings to the police as there is considerable mistrust of the police due to their limited capability, questionable commitment and their actual involvement.

Kidnapping in the Philippines has been heavily concentrated in two geographical locations – Manila and its environs, and Mindanao, a large southern island in the archipelago. It has always involved ransoms although in Mindanao it has often been interwoven with politics. Major targets in both places have been Filipino-Chinese families involved in business although foreigners, government officials, religious personnel and Filipinos have also been kidnapped. The Filipino-Chinese have been especially victimized because they are seen to have the resources to finance ransom payments and are more likely to pay. They often mistrust the police, have long experience of extra-legal pressures from officials for financial 'favours' and the kidnappers feel that popular sentiment is not particularly supportive of the Filipino-Chinese community (Turner 1995a).

In the Manila region, kidnapping is usually undertaken by criminal gangs who view kidnapping as a profitable illicit enterprise that can have high returns and a low risk of detection. This has often proved to be the case because there have been many allegations of official involvement, especially by police and military personnel. Such involvement has varied from direct participation to indirect aiding and abetting. Most kidnappings in Manila have been perpetrated by domestic criminals, but groups from Hong Kong, Taiwan and the People's Republic of China also appear to have been involved. In recent years, this has especially involved kidnapping Chinese workers in Philippine Offshore Gambling Operations (POGOs) which provide online gambling to customers in China where gambling is illegal. In 2022, the police identified 'at least' five foreign groups engaged in POGO-linked kidnapping (Cabalza 2022).

In Mindanao, the situation is more complex due to the frequent intrusion of politics into criminal practices and to the broader interactions of the kidnappers with communities in the environment in which they operate. Gutierrez (2013) recommends that we view Mindanao's kidnappers in business terms. Hence, kidnapping is an enterprise, albeit an illicit one, and the kidnappers are entrepreneurs who are linked to other relevant actors who are either collaborators or competitors. The collaborators can be local communities with kinship and friendship links to the kidnappers which make for reciprocity especially if the kidnappers disburse a portion of their income among the community. Moreover, the fear of heavily armed men encourages a spirit of cooperation. The kidnappers also seek links with local power structures. In Mindanao, this has often been local politicians, especially 'warlords,' and other officials but there has also been engagement with the Moro National Liberation Front (MNLF) and the Moro Islamic Liberation Front (MILF). These groups started out as armed secessionist organizations devoted to securing an independent homeland for the Muslim groups that are indigenous to Western and Central Mindanao (Turner 2008). Major conflict in the 1970s and 1980s resulted in considerable loss of life and property as well as population displacement. This was followed by uneasy truces with a succession of presidents, but sporadic low-level conflicts continued until a final peace settlement was made in 2019. The rebel groups were important and heavily armed political actors and many members of the kidnap groups originated from their ranks or at least were linked by kinship. Thus, a complex web of inter-personal relations binds the kidnap gangs to the broader environment and provides some security that reduces the risks posed by their criminal enterprises.

There are other environmental factors which have contributed to the high incidence of kidnapping in Western and Central Mindanao over many years. Until recently the state has been weak and lacking in capacity. It has failed to provide adequate services including justice and security, a situation that has contributed to the region being one of the poorest and least developed in the Philippines with a large pool of underemployed young men. Both tradition and recent conflict have created a proliferation of firearms. In such a context, kidnapping can become a viable and attractive business.

Some of Mindanao's kidnapping gangs have no political motivations. For example, the Pentagon Gang, which originated and largely operated in Central Mindanao from the late 1980s to the early 2000s and was led by a succession of former rebel commanders, had no political agenda (Santos and Santos 2010). Many successors in Mindanao's kidnapping business have shared this characteristic. However, the most infamous group of kidnappers in Mindanao, the Abu Sayyaf Group (ASG), commenced its abductions by making strong declarations of its political justifications and objectives, although it always demanded ransom payments, sometimes framed in terms of 'expenses' for the board and lodging of its victims.

The ASG first came to notice in 1992 when two Christian clerics were gunned down and a high school bombed in Zamboanga City in Western Mindanao (Turner 1995b). This was the start of a campaign to establish an independent Islamic state in Mindanao. Kidnappings of religious personnel followed with the ASG making both political and financial demands. Over the next decade or so, the ASG mounted a series of high-profile kidnappings often involving foreigners in Western Mindanao and even at sea. These activities and the ASG's political ideology led to the ASG being labelled a terrorist organization. But some analysts have argued that it was not a formal organization and that much of the kidnapping could be regarded as banditry rather than the pursuit of a terrorist political agenda (Ugarte 2008; Ugarte and Turner 2011; Vitug and Gloria 2000). It is best to visualize the ASG in terms of a complex shifting network of inter-personal relations that link kin groups with officials, police and military personnel, MILF and MNLF commanders and their followers, and Islamists. The nodes in the network are fluid and amenable to rapid change with a network only coming to life when mounting kidnapping operations. This successful mode of organizing enabled the different components of the ASG to operate for well over a decade in Western Mindanao, despite the efforts of a massive military force to wipe it out.

The resolution of kidnappings in Mindanao is generally achieved by the payment of ransoms although there have been cases where the victims have been killed. The negotiations leading to release and ransom payment take place well away from the public gaze and little is known about the process involved and the actual amounts paid. What is clear is that officials, especially politicians, are swift to seize the opportunity to act as negotiators. This can help to build their political capital and also provide them with financial gains by taking a cut of the ransom. While estimates of the ransoms paid can be found for many countries regarded as kidnapping hotspots, the figures must be treated with great caution as the parties involved rarely if ever reveal the exact sums. Governments also remain tight-lipped as they do not wish to encourage the illicit industry. Details of the multiple ways in which kidnapping is dealt with by societies, governments and private sector organizations across the world is presented in Box 7.1.

BOX 7.1 COMBATTING KIDNAPPING

Kidnapping for ransom as an attractive illicit business has grown considerably in recent decades as people travel much more for work and pleasure and criminal gangs and terrorist organizations have seized the opportunity to engage in this enterprise. So, what steps have been taken to combat this criminal business?

Governments

- Governments issue warnings to citizens travelling to foreign countries including up-to-date security briefs.
- Foreign missions of countries provide assistance to the families of kidnap victims.
- Governments in countries where kidnapping occurs use their law enforcement agencies to resolve incidents but there are often problems of effectiveness.
- There is a limit to what governments can do as many take a hardline stance against kidnapping and do not pay ransoms (some have more flexibility).

Individuals

- Individuals are expected to take responsibility for their own safety and to practise behaviours that make them hard targets e.g.

a   vary their personal routines;
b   keep a low profile;
c   avoid known kidnap zones;
d   travel by air rather than road;
e   have high-quality locks fitted to homes.

Insurance

- Insurance for kidnapping was first developed by Lloyd's of London following the 1932 abduction of the son of American aviator Charles Lindburgh – Lloyd's still dominates the market.
- There has been considerable growth in kidnap insurance since the 1970s with the increased incidence of organizations sending employees overseas for work.
- Insurance places an emphasis on prevention and involves security training.
- Costs vary according to the level of danger.
- If an insured person is kidnapped, the insurer will contract security consultants and negotiators to resolve the abduction.
- Insurers and their contractors generally prefer to minimize government involvement.

Human Trafficking

Human trafficking is a crime that is characterized by misery, exploitation and violence for its victims. Its antecedents stretch back to ancient civilizations including China and Cambodia in Asia, Africa, Europe and the pre-colonial Americas, all of which were involved in widespread use of slavery. In later years, the British engaged in slavery on an industrial scale when, over a period of almost 300 years, they transported over 12.5 million men, women and children from Africa to the Americas to satisfy the demand for labour in colonial plantations (Allain 2018, 3). Slavery was eventually abolished in many countries in the 18th and 19th centuries, although it was not until 1981 when it was made illegal everywhere (Smith and Kangaspunta 2012). Now, however, human trafficking is often depicted as 'modern-day slavery' (Bales 2007; Lee 2011; Anti-Slavery International 2023). However, a major difference between the old and the new manifestations of slavery is that the old models were considered legitimate and legal by the state while today's practices of human trafficking are illegal and constitute a type of illicit business run by criminals for profit.

While it is the illicit business characteristic of human trafficking that makes it important for this book, we should not lose sight of other perspectives that are essential for gaining a full understanding of this dark phenomenon. It is, of course, primarily viewed as a criminal problem for institutions and individuals involved in law enforcement. But for many others, NGOs for example, the focus is on the violation of human rights. In this approach it is the needs and experiences of the victims that take centre stage and rights violated can span a wide range – the right to liberty and security, the right not to be subject to torture and inhuman treatment, the right to freedom of movement, the right to just and favourable working conditions and fair compensation, and the right not to be subject to slavery, and forced and bonded labour (Burke et al. 2022, 12). One can also take a health perspective which looks at the adverse physical and psychological effects of human trafficking. Allied to this are approaches which deal with trafficking in terms of gender-based forms of discrimination and inequality. The subordination of women through patriarchal practices and their resulting disadvantaged socioeconomic positions in many countries makes women and girls especially vulnerable to human trafficking. The available statistics consistently demonstrate that females comprise a majority of persons trafficked. Finally, as with some other transnational crimes, human trafficking can be seen as a security risk because it sometimes provides an income for armed and extremist groups that enables them to bolster their power and military capacities, can lead to population displacement and community destabilization, and allow human trafficking gangs to become mired in other transnational crimes that contribute to making international borders more porous and dangerous (Bigio and Vogelstein 2019). Thus, human trafficking should be seen as a multidimensional and complex phenomenon.

Defining Human Trafficking

Human trafficking essentially refers to the economic exploitation of people. It covers a variety of instances and characteristics of such exploitation and is internationally defined in a protocol (the Palermo Protocol) to the United Nations (UN) Convention against Organized Crime of November 2000. The UN Office of Drugs and Crime (UNODC 2023) claims that it is 'the first legally binding instrument with an internationally recognized definition of human trafficking' with 181 UN member states having signed up to it as of 23 February 2023. The Protocol states that

> '[t]rafficking in persons' shall mean the recruitment, transportation, transfer, harbouring or receipt of persons, by means of the threat of the use of force or other forms of coercion, of abduction, of fraud, of deception, of the abuse of power or of a position of vulnerability or of the giving or receiving of payments or benefits to achieve the consent of a person having control over another person, for the purpose of exploitation.

The Protocol goes on to list examples of trafficking in persons and includes sexual exploitation, forced labour, slavery, servitude and organ removal.

It should be noted that there are other definitions of human trafficking which show minor variations and different interpretations of it between countries and cultures. What the law regards as human trafficking in one country might not be exactly the same in another. Further variations can be seen in its form, incidence and distribution over time and place. Thus, it can occur within a country or involve crossing international borders. It can be undertaken by organized crime groups (OCGs) which may also be involved in other transnational illegal activities such as drug trafficking. They are likely to run operations that transport large numbers of people. Alternatively, it can be instigated and perpetrated by family and friends and be on a small scale. The relations between those being trafficked and their traffickers and employers can range from extreme physical and psychological abuse, awful working conditions and severe economic exploitation – in other words, slavery – to 'fully consensual and collaborative arrangements between the parties' (Weitzer 2015, 239).

A final definitional consideration concerns something that is not human trafficking – migrant smuggling. According to another Protocol of the UN Convention against Transnational Organized Crime,

> [s]muggling of migrants shall mean the procurement, in order to obtain, directly or indirectly, a financial or other material benefit, of the illegal entry of a person into a State Party of which the person is not a national or a permanent resident.

The smuggler and the migrant engage in a commercial transaction that involves the would-be migrant paying the smuggler to facilitate their illegal entry into a country. However, a smuggled migrant can become a victim of human trafficking if that person is then forced to work in a job that is either illegal or whose conditions of employment are illegal and exploitative (Smith and Kangaspunta 2012).

The Extent of Human Trafficking

According to frequently cited statistics from international organizations, in 2016 there were 40.3 million victims of human trafficking or modern slavery and this represented an industry valued at US $150 billion (Toney-Butler et al. 2023). This gives some idea of the massive extent of human trafficking but, as with many illicit business statistics, these and others cited for human trafficking are often lacking in accuracy. Hard numbers that purport to show basic information on how many people have been trafficked or the financial worth of the illegal enterprise can be based on research which has questionable or obscure methodologies (Weitzer 2015). It is also extremely challenging for the researcher, as human trafficking is conducted in secrecy which means that the number of cases recorded will be below the number that actually occurs (Van Dijk and Campistol 2018). In addition, it is difficult to compare statistics across jurisdictions because of different legal definitions and methods of reporting and recording. The accuracy of such statistics is, however, of vital importance as effective policy to counter human trafficking needs to be based on reliable evidence. This is appreciated in many countries and by international law enforcement agencies and measures continue to be taken to achieve greater reliability (Goodey 2012).

As a demonstration of this, UNODC's *Global Report on Trafficking in Persons* focuses on the 'number of detected victims reported' – a fairly reliable figure – which is then broken down into categories such as age, gender and citizenship plus details of number and citizenship of persons investigated, arrests and prosecutions (UNODC 2022). Data are obtained from 141 countries representing 95% of the global population and are broken down into four regions, ten sub-regions and even smaller combinations of countries for which there are sufficient data. The baseline statistics from this publication are presented in Table 7.2.

The data reveal an upward trend in the number of detected victims reported over the period 2003–2019, although that was halted in 2020 by the COVID-19 pandemic when international borders were often closed and travel restricted. These developments appear to have had a particularly heavy impact on human trafficking for sexual exploitation. Nevertheless, in 2020, the detected victims per 100,000 population for sexual exploitation were the same as those for forced labour. For release from trafficking, the data show that in 41% of cases the initial action was taken by the victim. Only 28% of cases saw initial action taken by law enforcement institutions. Meanwhile, countries in sub-Saharan Africa and South Asia are convicting fewer traffickers and detecting fewer victims compared to the rest of the world; male victims, both men and boys, have been detected in greater numbers over the past decade; OCGs exploit more victims with more violence and

TABLE 7.2 Summary of Core Data and Indicators in the *Global Report on Trafficking in Persons 2022*

	2017	2018	2019	2020	2020 (or most recent)	Total 2017–2020
Number of detected victims reported	44,989	46,384	49,692	46,850	53,800	187,915
Number of detected victims for which age and sex was reported by member states	40,004	39,544	41,402	41,461	51,580	162,411
Number of detected victims for which a form of exploitation was reported by member states	36,218	39,112	40,527	36,628	45,258	152,485
Number of detected victims for which citizenship was reported by member states	26,111	29,899	39,599	34,968	38,709	130,577
Number of persons investigated/ suspected or arrested reported by member states	18,472	18,283	18,294	15,488	17,635	70,537
Number of persons prosecuted reported by member states	13,463	12,605	11,267	8,769	10,257	46,104
Number of persons convicted reported by member states	7,310	6,667	3,247	2,271	2,858	19,495
Number of persons convicted for which citizenship was reported by member states	3,038	2,197	1,488	2,894	3,409	9,617

Note: This table first appeared in UNODC (2022) *Global Report on Trafficking in Persons 2022*. New York: United Nations.

for longer periods of time; and women and children suffer greater violence at the hands of traffickers – three times higher than males.

This last finding requires further elaboration. Sex trafficking is regarded as the most common form of human trafficking and the victims are predominantly young and female (McCabe 2022). It is estimated that worldwide five million persons are trafficked for sex every year, of whom 20% are under the age of 18 years (Toney-Butler et al. 2023). While victims of sex trafficking are predominantly involved in prostitution, significant numbers are also recruited for pornography and bride trafficking. Some victims do not report their predicament for a variety of reasons. These include mistrust of law enforcement; lack of language skills in a foreign country; acceptance of 'debt bondage' that occurs when ruthless traffickers charge exorbitant sums for travel, food and accommodation that must be paid off; and fear of retribution by families if they have been involved in the recruitment of the trafficked person and received payment; and gender inequalities (Ezelio 2018).

Business Models of Human Trafficking

Like other illegal enterprises, human trafficking is concerned with making a profit. But the ways in which this profit is obtained reveal a variety of business models which reflect a range of interactions between traffickers, victims and numerous environmental factors. Models may vary by geographical region, types of trafficking, opportunities and risks, and traffickers' resources. Thus, some criminal groups specialize in the organ trade, while others focus on recruiting and exploiting child labour. Some trafficking is domestic, while many operations involve the movement of people across international borders. There are groups which rely heavily on violence, threat and fear, while others may utilize techniques that look more to persuasion and attraction. Some gangs are involved in multiple criminal activities and operate on a large transnational scale, while others are small with much more restricted trafficking activities. In short, human trafficking is conducted by OCGs using a variety of organizational structures and practices. Shelley (2010) has analysed these business models and has come up with six distinctive types which are set out below. However, the typology is not exhaustive. Additional types can be identified (see Box 7.2 for a new model that emerged in Southeast Asia during the COVID-19 pandemic). Furthermore, there are constant changes in the activities of human traffickers and existing models may undergo modification and new ones can emerge.

Trade and development model: Chinese traffickers

This model is based on the trafficking of people, historically mainly men, for work overseas. This form of trafficking is described as being 'integrated' with tight control over victims throughout the process of recruitment, transportation and work assignment. While some manifestations of this model may commence with people smuggling, the end result is normally debt bondage in which victims must work long hours for low pay to clear their debt to the traffickers. There may be variations on what happens on the payment of the debt with instances of both freedom for the debtors and of continuing enslavement. As traffickers in the original model sourced labour from a particularly poor region in China, it was in their interest to pay some attention to the welfare of their human capital to keep them working and minimally satisfied as this would help to maintain long-term profitability. The business model makes extensive use of the Chinese diaspora who serve as employers at foreign destinations such as the United States and Europe. The network design and operation of the Chinese traffickers bears some resemblance to the overseas Chinese business model for legitimate business that has characterized commercial linkages between mainland China and the Chinese diaspora (Kao 1993). The links are built on *guanxi*, dyadic ties based on trust that leads to tight social networks among different nodes. A final characteristic of the illicit Chinese trafficking business model is its strong reliance on the corruption of local officials who turn a blind eye to the traffickers' activities at all stages of the process.

BOX 7.2 THE EMERGENCE OF CYBER-SLAVERY IN SOUTHEAST ASIA

The restrictions on travel and business operations brought about by the COVID-19 pandemic shut down the thriving gambling businesses of Chinese gangs operating in Southeast Asia. Therefore the gangsters needed to move into other illicit businesses and one popular option has proved to be cyber scamming. If these scams are to target rich Western nations, then a workforce with English language skills and computer literacy are essential. Trafficking is the main means of assembling this workforce. Young people from Southeast Asia and elsewhere are lured into applying for highly paid jobs in fields such as marketing or currency trading through adverts in social media or personal contacts. Free travel and meals are added draws. But when the job-seekers reach Bangkok, the preferred entry point in Southeast Asia for the cyber scammers, they are whisked off by bus and dumped in fortified compounds with armed guards in either Cambodia, Myanmar or Laos. They are not allowed to go outside the compound. Their passports are confiscated, their contracts torn up and they are forced to learn the sales patter for particular scams. These trafficked victims are forced to work up to 14 hours per day trying to persuade mainly Americans, Europeans and Australians to sign up for fake romances or business opportunities. This process is colloquially known as 'pig-butchering,' and if the prisoners fail to meet their quotas or disobey the rules they are subject to violent punishments that can result in severe injury.

Knowledge of the cyber scam operations has been imparted through the testimonies of escapees. Actions of law enforcement in the host countries of Cambodia, Myanmar and Laos have been slow to come and when they do, it is pressure from neighbouring governments that has led to arrests and freedom for some cyber scam prisoners. One reason for this weak response is endemic corruption in the host countries which leads to officials at all levels turning a blind eye to the cyber scam operations. But as outside knowledge and outrage has grown, so too have estimates of the scale of the operations. From an original estimate of up to 10,000 victims, some organizations believe the figure to be as high as 100,000. While the May 2023 Association of Southeast Asian Nations (ASEAN) leaders' summit promised a regional approach to combating human trafficking and cyber crime, there are problems associated with the lack of standardized legislation, protocols and agreements, and foot-dragging by law enforcement in countries that have hosted this illicit business.

Source: Turner and McCarthy-Jones (2023)

Natural resource model: post-Soviet organized crime

The crime groups utilizing this model of human trafficking range in size from a few individuals to much larger organizations involved in a range of criminal activities. They traffic women and labour more generally but lack 'integrated' business models. This is reflected in their short-term profit orientation rather than with the longer-term viability of their business. Shelley (2010) likens their business practices to Russia's pre-revolutionary trade in natural resources and its contemporary focus on the sale of oil and gas. Thus, the crime groups treat their human victims as commodities to be traded. Other crime groups in foreign countries are often purchasers of the human cargo. Ex-military personnel, brutalized in wars overseas, have been used as enforcers and are ready to apply extreme violence to uncooperative victims. The traffickers recruit their victims from a variety of sources; some come from children's homes, others are bought from alcoholic parents, and abandoned street children are rounded up. The traffickers also make extensive use of social media. Meanwhile, infants sold for adoption are acquired from hospitals. Unlike the previous Chinese model where recruitment occurs within communities, in the post-Soviet model current victims have no links to previous ones. However, they do share the use of corruption of officials to ensure that business is not disrupted.

Violent entrepreneur model: Balkan crime groups

The focus of groups covered under this business model is the trafficking of women although the groups may also traffic other commodities such as drugs and arms. Shelley describes the crime groups as 'opportunistic' because of their emergence under particular circumstances in both source and recipient countries. The Balkan Wars left many women vulnerable to exploitation. Similarly, the loosening of state controls and difficult economic conditions in Eastern Europe and the Soviet Union led to the creation of another group of women who could be preyed upon. In recipient countries, the Balkan gangs found they could oust existing brothel operators with a combination of market power and extreme force. Indeed, violence is a defining characteristic of this business model and is evident at all stages of the trafficking process. At least in their initial formation, former members of the police and other organizations in states' security services are evident. The criminal groups operate within families and are largely controlled by men. They are described as employing an integrated business model that sees control of victims from recruitment through to their work in brothels. The groups maintain links with other criminal organizations in Eastern Europe and the former Soviet Union. The prime market focus for Balkan crime groups is the lucrative European market for the provision of sexual services. The criminal operations may be interconnected with legitimate businesses for some services such as transport and banking, and in their home countries criminal groups using the Balkan model may invest profits in legal businesses.

American pimp model: high consumption and small savings

Shelley (2010) assigns this business model exclusively to the United States. Furthermore, it only applies to human trafficking of females for sexual exploitation. The traffickers are identified as American-born and operating on a small scale but in loose, mutually supportive networks. The 'pimps' recruit young, vulnerable American women who are often homeless or 'throwaway children' and who have already experienced sexual violence. These victims respond positively to affection and promises of a lavish lifestyle, but once they have been recruited they are subject to coercion and violence. They may also become drug dependent, a habit that tightens the pimps' control over their victims. The loose networks of pimps often engage in price-fixing to maintain uniform prices in a particular geographical area. Costs are kept low with the venues for sex being places such as cheap motel rooms, pimps' homes, adult clubs and car parks. By contrast, the pimps enjoy a lifestyle of lavish consumption and are disinclined to save, which Shelley (2010) alleges conforms to broader American patterns of consumption and investment. Until recently, pimps have been romanticized in American pop culture and the hardship endured by their victims overlooked.

Supermarket model: low cost and high volume

This model which focuses on illegal migration from Latin America into the United States across the Mexican border is based on maximizing profits from a high volume of transactions – cheap prices through economies of scale. The key to the human trafficking supermarket model is dealing with large numbers of would-be migrants to reduce unit costs. The trafficking gangs may have diversified from drugs and other criminal activities to seize the lucrative opportunities offered by thousands of Latin Americans trying to enter the United States. It was estimated that, in 2021, Mexican crime groups made profits of US $2.6 billion from human trafficking (Dinan 2022). Prices have risen considerably since Shelley (2010) wrote her book with traffickers now charging US $8,600 for Mexicans and US $11,500 for those from El Salvador, Honduras and Guatemala – up by US $2,000 since 2019 (Dinan 2022). The traffickers blame this on rising production costs such as petrol, employees' remuneration, logistics and presumably bribery as the latter is important to facilitate the large-scale movement of people. While the amounts that would-be migrants must pay to crime gangs to facilitate their entry into the United States may seem low to people in wealthy countries, they can be as much as an individual earns in one or two years in the migrants' countries of origin. Most of the border-crossings constitute people smuggling but there are certainly many cases of people being forced into servitude, for example in prostitution or agricultural labour. This is usually because those wanting to be smuggled may be unable to pay the trafficking fees and have to work off their debts to the traffickers.

Traditional slavery with modern technology: trafficking out of Nigeria and West Africa

Nigerian crime groups' human trafficking activities include women for sexual exploitation in Europe, the Middle East and North Africa and children for forced labour in Nigeria and the West African region. Child labour is in demand for domestic work, small commercial establishments, begging and mining. The crime groups in Nigeria have bases in family and ethnic links. Their overseas linkages are through the Nigerian diaspora. In Italy, which houses the largest Nigerian community in Europe, the Nigerian crime groups have joined forces with the domestic mafia organizations. The human trafficking of women for sexual exploitation has been based in the Edo region of Nigeria where Benin City is seen as the centre of operations. Women, sometimes previous victims, can be used to sign up newcomers. Recruitment occurs not only in Nigeria but may go further afield into neighbouring West African countries. This also applies to children who may be sourced from and sold to work in these countries. Human trafficking may also have the assent of the families of the trafficked persons who receive payment for them from the traffickers. The 'contracts' entered into are seen as enforceable by the trafficked persons and are used to gain victim compliance. Only small sums are obtained by the families as the bulk of the profits accrue to the OCGs. The criminal enterprise is greatly assisted by extremely high levels of corruption in Nigeria, low law enforcement capability and a poorly performing bureaucracy. Shelley's (2010) characterization of the business model as combining tradition and modernity relates to the use of traditional practices of Nigerian societies, such as magic to gain psychological control of victims, juxtaposed with modern transport and communication.

Understanding different models of human trafficking is important for law enforcement agencies in their efforts to prevent it from occurring. The UN trafficking protocol specifies a three-pronged approach known as 'the 3 Ps': *prevention* of the crime, *prosecution* of the trafficker and *protection* for the victims. A fourth 'P' – partnership – has been added more recently (Burke et al. 2022). Partnerships can involve diverse members spanning the range between local, national and international and involving government and civil society organizations. While the '4 Ps' approach provides an overall framework for anti-trafficking action, the organizations concerned need to design specific action plans to disrupt and close down particular business models. A one-size-fits-all approach will not suffice. Understanding how a model works and what factors lead to victim recruitment can form the basis of more effective anti-trafficking initiatives.

Conclusion

Despite government and UN commitment to address human trafficking and kidnap-for-ransom, these two multifaceted criminal enterprises have continued to grow in size as have the profits reaped by the gangs involved. The gangs engaged in these crimes have created diverse business models with innovation enabling them to match their objectives, capacities and organizational environments. Such innovation has also led to increases in the range of their targets. Furthermore, kidnap-for-ransom and human trafficking are evident across the globe although kidnap-for-ransom is overwhelmingly a domestic concern, the entire business process occurring within a country and especially where the state is weak. By contrast, human trafficking is often, but by no means exclusively, transnational in character and involves a range of actors undertaking a variety of roles; victims of human trafficking frequently end up in rich countries in which the state is relatively strong but where the criminals are still able to keep away from the gaze or attentions of law enforcement agencies. But one should not underestimate the complexity and difficulty of combating these crimes especially where trust in law enforcement is low and, for human trafficking, where substantial markets for sexual exploitation and forced labour provides a strong incentive for criminal gangs. The '4 Ps' form a useful framework for human trafficking but, as with kidnap-for-ransom, there is a need for law enforcement responses to be tailored to specific situations. Sometimes, effective solutions require profound changes in society and state, matters which go way beyond law enforcement agencies' remit.

References

Allain, J. (2018) 'Genealogies of human trafficking and slavery.' In R. Piotrowicz, C. Rijken and B.H. Uhl (eds) *Routledge Handbook of Human Trafficking*, pp. 3–12. London: Routledge.

Anti-Slavery International (2023) Anti-Slavery International website. Available at https://www.antislavery.org.

Assanvo, W. and Okereke, D. (2019) 'Nigeria's kidnapping crisis.' *Enact Observer*, 1 February. Available at https://enactafrica.org/enact-observer/nigerias-kidnapping-crisis.

Bales, K. (2007) *Ending Slavery: How We Free Today's Slaves*. Berkely, CA: University of California Press.

Bigio, J. and Vogelstein, R. (2019) 'The security implications of human trafficking.' Discussion Paper, October. New York: Council on Foreign Relations.

Bles, M. and Low, R. (1987) *The Kidnap Business*. London: Pelham.

Burke, M., Krolikowski, T., White, S. and Alabase, N. (2022) 'Introduction to human trafficking.' In M. Burke (ed.) *Human Trafficking: Interdisciplinary Perspectives*, pp. 3–31. New York: Routledge.

Cabalza, D. (2022) 'PNP: At least 5 groups may be into Pogo-link kidnappings.' *Philippine Daily Inquirer*, 17 September. Available at https://newsinfo.inquirer.net/1665660/pnp-at-least-5-groups-may-be-into-pogo-linked-kidnappings#:~:text=MANILA%2C%20Phi lippines%20—%20The%20Philippine%20National%20Police%20is,syndicates%20belie ved%20to%20be%20operating%20in%20the%20country.

Chinwokwu, E. and Michael, C. (2019) 'Militancy and violence as a catalyst to kidnapping in Nigeria.' *International Journal of Police Science and Management* 21 (1) 17–35.

Clutterbuck, R. (1978) *Kidnap and Ransom: The Response*. London: Faber and Faber.

Dinan, S. (2022) 'Hidden inflation on Biden's watch: Prices in migrant smuggling economy soar to $2.6 billion.' *Washington Times*, 2 October. Available at https://www.washingtontimes.com/news/2022/oct/2/cartels-collect-26-billion-smuggling-profit-border/.

Ezelio, J. (2018) 'Trafficking in human beings in the African context.' In R. Piotrowicz, C. Rijken and B.H. Uhl (eds) *Routledge Handbook of Human Trafficking*, pp. 52–67. Abingdon: Routledge.

Finkelhor, D., Hotaling, G. and Sedlak, A. (1992) 'The abduction of children by strangers and non-family members: Estimating the incidence by multiple methods.' *Journal of Interpersonal Violence* 7 (2) 226–243.

Goodey, J. (2012) 'Data on human trafficking: Challenges and policy context.' In J. Winterdyk, B. Perrin and P. Reichel (eds) *Human Trafficking: Exploring the International Nature, Concerns and Complexities*, pp. 39–56. Boca Raton, FL: CRC Press.

Gutierrez, E. (2013) 'Bandits, villains and bosses: Kidnappers of the Southern Philippines.' In F. Lara, Jr and S. Schoofs (eds) *Out of the Shadows: Violent Conflict and the Real Economy of Mindanao*, pp. 118–144. London: International Alert.

Heard, B. (2019) *Kidnapping and Abduction: Minimizing the Threat and Lessons in Survival*. Boca Raton, FL: CRC Press.

Kao, J. (1993) 'The worldwide web of Chinese business.' *Harvard Business Review* 71 (2) 24–36.

Lee, M. (2011) *Trafficking and Global Crime Control*. London: SAGE.

McCabe, K.A. (2022) 'Sex trafficking: Yesterday and today.' In M.C. Burke (ed) *Human Trafficking: Interdisciplinary Perspectives*, pp. 77–95. Routledge: New York and Abingdon.

Okoli, A. (2022) 'Who's at risk of being kidnapped in Nigeria?' *The Conversation*, 17 June. Available at https://theconversation.com/whos-at-risk-of-being-kidnapped-in-nigeria-184217.

Onuoha, F. and Akogwu, J. (2022) 'From terrorism to banditry: Mass abductions of schoolchildren in Nigeria.' ACCORD Conflict Trends 2022/1. Available at https://www.accord.org.za/conflict-trends/from-terrorism-to-banditry-mass-abductions-of-schoolchildren-in-nigeria/.

Pérouse de Monclos, M.-A. (ed.) (2014) *Boko Haram: Islamism, Politics, Security and the State in Nigeria*. Ibadan: IFRA-Nigeria.

Santos, S.M., Jr and Santos, P.V. (2010) 'Pentagon gang and other obscure Moro armed groups.' In S. Santos, Jr and P. Santos (eds) *Primed and Purposeful: Armed Groups and Human Security Efforts in the Philippines*, pp. 393–403. Geneva: Small Arms Survey and South-South Network for Non-state Armed Group Engagement.

Schiller, D. (1985) 'The European experience.' In B. Jenkins (ed.) *Terrorism and Personal Protection*, pp. 46–63. Boston, MA: Butterworth.

Shelley, L. (2010) *Human Trafficking: A Global Perspective*. Cambridge: Cambridge University Press.

Smartraveller (2023) 'Reducing the risk of kidnapping.' Department of Foreign Affairs and Trade, 4 January. https://www.smartraveller.gov.au/before-you-go/safety/kidnapping.

Smith, C.J. and Kangaspunta, K. (2012) 'Defining human trafficking and its nuances in a cultural context.' In J. Winterdyk, B. Perrin and P. Reichel (eds) *Human Trafficking: Exploring the International Nature, Concerns and Complexities*, pp. 19–38. Boca Raton, FL: CRC Press.

The Star (2022) 'Kidnapping rampant again in the Philippines.' 14 September. Available at https://www.thestar.com.my/aseanplus/2022/09/14/kidnapping-rampant-again-in-the-philippines-inquirer.

Toney-Butler, T.J., Ladd, M. and Mittel, O. (2023) 'StatPearls.' National Library of Medicine, National Center for Biotechnology Information. Available at https://www.ncbi.nlm.nih.gov/books/NBK430910/.

Turner, M. (1995a) 'The kidnapping crisis in the Philippines 1991–1993: Context and management.' *Journal of Contingencies and Crisis Management* 3 (1) 1–11.

Turner, M. (1995b) 'Terrorism and Secession in the Southern Philippines: The rise of the Abu Sayyaf.' *Contemporary Southeast Asia* 17 (1) 1–19.

Turner, M. (1998) 'Kidnapping and politics.' *International Journal of the Sociology of Law* 26 (2) 145–160.

Turner, M. (2008) 'Resolving self-determination disputes through complex power-sharing arrangements: The case of Mindanao, southern Philippines.' In M. Weller and B. Metzger (eds) *Settling Self-determination Disputes: Complex Power-sharing in Theory and Practice*, pp. 161–192. Leiden: Martinus Nijhoff.

Turner, M. and McCarthy-Jones, A. (2023) 'Cyber slavery starts up in Southeast Asia.' *East Asia Forum*, 14 June. Available at https://www.eastasiaforum.org/2023/06/14/cyber-slavery-starts-up-in-southeast-asia/.

Ugarte, E. (2008) 'The phenomenon of kidnapping in the southern Philippines: An overview.' *South East Asia Research* 16 (3) 293–341.

Ugarte, E. and Turner, M. (2011) 'What is the Abu Sayyaf? How labels shape reality.' *Pacific Review* 24 (4) 397–420.

United Nations Office of Drugs and Crime (UNODC) (2022) *Global Report on Trafficking in Persons 2022*. New York: United Nations.

United Nations Office of Drugs and Crime (UNODC) (2023) *The Protocol*. UNODC website. Available at https://www.unodc.org/unodc/en/human-trafficking/protocol.html.

Van Dijk, J. and Campistol, C. (2018) 'Work in progress: International statistics on human trafficking.' In R.W. Piotrowicz, C. Rijken and B.H. Uhl (eds) *Routledge Handbook of Human Trafficking*. pp. 381–394. Abingdon: Routledge.

Vitug, M. and Gloria, G. (2000) *Under the Crescent Moon: Rebellion in Mindanao*. Quezon City: Ateneo Center for Social Policy and Public Affairs and Institute for Popular Democracy.

Weitzer, R. (2015) 'Human trafficking and contemporary slavery.' *Annual Review of Sociology* 41, 223–242.

8

ILLICIT BUSINESS AND THE ENVIRONMENT

Introduction

We are now living in the Anthropocene, an unofficial unit of geological time that describes a period in which human activity has become the dominant influence on the Earth's environment (Johnson et al. 2022; Bergquist 2019). Scientific enquiry has overwhelmingly and repeatedly proved that over the past two centuries global warming, habitat loss, flora and fauna extinction, and altered chemical compositions of the atmosphere, oceans and soils have in large part been caused by human activities. The transition to the Anthropocene has been in progress since the mid-18th century when the Industrial Revolution ushered in dramatic changes to what human beings produce and how they produce it. Industry, agriculture and natural resource extraction have all caused major environmental damage and continue to do so. But, for the most part, these business undertakings have been operating legally. The harm they have caused has generally not broken the law despite their devastating impact on the environment.

In this chapter, the focus is on illicit business and the adverse effect it can have on the environment, society and the economy. These are enterprises that operate outside of state authorities and the law. But also included are legal entities which intentionally flout the law by regularly and systematically engaging in business practices that are illegal and which cause environmental damage. Environmentally destructive illicit businesses and business practices can be found in a broad range of human endeavours including wildlife trafficking, logging, fishing, mining, drug production, waste dumping and manufacturing. The participants in these businesses have little or no care for the environment in their pursuit of profits. Their impact can be considerable and can include pollution of the air, land and water, destruction of natural ecosystems, exploitation of workers and threats to the livelihoods of persons living

DOI: 10.4324/9781003293620-8

near the illegal operations. Growing concern over these planetary problems has been driven by environmental activists and civil society organizations and has given rise to 'the green criminological perspective' (Walters 2015). However, this perspective is in its infancy and there is no common agreement on a set of indicators that measures the impact of illicit business on the environment.

While there are similarities between the various forms of illicit business and its adverse effects on the environment, there are also differences. These similarities and differences will be examined in the rest of the chapter in which we explore two types of illicit business and their effects on the environment and society. These are the extractive industries of fishing and wildlife trafficking. Note that in each of these industries there are legal enterprises that operate within the requirements of prevailing laws and regulations.

Fishing

Fisheries are a vital industry for human nutrition and employment. In 2015, it was estimated that 3.2 billion people received 20% of their average per capita intake of animal protein from fish (FAO 2022). For some developing countries and small island states the figure can be 50% or more. Global consumption of fisheries products is rising; it increased from 9.9 kg per capita in the 1960s to 20.2 kg per capita in the 2020s (FAO 2022). In 2020, the global primary fisheries sector employed an estimated 58.5 million persons either full-time or part-time while, when subsistence production and secondary employment are included, 600 million households depended for their livelihoods at least partially on fisheries and aquaculture. But there are some disturbing trends. There has been a significant decline of fish stocks. In 2014, the Food and Agriculture Organization of the United Nations (FAO) reported that 90.1% of global fish stocks were fully exploited or over-exploited, while in 2019 only 64.6% of fish stocks were within biologically sustainable levels (FAO 2014, 2022). One of the main threats to maintaining fish stocks is the business of illicit fishing known as illegal, unreported and unregulated (IUU) fishing which is broadly defined as 'fishing activities that contravene regional, national or international fisheries conservation or management measures, or occur outside the reach of these laws and regulations' (TRACIT 2019, 63). While there are three components to IUU – the illegal, the unregulated and the unreported – they are interrelated. The true extent of IUU fishing is unknown, but it has been estimated that it could be as much as US $36 billion per annum. What is known is that there is considerable incentive to engage in IUU fishing as profits are high for the big operators who account for most of the illicit catch.

Illegal fishing involves 'activities conducted by national or foreign vessels in waters under the jurisdiction of a State, without the permission of that State, or in contravention of its laws and regulations' (TRACIT 2019, 63). It is seen in practices such as fishing without a licence; fishing in a closed or protected area; keeping undersized fish; using banned fishing gear; and illegally transshipping fish (World Ocean Review 2013). It occurs chiefly in the waters of developing countries where the state's capacity to prevent illegal fishing is severely constrained by lack of resources to assert control over its seas and corruption of responsible officials. This has been the case in West Africa which has been described as the 'epicenter' of illegal fishing owing to its rich fishing grounds that act as magnet for extensive illegal fishing on an 'industrial' scale with many vessels even making the long voyage from the People's Republic of China and Taiwan to participate in the indiscriminate plunder (Skrdlik 2022). Local artisanal fisheries have been badly affected by depleted fish stocks, yet up to 25% of local jobs are related to fishing. Furthermore, the region could be losing up to US $9.4 billion per year in illegally taken fish, a huge amount for the poor countries of the region.

Unreported fishing occurs when fishing activities are not reported or are misreported to the national authorities or to Regional Fisheries Management Organisations (RFMOs) when the illicit activities take place within the jurisdiction of those bodies. These include only reporting a portion of the catch so as to keep it within the quota; failing to disclose the harvesting of non-targeted species; the total avoidance of reporting; making false recordings of the location of fishing activities; inaccurately calculating the amount of fish transshipped at sea; and offloading fish at 'ports of convenience,' so named because of their low regulatory and inspection standards.

Unregulated fishing is a broad term that includes 'fishing conducted by vessels without nationality, or those flying the flag of convenience of a country not party to a RFMO within the jurisdiction of that RFMO' (TRACIT 2019, 63). Some unregulated fishing may not explicitly break the law; for example, fishing in an area where no conservation measures are in place or just outside the boundary of a marine reserve. Such actions are not illegal but can be viewed as circumventing or violating the spirit of the law. Much unregulated fishing occurs on the high seas in areas beyond countries' exclusive economic zones – 200 nautical miles from the shoreline – where there are no applicable conservation measures. Although many states have declared their support for the conservation of marine resources, under international law they are reluctant to enforce those laws due to the high cost involved, legal uncertainty and diplomatic issues relating to such actions. This discarding of global responsibilities has been likened to another 'tragedy of the commons' in which various economic actors have unrestricted access to a finite resource leading to its over-exploitation (Phelps Bondaroff et al. 2015).

While some illicit fishing activities are undertaken by artisanal fisherfolk to secure their livelihoods and survival in the face of declining fish stocks and catches (see Box 8.1), the big players responsible for the vast majority of IUU activities can be seen as utilizing practices that are consistent with transnational organized crime. They violate rules and regulations in a systematic and highly coordinated manner. Their fishing expeditions are highly planned and involve multiple actors including financiers, vessel owners, ship captains, crews and onshore participants who feed the illegal catches into the market. Illicit fishing involves a lengthy supply chain. Phelps Bondaroff et al. (2015, 37) allege that the activities of major IUU operators are 'more likely to target the most vulnerable and most valuable species and can include environmental offences, theft, fraud, quarantine violations, tax evasion, and serious crimes against people, including murder.'

BOX 8.1: DYNAMITE FISHING: SHORT-TERM WIN, LONG-TERM LOSS

While our discussion of IUU fishing has focused on highly organized criminal networks of transnational scope, there are also poor actors who engage in illegal fishing to secure their survival. These are the dynamite or blast fishermen who can be found in parts of Southeast Asia, South Asia and Africa. This mode of fishing involves throwing dynamite into the water to kill a large number of fish quickly and cheaply. It is illegal in most countries. In Sri Lanka, only two people, one boat and an oxygen cylinder are needed to catch fish in this manner, compared to the 25 people and multiple nets needed for traditional fishing – and the catch for the dynamite fishermen is higher. In the Philippines, poor fishermen create homemade bombs from ammonium nitrate crammed into old bottles with fuses protruding from the neck. Not only is dynamite fishing illegal in the Philippines but also the sale of ammonium nitrate is banned. It is nevertheless available. As in Sri Lanka, the Filipino blast fishers say that they use this method because of its efficiency in the context of declining fish stocks. They perceive a need to do it to safeguard their livelihoods. However, the gains are short term as dynamite fishing destroys the food chain and the coral reefs where fish reside and breed. Everything within the blast area radius of the bomb is killed – and in some cases the fishermen themselves receive serious injuries from their improvised bombs. In the long term, the reefs and their fish stocks will be decimated, thus threatening poor fishing communities with destitution. While top-down regulation has a part to play in eliminating dynamite fishing, it is of limited effect. It is vitally important to engage local communities and local authorities in more effective marine management. Creating alternative employment opportunities is also essential for the survival of reef ecosystems and poor coastal communities.

Sources: Attanayake (2023); Almendral (2018); ReefCause Team (2021).

As with other large-scale illicit businesses, a major theme in the case of the big players involved in IUU fishing are concerned with evasion in various forms. There are practices designed to avoid taxes such as dodging import and export duties, failure to account for income tax on profits, non-payment of social security for workers and undervaluation of products through mislabelling (Phelps Bondaroff et al. 2015). Some types of evasion may be more specific to fishing such as tampering with automatic identification systems so that fishing vessels cannot be tracked when they 'go dark.' Where they are fishing and where they are going to are obscured. There have even been cases of hacking to create 'ghost ships' where there are no vessels. Great efforts are made by the illicit business operators to disguise the ownership of fishing vessels. One common method is to use 'flags of convenience,' That is, ships are registered in countries that have lax requirements and/or provide little or no supervision of the vessels. Sometimes a single vessel may acquire multiple names and so receive multiple fishing permits. Ship names can be painted over to avoid identification. Owners and operators change ships' names, sometimes frequently, to confuse regulators and enforcers. Ships' ownership is often obscured through complex webs of companies located in multiple countries whose disclosure and tax regimes are favoured by transnational crime organizations. Another important evasive practice is the process of 'fish laundering' through a combination of transshipment and 'ports of convenience.' Transshipment occurs when fish are collected at sea by a refrigerator ship that services a fleet of smaller fishing vessels. Fish that are legally caught can then be mixed with illegal catches. The refrigerator ships then seek ports of convenience where there is minimal inspection and the fish can pass into the global supply chain.

We have seen how illicit fishing contributes considerably to environmental damage and how the industry is characterized by multiple criminal practices to avoid tax and financial responsibilities. The industry has also known to be involved in illegal labour practices that are sometimes said to be an example of modern slavery (Wilhelm et al. 2020; Stringer et al. 2022). Although the UN's Sustainable Development Goal 8 seeks to eradicate modern slavery, forced labour and human trafficking in order to protect labour rights and to promote safe and secure working environments, these aims are far from being achieved in IUU fishing. The International Labour Organization has declared forced labour and human trafficking in fisheries to be a 'severe problem' (ILO 2023). Victims have described a variety of illegal practices that violate labour laws and human rights including failure to attend to crew illnesses and injuries; psychological and sexual abuse; physical abuse including whipping and beating; low pay; long periods at sea sometimes lasting for months; unsafe working conditions; excessively long working hours; withholding pay; confiscation of personal identification; scarce or inadequate food; and working against one's will. There have even been accusations of murder. Migrant workers in particular are exploited. They are often tricked or coerced into signing on to work on fishing vessels and then find themselves in debt to ship operators (White 2023; Phelps Bondaroff et al 2015; Studeman 2023; Global Fishing Watch 2023). Labour exploitation is driven by the drive for profit in IUU fishing coupled with the situation of those being exploited (Yea and Stringer 2021). One part of the situation is the weak economic and power position of the migrant worker, but the other is that the fishing vessel can be seen as a 'total institution' in which exploitation can thrive. A total institution is a closed social system cut off from the wider society and governed by strict norms, rules and schedules that are determined by a single authority (Davies 1989). A distant-water fishing vessel fits this description with some operators and officers able to enforce brutal exploitative regimes on workers who are trapped on fishing vessels for long periods under the single authority of the officers.

A final question is what can be done to put an end to IUU fishing and the environmental destruction and labour exploitation that accompanies it? There is widespread knowledge of these problems and numerous treaties, declarations and agreements have been put in place at the international and regional level as have national legislation and rules all of which seek to create a sustainable global fisheries industry. However, more needs to be done to push 'flag of convenience' nations into action and ensure that the private sector, especially multinationals, use their market power to bring improved governance to the fisheries sector. Increasing the capacity of developing countries to police their waters and ports to prevent IUU and the damage it causes to their economies is another key task. Research is also required and has been greatly aided in recent years by the Illegal Unreported and Unregulated Fishing Risk Index that provides systematic measures of countries' vulnerability to, the prevalence of and responses to IUU fishing (Macfadyen and Hosch 2023). The Index provides data for all 152 coastal countries of the world according to 40 indices. In 2023, China was again the worst-performing country and Asia the worst-performing region, and while 54 countries had improved their scores from 2019 and 2021, 93 had worse scores. This is bad news for the planet and emphasizes the need to take more concerted action to tackle the devastating problem of IUU fishing.

Wildlife Trafficking

In 2023, the *Global Risk Report* published by the World Economic Forum (WEF) listed 'biodiversity loss and ecosystem collapse' as one of the major global risks of the coming decade (WEF 2023). The WEF ranked this risk the fourth highest out of 32 risks in terms of impact and severity, thus emphasizing the seriousness of it. Alarmingly, in terms of risk preparedness, biodiversity loss and ecosystem collapse was in 29th position out of 32 listed risks. Such concern from an elite economic organization clearly indicates the seriousness and scale of the problem. However, this is not new knowledge. Scientists, environmental non-governmental organizations and 'green' politicians have tirelessly issued reports, data and warnings for many years about the ecological damage being done to the planet. One contributor to this sorry state of affairs is the illegal trade in wildlife. But there are many legal activities that have even greater impacts; for example, clearing land for agriculture, forestry, urban growth and mining. Nevertheless, our concern is with the illicit trade in wildlife.

Wildlife trafficking is allegedly one of the most profitable criminal activities around the globe (TRAFFIC 2024). Sollund (2013) claims that it is the second largest type of illicit trade. Estimates of the value of the trade range from US \$5 billion to US \$23 billion but nobody really knows the true amount as transactions are clandestine and prices all depend on where an actor sits in the global supply chain – poacher, transporter, broker, user (GFI 2017). Nevertheless, the respected International Union for the Conservation of Nature (IUCN) Red List of threatened species for 2023 reports significant increases in volume and value of trade in wild species with almost every country in the world having active participants in the business. This particular illicit trade often comes at a high cost. According to TRAFFIC (2023), the illicit trade in wildlife 'fuels biodiversity loss, environmental degradation, economic loss and corruption.' There is also the intrinsic loss of components of our natural environment as well as cultural and aesthetic suffering and deprivation. In statistical terms IUCN (2023) records 44,000 species that are currently threatened by extinction; that is, 28% of 157,000 species on IUCN's list. Furthermore, there has been no reduction in the rate at which species are moving towards extinction. This can be explained in terms of the growth in number, volume and value of wild species entering the global supply chain.

While many of us are familiar with the illegal poaching of elephants for their ivory tusks, rhinoceroses for their horns (see Box 8.2) and tigers for their skins and bones, there are many more species being illegally traded. Wildlife can be defined as 'all non-human animals, plants and fungi which form part of a country's natural environment or which are visitors in a wild or captured state' (Nurse and Wyatt 2020, 5). Wildlife trafficking involves 'the illegal trade, smuggling, poaching, capture, or collection of endangered species, protected wildlife … derivatives or products thereof' (South and Wyatt 2011, 542). As can be seen from these definitions the term wildlife does not simply denote animals. It also includes birds, reptiles, plants and fungi, all of which are subject to illicit trade. For example, it has been claimed that Colombia accounts for 10% of the earth's biodiversity (Sollund 2019, 146). It is also a country which has been involved in supplying the illegal wildlife trade. Interviewees in a detailed study by Sollund (2019) listed a large number of species including turtles/tortoises; macaws, parrots, canaries and other songbirds; reptiles, insects and fish; monkeys and *tigrillos*; and the skins of crocodiles and mammals. The end uses were as pets, food and skins.

BOX 8.2: SAVING THE WHITE RHINO

The African Southern white rhinoceros was nearly brought to extinction by European hunters in the 19th century but conservation efforts restored their numbers to around 21,000. But from 2012 Southern white rhino numbers began to decline. This was because of increased poaching resulting from rising demand for rhino horn in Vietnam and, to a lesser extent, China. It is an illicit trade that was banned internationally in 1977 with later supporting domestic legislation in Vietnam and China. The increased demand has been driven by two factors. The first is the belief that rhino horn has efficacious medicinal properties that can cure hangovers, give respite to those with potentially terminal illnesses, and more. Furthermore, wild rhino horns are preferred to the farmed variety. However, there is absolutely no scientific basis for these claims.

Rhino horn is made of keratin, the same material as human hair and nails; and as an ecologist at the London Zoological Society once remarked, 'you might as well chew your fingernails.' China removed rhino horns from the ingredients listed in traditional Chinese pharmacopeia in 1993. The second factor – rhino horn as a status symbol – is linked to rising conspicuous consumption with increased affluence, especially in Vietnam. The horn can be carved into jewellery and other trinkets which can be perceived as a display of wealth. Horn in its powdered form might also be given to terminally ill relatives to show that everything that can be done to save them has been done. This is because rhino horn is an extremely valuable commodity with the figure of US $100,000 per kg sometimes cited, although environmental groups involved in saving rhinos do not want the market prices publicized as this might encourage further poaching. However, it has proved to be very challenging to reduce demand, especially in Vietnam. Interviews with Vietnamese purchasers of rhino horn products reveal little or no concern about the trade. The poaching of rhinos is remote from them and is not undertaken by them. There also seems to be low levels of concern about the legal repercussions of being involved in the trade. Purchasers perceive the police to have little interest in the trade in rhino products, an observation borne out by the facts. Other actors in the global supply chain that starts with poaching or stealing from stockpiles in Africa and ends up in dealers' hands in Vietnam also perceive the profits to outweigh the risks. As Southern white rhino numbers continue to fall it should be noted that of the four other types of rhinoceros, three are on the critically endangered list. A footnote to the illicit trade in rhino horn is that it has never been used as an aphrodisiac in East Asia. That is a Western media myth.

Sources: Ritchie (2021); Hsu (2017); Dang and Nielson (2019).

It should be noted that while there has been growing concern about illegal wildlife trafficking, the trade in fauna has received the greatest attention in the literature on the subject and in anti-trafficking policy. Flora have been somewhat neglected. This has been attributed to 'plant blindness,' whereby plants are ranked as being inferior to animals (Marguiles et al. 2019). Yet a wide variety of plant species are illegally traded for the production of oils, perfumes and medicines, and for ornamental purposes. Some species are threatened. For example, 31% or more of all cacti species are threatened, 47% of which are traded. Cycads, prehistoric palm-like plants, are now seen as the most endangered group of plant species, while orchids are also under threat through trade (IUCN 2018). There are 900 species of timber that are similarly threatened (Marguiles et al. 2019). Some of the trade in threatened plant species is undertaken via legal channels, but it appears that much of it flows through illegal channels.

Wildlife trafficking is a crime but until relatively recently in our history this was not necessarily the case. Indeed, some species were legally hunted to extinction, for example, the dodo on Mauritius to provide meat for sailors and Schomburgk's deer eliminated by commercial hunting in its native Thailand (Wittig 2016). The perception of wildlife trafficking as a crime has been linked to the growth of the conservation movement in North America and Europe in the 20th century which prompted official concern leading to the regulation of the legal trade in wildlife at the national and international level. Much of the trade in wildlife and wildlife products remains legal, but the attraction of high profit margins and the presence of demand for a wide range of these items has led to the growth of illicit trade and the involvement of organized crime (Wittig 2016). As the inter-governmental Financial Action Task Force (2020) has observed, 'the illegal wildlife trade is a major transnational organised crime which generates billions of dollars of criminal gains each year.' But how is it organized?

The Australian Transaction Reports and Analysis Centre (AUSTRAC), a government agency tasked with combating financial crime, has provided an insight into the network of actors and their transactions that have characterized wildlife crime in Australia (AUSTRAC 2020). Reptiles are by far the most common internationally trafficked Australian live animal with prices overseas being up to 28 times more than domestic ones. It is, however, illegal to export living Australian fauna for commercial purposes. There are 900 reptile species native to Australia of which 90% are not found elsewhere (Meneguzzi 2021). This enhances their novelty value and increases their attraction as exotic pets. China, Hong Kong and Taiwan have been identified as the major markets for these reptiles, although there is a global market for them too (AUSTRAC 2020). Relatively low penalties for wildlife trafficking compared to trafficking in drugs or people reduces the risks for those involved. The wildlife trafficking system showing the major actors and their transactions can be seen in diagrammatic form in Figure 8.1. The network comes to life with an overseas trader sourcing reptiles for the exotic pet market. For this, the trader needs a contact in Australia, referred to as a coordinator in Figure 8.1, who we might recognize as a broker from earlier chapters. The broker fills a structural hole that enables otherwise disconnected actors to cooperate in the criminal venture. Funds are either transmitted directly or via 'money mules' from the trader to the coordinator who can buy the reptiles on the legal domestic market or finance poaching. The coordinator may pack and post the reptiles or pay a courier to transport them. As with many networks it is the broker (coordinator) who makes the operation work. Coordinators can be based in Australia or overseas. According to AUSTRAC (2020), those operating in Australia are adept at remaining anonymous, while some overseas coordinators have been identified through online advertising of Australian reptiles for sale. Couriers generally send the parcels containing the animals overseas or pack them in their travel bags. Students and short-term visa holders are typically employed in the courier role. The parcels they send overseas are

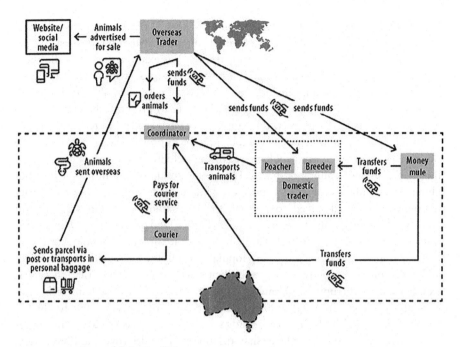

FIGURE 8.1 The Wildlife Trafficking System
Source: AUSTRAC (2020).

generally paid for with cash to avoid identification. The poachers may be local or from overseas. Their detection is extremely difficult in the vastness of the Australian outback where the resident population is sparse. Other actors may also enter the network such as pet store owners and transport operators. AUSTRAC (2020) notes that people involved in wildlife trafficking may also commit other crimes such as identity and financial fraud.

As can be seen, wildlife trafficking from Australia can be classified as an organized crime. This is similar elsewhere. There may be some opportunism involved but the networks required to facilitate wildlife trafficking and the amounts trafficked indicate high levels of organization across international borders. But what is being done to stop this illicit business? The primary instrument is the Convention on International Trade in Endangered Species of Wild Fauna and Flora, commonly known as CITES. It is an international agreement between governments and regional bodies that aims to ensure that trade in wild animals, plants and products derived thereof does not threaten the survival of species (CITES 2024). Currently, there are 184 states that are parties to the agreement; in other words, most of the countries in the world. CITES arose from international discussions about conservation in the 1960s but it was not until 1973 that the Convention was finally agreed. Today, more than 40,000 species are listed for varying degrees of protection under CITES. While states and regional organizations adhere voluntarily to CITES, it is legally binding. However, each state party to the agreement must enact its own domestic legislation to implement CITES at the national level. For example, in Australia there is the Environment Protection and Biodiversity Conservation Act 1999; in Kenya, the Wildlife Management and Conservation Act Revised Edition 2022; while in Peru, the Constitution obligates the state to promote the conservation of biodiversity and is legislated through the Forestry and Wildlife Law.

Although CITES represents a laudable attempt to protect the environment and the species in it, there are problems regarding wildlife trafficking. The first and most obvious shortcoming is that CITES is not an anti-crime measure. It is not about combating the illicit business of wildlife trafficking. It is a regulatory instrument largely designed to manage the legal trade in wildlife and not to combat organized crime (Harvey 2016). The second problem is that of the implementation of CITES and national legislation to control wildlife trade. In many countries, especially in the developing world, there are insufficient resources and capacities to properly address the illicit wildlife trade. The situation can be exacerbated by corruption. Organized crime groups have been able to bribe officials at all levels – from government ministers to park rangers – but for higher level officials in East African case studies identified by Wittig (2016), investigations can be abandoned, evidence may disappear or be destroyed, and no arrests or prosecutions are ever made. Documents can be forged or switched by customs officials and false identity cards can be used (Wyatt et al. 2018). Wild-caught species can be laundered through captive-breeding facilities (Harvey 2016). In short, powerful supply-side actors are able to exploit weak governance and law enforcement in the pursuit of illegal profits (Cooney et al. 2021). Corruption can occur at all stages of the illicit value chain. A third issue is that illegal trade income at the bottom end of the value chain may be supporting poor households with few other income-earning possibilities. Fourth, demand for illegally sourced wildlife may be longstanding and deeply entrenched. If the species is greatly threatened, this could have the perverse effect of raising prices through scarcity, thus increasing the attraction of poaching (Cooney et al. 2021).

An important driver of the increase in wildlife trafficking since the early 2000s has been the internet. Like legitimate businesses that have revolutionized the retail trade through the internet, so too have illicit businesses seized the opportunities offered to them by this technology to increase the volume and variety of trade and, of course, profits. Lavorgna (2014) has listed the opportunities offered by the internet to facilitate and boost wildlife trafficking:

- *Communicative and managerial opportunities:* communication has been facilitated by email, social media and messaging apps among traders, between traders and customers and more generally among all actors in the trafficking network.
- *Informational and technical opportunities:* providing access to useful practical information (e.g. feeding a reptile or accessing legal frameworks) and

finding solutions to problems (e.g. translating adverts into other languages or tracking shipments).

- *Organizational and relational opportunities:* facilitating the organization of the criminal network, perhaps even removing actors to increase network efficiency.
- *Promotional opportunities:* indicating the availability for sale of wildlife and their products
- *Persuasive opportunities:* to reassure buyers about the reliability of the trade and validity of the products being sold.

The internet is thus a leading tool for making criminal networks engaged in wildlife trading function more efficiently and effectively. In short, it is good for business. For example, a Thai study of the critically endangered bowmouth guitarfish found 977 items online including on Facebook Marketplace, eBay and Lazada (Pytka et al. 2023). The fish's spine and brows are used to make amulets that are believed to have protective qualities, although there is no scientific evidence to support this. In 2018, IUCN found 365 protected plant species openly traded on Amazon and eBay (IUCN 2018). In a six-week study in 2021, investigators in America found nearly 2,000 adverts for almost 2,400 animals, derivatives or products of species protected under the Endangered Species Act (IFAW 2021). The online illicit trade is 'hidden in plain sight.' However, action has been taken through the formation of the Coalition to End Wildlife Trafficking Online with 47 companies signing up including Meta, eBay, TikTok and Alibaba (Wang 2024). But there has been very limited success. For example, Facebook joined the Coalition in 2018, but two years later wildlife traffickers were still 'easily and openly operating on the platform' and 'wildlife trading for multiple endangered species had increased since 2018 (Paul et al. 2020, 7).

A final observation on wildlife trafficking is that it can be linked to other forms of illicit business and terrorist groups. For example, connections have been made between wildlife and drug trafficking (van Uhm et al. 2021). In a comprehensive overview of the relevant literature it was found that the overlap or convergence of other types of illicit business could be either 'active' or 'passive' (Anagnostou and Doberstein 2022). The active mode occurs when criminal actors are seeking to diversify their businesses in general or specifically through 'contraband barter trade,' different commodities are shipped together, wildlife traffickers are taxed by other criminal organizations and 'threat finance' is demanded by heavily armed non-state armed groups. Passive convergence occurs incidentally through environmental factors such as shared trafficking routes, the use of a common port or operating in a jurisdiction characterized by weak governance. Terrorist groups have also been accused of wildlife poaching to feed their combatants and to generate funds to enable them to continue their armed conflicts. For example, several insurgent groups – Al-Shabaab in Somalia, the Janjaweed Arab militia in Sudan, the Seleka rebels in the Central African Republic and the Lord's Resistance Army in Central Africa and East Africa – have been involved in the slaughter of elephants in Africa for both of these purposes (Felbab-Brown 2018; Haenlein et al., 2016). But the literature on the subject has featured myths and unfounded assumptions, and has probably exaggerated the role of militant groups. There is certainly evidence to prove their participation but their activities represent only a small proportion of the global wildlife trade (Felbab-Brown 2018). Furthermore, counter-insurgency forces have also been known to participate in poaching. Whether it is the latter or the insurgent organizations doing the actual poaching, they will need to link up with criminal networks to get the products into global supply chains.

Conclusion

There is no doubt that human beings have caused extensive damage to the environment of planet Earth, usually legally. However, criminals ranging from poor fishermen in the tropics to well-funded multinational networks have contributed to this appalling state of affairs. As we have seen in this chapter, illicit businesses plunder marine life and poach threatened terrestrial species in the pursuit of profits or for their survival. Vulnerable people may also be exploited and their long-term livelihoods put at risk. There are international agreements and national laws and regulations in place which make these activities illegal. However, their implementation is often patchy in developing countries that suffer from weak governance and widespread corruption. But we cannot simply put all the blame onto these developing countries. There are market demands from high- and middle-income countries that make these trades profitable and worth the risk for criminals.

References

Almendral, A. (2018) 'Dynamite fishing decimates entire ocean food chain in the Philippines.' SBS, 19 June. Available at https://www.sbs.com.au/news/article/dynamite-fishing-decimates-entire-ocean-food-chains-in-the-philippines/y1e1yth62.

Anagnostou, M. and Doberstein, B. (2022) 'Illegal wildlife trade and other organized crime: A scoping review.' *Ambio* 51, 1615–1631.

Attanayake, D. (2023) 'Everything is destroyed': Dynamite use sends shockwaves through fishing industries.' *The Guardian*, 7 September. Available at https://www.theguardian.com/environment/2023/sep/07/everything-is-destroyed-dynamite-use-sends-shockwaves-through-fishing-industries-sri-lanka.

Australian Transaction Reports and Analysis Centre (AUSTRAC) (2020) *Stopping the Illegal Trafficking of Australian Wildlife*. Sydney: AUSTRAC.

Bergquist, A.-K. (2019) 'Renewing business history in the era of the Anthropocene.' *Business History Review* 93 (1) 3–24.

Convention on International Trade in Endangered Species of Wild Fauna and Flora (CITES) (2024) CITES website. Available at https://cites.org/eng/disc/text.php.

Cooney, R., Challender, D.W.S., Broad, S., Roe, D. and Natusch, D.J.D. (2021) 'Think before you act: Improving the outcomes of CITES listing decisions.' *Frontiers in Ecology Evolution* 9.

Dang, V.H.N. and Nielson, M.R. (2019) 'We asked people in Vietnam why they use rhino horn. Here's what they said.' *The Conversation*, 30 April. Available at https://theconversation.com/we-asked-people-in-vietnam-why-they-use-rhino-horn-heres-what-they-said-116307.

Davies, C. (1989) 'Goffman's concept of the total institution: Criticisms and revisions.' *Human Studies* 12 (1/2) 77–95.

Felbab-Brown, W. (2018) 'Wildlife and drug trafficking, terrorism, and human security.' *Brookings Commentary*, 8 November. Available at https://www.brookings.edu/articles/wildlife-and-drug-trafficking-terrorism-and-human-security/.

Financial Action Task Force (2020) *Money Laundering and the Illegal Wildlife Trade*. Paris: Financial Action Task Force.

Food and Agriculture Organization of the United Nations (FAO) (2014) *The State of the World's Fisheries and Aquaculture: Opportunities and Challenges*. Rome: FAO.

Food and Agriculture Organization of the United Nations (FAO) (2022) *The State of the World's Fisheries and Aquaculture 2022: Towards Blue Transformation*. Rome: FAO.

Global Financial Integrity (GFI) (2017) *Transnational Crime in the Developing World*. Washington, DC: GFI.

Global Fishing Watch (2023) 'Following forced labour in the world's fishing fleets.' Global Fishing Watch website. Available at https://globalfishingwatch.org/blog/new-study-unveils-risk-of-forced-labor-in-fisheries.

Haenlein, C., Maguire, T. and Somerville, K. (2016) 'Poaching, wildlife trafficking and terrorism.' In C. Haenlein and M.L.R. Smith (eds) *Poaching, Wildlife Trafficking and Security in Africa*, pp. 58–76. Abingdon: Routledge for the Royal United Services Institute for Defence and Security Studies.

Harvey, R. (2016) 'What is CITES and why should we care.' *The Conversation*, 19 September. Available at https://theconversation.com/explainer-what-is-cites-and-why-should-we-care-65510.

Hsu, J. (2017) 'The hard truth about the rhino horn "aphrodisiac".' SCI AM, 5 April. Available at https://www.scientificamerican.com/article/the-hard-truth-about-the-rhino-horn-aphrodisiac-market/.

International Fund for Animal Welfare (IFAW) (2021) *Digital Markets: Wildlife Trafficking Hidden in Plain Sight*. Washington, DC: IFAW.

International Labour Organization (ILO) (2023) 'Forced labour and human trafficking in fisheries.' Available at https://www.ilo.org/global/topics/forced-labour/policy-areas/fisheries/lang–en/index.htm.

International Union for Conservation of Nature (IUCN) (2018) 'Illegal wildlife trade endangers plants – but few are listening.' 9 October. Available at https://www.iucn.org/news/species/201810/illegal-wildlife-trade-endangers-plants-few-are-listening.

International Union for Conservation of Nature (IUCN) (2023) *IUCN Red List of Threatened Species 2023*. Available at https://www.iucnredlist.org/en.

Johnson, A., Hebdon, C., Burrow, P., Chatti, D. and Dove, M. (2022) 'Anthropocene.' In *Oxford Research Encyclopedia of Anthropology*. Oxford: Oxford University Press. Available at https://oxfordre.com/anthropology/display/10.1093/acrefore/9780190854584.001.0001/acrefore-9780190854584-e-295.

Lavorgna, A. (2014) 'Wildlife trafficking in the Internet age.' *Crime Science* 3 (5).

Macfadyen, G. and Hosch, G. (2023) *The Illegal Unreported and Unregulated Fishing Risk Index: 2023 Update*. Poseidon Aquatic Resource Management Ltd and the Global Initiative Against Transnational Organized Crime.

Marguiles, J.D., Bullough, L.-A., Hinsley, A., Ingram, D.J., Cowell, C., Goettsch, B., Klitgard, B.B., Lavorgna, A., Sinovas, P. and Phelps, J. (2019) 'Illegal wildlife trade and the persistence of "plant blindness".' *PPP Plants People Planet* 1 (3) 173–182.

Meneguzzi, J. (2021) 'Bound, gagged, posted: Investigating Australia's cruel and corrupt illegal wildlife trade.' *Australian Geographic*, 23 December. Available at https://www.australiangeographic.com.au/topics/wildlife/2021/12/australias-illegal-wildlife-trade/.

Nurse, A. and Wyatt, T. (2020) *Wildlife Criminology*. Bristol: Policy Press.

Paul, K.A., Miles, K. and Huffer, D. (2020) *Two Clicks Away: Wildlife Sales on Facebook*. Alliance to Counter Crime Online.

Phelps Bondaroff, T.N., van der Werf, W. and Reitano, T. (2015) *The Illegal Fishing and Organized Crime Nexus: Illegal Fishing as Transnational Organized Crime*. GI-TOC and The Black Fish.

Pytka, J.M., Moore, A.B.M. and Heenan, A. (2023) 'Internet trade of a previously unknown wildlife product from a critically endangered marine fish.' *Conservation Science and Practice* 5 (3) e12896.

ReefCause Team (2021) 'The harmful effects of dynamite fishing on coral reefs.' 11 April. Available at https://conservation.reefcause.com/the-harmful-effects-of-dynamite-fishing-on-coral-reefs/.

Ritchie, H. (2021) 'The state of the world's rhino populations.' Our World in Data, 30 November. Available at https://ourworldindata.org/rhino-populations.

Skrdlik, J. (2022) 'Report: West Africa is the global epicenter of illegal fishing.' Organized Crime and Corruption Reporting. Available at https://www.occrp.org/en/daily/16963-report-west-africa-is-the-global-epicenter-of-illegal-fishing.

Sollund, R.A. (2013) 'Animal trafficking trade: Abuse and species injustice.' In R. Walters, D.S. Westerhuis and T. Wyatt (eds) *Emerging Issues in Green Criminology*, pp. 79–82. London: Palgrave Macmillan.

Sollund, R.A. (2019) *The Crimes of Wildlife Trafficking: Issues of Justice, Legality and Morality*. Abingdon: Routledge.

South, N. and Wyatt, T. (2011) 'Comparison of the illicit wildlife and drug trades: An exploratory study.' *Deviant Behavior* 32 (6) 538–561.

Stringer, C., Burmester, B. and Michailova, S. (2022) 'Modern slavery and the governance of labor exploitation in the Thai fishing industry.' *Journal of Cleaner Production* 371, 15 October, 133645.

Studeman, M. (2023) 'China's rampant illegal fishing is endangering the environment and global economy.' *Newsweek*, 24 January. Available at https://www.newsweek.com/chinas-rampant-illegal-fishing-endangering-environment-global-economy-opinion-1776034.

Transnational Alliance to Combat Illicit Trade (TRACIT) (2019) *Mapping the Impact of Illicit Trade on the Sustainable Development Goals*. Available at https://euipo.europa.eu/tunnel-web/secure/webdav/guest/document_library/observatory/documents/reports/2019_Mapping_The_Impact_Of_Illicit_Trade/2019_Mapping_The_Impact_Of_Illicit_Trade_EN.pdf.

TRAFFIC (2024) TRAFFIC website. Available at https://www.traffic.org.

Van Uhm, D., South, N. and Wyatt, T. (2021) 'Connection between trades and trafficking in wildlife and drugs.' *Trends in Organized Crime* 24, 425–446.

Walters, R. (2015) 'Organized crime and the environment.' In G. Bruinsma and D. Weisburd (eds) *Encyclopedia of Criminology and Criminal Justice*. pp. 3368–3375. New York: Springer. Available at https://link.springer.com/referenceworkentry/10.1007/978-1-4614-5690-2_285.

Wang, M. (2024) 'How social media helps wildlife trafficking thrive in plain sight.' *Popular Science*, 9 March. Available at https://www.popsci.com/environment/social-media-endangered-animals-for-sale/.

White, C. (2023) 'Seafood working group urges downgrade of Thailand, Taiwan in forthcoming US Trafficking in Persons Report.' SeafoodSource, 5 June. Available at https://www.seafoodsource.com/news/environment-sustainability/seafood-working-group-urges-downgrade-of-thailand-taiwan-in-forthcoming-us-trafficking-in-persons-report.

Wilhelm, M., Kadfk, A., Bhakod, V. and Skattang, K. (2020) 'Private governance of human and labor rights in seafood supply chains: The case of the modern slavery crisis in Thailand.' *Marine Policy* 115, May, 103833.

Wittig, T. (2016) 'Poaching, wildlife trafficking and organised crime.' In C. Haenlein and M. L.R. Smith (eds) *Poaching, Wildlife Trafficking and Security in Africa*, pp. 77–101. Abingdon: Routledge for the Royal United Services Institute for Defence and Security Studies.

World Economic Forum (WEF) (2023) *The World Economic Forum Global Risk Report 2023*. Geneva: WEF.

World Ocean Review (2013) 'WOR 2: The future of fish: The fisheries of the future – illegal fishing.' Available at https://worldoceanreview.com/en/wor-2/fisheries/illegal-fishing/.

Wyatt. T., Johnson, K., Hunter, L., George, R. and Gunter, R. (2018) 'Corruption and wildlife trafficking: Three case studies involving Asia.' *Asian Journal of Criminology* 13, 35–55.

Yea, S. and Stringer, C. (2021) 'Caught in a vicious cycle: Connecting forced labour and environmental exploitation through a case study of Asia-Pacific.' *Marine Policy* 134, Dec., 104825.

9

STATE-LED ILLICIT BUSINESS

Introduction

In this chapter we explore a new area in the study of illicit business and organized crime that deals with the complex yet intriguing idea of state-led illicit business. Traditionally, organized crime and illicit business were understood as the product of individuals and groups seeking to engage in profit-based activities that were proscribed by the state. As such, the relationship between illicit business and the state has been perceived as oppositional, but what if the two parties engage in cooperation? Lupsha (1996) proposed that this relationship could be understood as existing in three stages: predatory, parasitic and symbiotic. In the predatory stage, organized crime groups (OCGs) are in direct competition and/or conflict with the state, motivated by a 'winner takes all' mentality, meaning that their actions always come at a cost to the state. In the second stage, OCGs adopt strategies to leverage the state's resources while minimizing the cost to the state. During the final stage the relationship can be conceptualized as symbiotic. In this environment, OCGs have moved from competing to cooperating with the state to varying degrees. Both the criminal group and state share mutual interests and can derive significant benefits from their collaborative efforts.

Another way to explore the symbiosis of criminal groups and the state is to move beyond an examination of differing relationships between the two, and instead undertake a closer examination of the state itself. State classification has generated a number of important contributions with the majority emerging from work in political science. These have included 'soft states' (Myrdal 1968), states classified by their 'degree of government' (Huntington 1968), 'weak states' struggling with strong societies (Migdal 1988), 'failed states' (Rotberg 2004), 'collapsed states' (Zartman 1995) and 'kleptocracies'

DOI: 10.4324/9781003293620-9

(Andreski 1968). McCarthy-Jones and Turner (2022, 1195) point out that 'this classificatory pursuit has especially involved developing and post-communist countries where the state has evolved into a variety of forms.' These environments are dynamic, change frequently and, in some cases, experience protracted periods of volatility. As a result, more recent contributions have pointed to the existence of another state formation, the 'mafia state.'

Until recently, this term has been attributed to over 20 countries including, but not limited to, the Russian Federation, Hungary, Bulgaria, Azerbaijan, Ukraine, Montenegro, Venezuela, Cambodia, the Democratic People's Republic of Korea (North Korea), South Africa, Nigeria and Guinea-Bissau. In most cases the term has been applied indiscriminately, and in some cases disparagingly, to criticize specific governments without substantial qualification for the use of the term.

Defining the Mafia State

While many characterizations of states as 'mafia states' fail to list the criteria that justify that classification, contributions from Naím (2012) and Magyar (2016) have attempted to provide more precise reasoning for the use of the term. Naím (2012, 101) highlights the 'fusing of governments and criminal groups' so that the interests of organized crime and government become 'inextricably intertwined.' He identifies examples of alliances between criminal groups and the state, arguing that governments have undergone a process of criminalization in countries including Russia, Kosovo, Bulgaria, Afghanistan, Guinea, Venezuela, Mexico, Pakistan and North Korea. However, Naím's work actively avoids providing a working definition of a mafia state because 'they defy easy categorization' (Naím 2012, 101).

In contrast, Magyar (2016) provides a more substantial assessment of a mafia state through an in-depth analysis of Hungary under President Viktor Orbán. Magyar (2016) acknowledges that even though the mafia state is inherently authoritarian it should still be considered as a 'stand-alone' variant. In this conceptualization, élite control of politics and business is achieved through networks of associates often possessing blood ties. Thus, the organizational structure mimics that of the Italian mafia which creates strong organizational loyalty through blood ties. Magyar (2016, 71) describes this structure as a 'pyramid-like order' in which the president sits at its summit. Rather than focusing on criminal groups, Magyar (2016) paints a vivid picture of 'upperworld' corruption that is highly organized by both political and economic members of the élite. However, the distinctiveness of Magyar's concept of the mafia state is based on specific environmental conditions that emerged after the collapse of Soviet Union. The post-communist countries undoubtedly possess similar experiences, but this also limits its explanatory power for states that sit outside of this particular historical experience. Therefore, a 'procedural minimum' definition is required in order to bring clarity to the term and precision to its application. McCarthy-Jones and Turner (2022, 1998) argue that

> as a general definition, the mafia state is run as a criminal organization in which the country's political leader presides over a network of family and friends who make private gains from state action. However, in one variation, the mafia state can be engaged in cooperation with organized crime groups outside of the state. This relationship involves state personnel from the top leadership down participating in, possibly even taking over, illicit activities normally associated with organized crime.

This definition extends the concept of the symbiotic relationship and shows that in some cases the state may choose to completely co-opt criminality, whereby the state shifts from a collaborative role and evolves into the dominant actor in criminal activities. Beyond their general definition, McCarthy-Jones and Turner (2022) have identified three subtypes of mafia states and their associated characteristics (see Table 9.1). Sub-type 1 relates to a mafia state that is heavily engaged with organized crime in line with Naím (2012); sub-type 2 refers to mafia states that operate with minimal engagement with criminal groups in line with Magyar (2016), while sub-type 3 represents a hybrid formation of sub-types 1 and 2.

As the three sub-types show, the relationship between organized crime and the state is complex and varied. Sub-types provide an overview of the central characteristics of a mafia state, but they do not help to explain the causes of the nexus between criminal groups and the state. This is why identifying critical junctures in a country's history can hold great explanatory power by pinpointing specific events that have contributed to a deepening of the nexus. These critical junctures could be the result of endogenous or exogenous factors that impact the political, economic, societal and security landscapes of a nation, creating openings for significant change to occur (Capoccia 2016). Accordingly, decision-making and policymaking processes are often radically altered to accommodate rapidly changing environmental conditions. During these periods, there are significant departures from the status quo that modify or fundamentally change the future trajectory of a country. The consequence of these departures from the status quo is that sometimes the separation between the state and criminal groups or criminal activities is reduced, and as a reflection the nexus between the state and criminality increases. To illustrate how this unfolds, we now turn to examine three case studies of state-led illicit business: North Korea, Venezuela and the Syrian Arab Republic. All three have been accused as operating as mafia states, and yet there are clear distinctions between each case. However, all three cases possess similarities that should be considered as causal factors for the emergence of state-led illicit business in different parts of the world. A historical approach is adopted for the case studies to show how sequences of events often over decades eventually led to the emergence of political regimes which rely heavily on illicit business for their survival.

TABLE 9.1 Sub-types of the Mafia State

Characteristics	Sub-type 1 With Organized Crime Groups	Sub-type 2 Without Organized Crime Groups	Sub-type 3 Hybrid
State is engaged with organized crime groups	Heavily engaged	Little or no engagement	Somewhat engaged
Likely political regime	Authoritarian with opposition oppressed by violent means	Semi-authoritarian with opposition weakened	Authoritarian with opposition weakened so cannot win elections
Accountability institutions	Abolished or replaced and staffed by regime loyalists	Weakened but can still make some independent decisions	Subservient to the political regime
Coercive forces of the state	Loyal to the state and benefits materially from participation in mafia state activities	Loyal to the state but little or no material benefit from mafia state activities	Loyal to the state and possible material benefit for a select few from mafia state activities
Criminal groups and state authority	State cedes authority to organized crime groups for certain illegal activities and public order in particular areas but the state retains overall control	Little or no state cooperation or ceding of authority	State allows selected criminal groups to operate illicit business and uses them as proxies in some circumstances
State capability	Weak state unable to deliver expected public goods	State delivering expected public goods	State likely to deliver expected public goods
Exemplar	Venezuela under Nicolás Maduro	Hungary under Viktor Orbán	Russia under Vladimir Putin

Source: McCarthy-Jones and Turner (2022).

Note: This table first appeared in McCarthy-Jones, A. and Turner, M. (2022) 'What is a "Mafia State" and how is one created?' *Policy Studies* 43(6) 1195–1215.

North Korea

North Korea is an isolated and reclusive country. It is often described as a 'hermit kingdom' that does not participate in the international financial system and does not possess global trading partners in a conventional sense (Lankov 2022). During the Cold War, North Korea relied on support from its traditional allies Russia (the former Soviet Union) and China to overcome its economic isolation. However, by the 1980s, this support was in decline as these nations focused on their own economic development through participation in global economic and political forums.

Today, North Korea is considered a pariah state by the international community and is subject to numerous sanctions due to its unilateral nuclear development programme (UNSC 2021). In 2022, the United Nations (UN) reported that North Korea's trade in goods amounted to US $1 billion and that in that year over 99% of its imports came directly from the People's Republic of China with which it shares a land border (UNDESA 2023). Yet over the decades the dynastic rule of North Korea by the Kim family has managed to withstand mounting pressure from the international community to conform to global agreements and norms and, to this day, the regime under the leadership of Kim Jong-un maintains an iron grip over the country and its population. It continues to fund its nuclear development programme and members of the Kim regime are frequently seen in photographs that feature ostentatious displays of wealth, while poverty and severe deprivation are widespread among the population (Walcott 2020). This strange situation raises the question: what explains the regime's survival? One vital contributing factor is a North Korean government agency known as Bureau 39 or Office 39. While most people outside North Korea are unlikely to have heard of this organization, the work of Bureau 39 is the most important part of the North Korean state apparatus for maintaining the regime's survival. It supplies the regime with its funds through illegal activities.

The history of Bureau 39 can be traced back to critical junctures that occurred in 1970s and 1980s. A series of failed development plans under the then ruler, Kim Il Sung, the suppression of consumerism and private wealth in North Korean society, and the establishment of a permanent 'wartime' economy led to the accumulation of unserviceable foreign debt. The regime's inability to manage this debt had a cascade effect on the economy that brought the country close to default in 1974. This severely diminished the government's borrowing capacity, thus creating a significant cash reserve problem. The result was increasing isolation from the international community which was the 'natural consequence of the Kims' dogged insistence on destructive policies' (Eberstadt 2015, 1). It was during this era that Bureau 39 was established with a mandate to address the state's growing cash crisis.

Initially, the work of Bureau 39 was proposed as the solution to what was considered to be a short-term problem. However, in the late 1980s, North Korea's cash supply issues intensified when China and members of the Soviet Union refused to honour barter systems that previously had been accepted as a method of payment for imports from each country (Armstrong 2005). This proved to be the catalyst for the expansion of Bureau 39's illicit business activities. For example, Bureau 39 was the department responsible for developing counterfeit US $100 bills known as 'supernotes.' The quality of the forged notes was almost unprecedented, making detection extremely difficult, and so for a time they provided the regime with a sizable source of income (Carney 2018). This type of illicit business scheme aligned with Bureau 39's mandate, which was to operate as the central government agency tasked with generating and managing foreign currency for the regime (Hurst 2005). To this day it controls all the economic channels that can bypass sanctions and generate revenue for the regime. As Katzeff Silberstein (2023, 1) points out, 'sanctions-evading actions are not rare events, but are institutionalised within North Korea's economy.'

To evade detection the regime has often utilized its diplomatic networks and infrastructure to assist its illicit revenue raising schemes. For example, North Korea has a long history dating back to the 1970s of using its diplomatic resources to provide the logistical support for the trafficking of drugs, conflict diamonds, gold, ivory, counterfeit currency, pharmaceuticals, tobacco and cigarettes (GI-TOC 2017, 4). The Global Initiative Against Transnational Organized Crime asserts that this practice continues to be used in various parts of the world, particularly in Africa (GI-TOC 2017). According to a report published by GI-TOC (2017, 12), 'North Korea's African embassies form a nexus of illicit trade in rhino horn, ivory, cigarettes and minerals.'

Bureau 39 is also heavily involved in the export of North Korean labour as a means of generating income. This has become particularly evident in relation to textile industries abroad, particularly those in China. It has been claimed that North Korean textile workers operating in factories in Dandong, China, are expected to work up to 18 hours a day without any leave entitlements and a large portion of their pay is garnished by the North Korean government (Breuker and van Gardingen 2019). They are unable to leave their workplaces without permission and they are subjected to constant surveillance which amounts to a form of 'state-sponsored forced labour' (Pattisson 2020). These workers create products that are exported and sold on the international market. For example, during the COVID-19 pandemic, personal protective equipment products made by North Korean workers in Dandong were purchased by countries including Germany, Italy, Japan, South Africa, South Korea, Myanmar, the Philippines and the United States (Pattisson 2020). Detecting the source of labour is difficult because many of these export companies masquerade as legal Chinese businesses, when in fact they are operated by the North Korean state. Further complicating matters is that beyond these shadow companies, many legal Chinese textile businesses use North Korean labour to produce their end products. This demonstrates the ease with which international supply chains can be infiltrated with products made from exploitative indentured forms of labour (Breuker and van Gardingen 2019).

The scale of Bureau 39's activities, estimated to be in the billions of US dollars each year, has enabled the regime to almost completely bypass the effects of economic sanctions (Bechtol 2018). Not only has Bureau 39 provided the funds that allow the regime to control its population both inside and outside of the country, but it has also enabled North Korea to guarantee its survival through the state's total co-option of criminality. Kan et al. (2010, vii) clarify this process when they argue that

> North Korea practices a form of 'criminal sovereignty' that is unique in the contemporary international security arena. North Korea uses state sovereignty to protect itself from external interference in its domestic affairs

while dedicating a portion of its government to carrying out illicit international activities in defiance of international law and the domestic laws of numerous other nations. The proceeds of these activities are then used in a number of ways to sustain North Korea's existence and to enable other policies. For example, criminal proceeds are distributed to members of the North Korean elite (including senior officers of the armed forces); are used to support Kim Jong-il's personal lifestyle; and are invested in its military apparatus.

More recently, the North Korean government and members of Bureau 39 are reported to be heavily involved in illicit activities related to cryptocurrencies. According to Kim et al. (2022, 3), North Korea has developed a system that draws on 'over-the-counter virtual asset brokers, many of whom are in third party countries like China' to exploit the anonymity provided by peer-to-peer services to launder illicit funds that are then changed into cryptocurrencies. These schemes combine the expertise of brokers located in countries across the Asia-Pacific that work in tandem to move millions of dollars out of the national banking systems in these countries and into North Korea. According to the a report published by the UN Panel of Experts (UNSC 2021, 51),

> the Democratic People's Republic of Korea continues to access international financial systems through joint ventures, offshore accounts, shell companies, virtual asset service providers (e.g. cryptocurrencies) and overseas banking representatives. The illicit revenue generated from sanctions evasion activities and laundered through these networks both directly and indirectly supports the country's weapons of mass destruction and ballistic missile programmes.

The same UN Panel of Experts assessed the value of virtual assets stolen by North Korea between January 2019 and November 2020 to be just over US $316 million (UNSC 2021, 56). This demonstrates the lucrative revenue stream provided to the North Korean regime through its development of cyber capabilities for the purposes of its illicit business activities. In 2024, the Panel of Experts on the Democratic People's Republic of Korea claimed that over the past few years the North Korean regime has engaged in large-scale theft of approximately US $3 billion in cryptocurrencies to fund its nuclear weapons program (Martin 2024). As we will discuss in Chapter 10, the North Korean regime has also been linked to several cybercrime groups. These groups have developed sophisticated cyber operations that aim to advance the interests of the regime and provide new and lucrative forms of revenue raising capabilities for North Korea's state-led illicit business activities.

North Korea provides a novel example of how state-led illicit business can operate. It shows that exclusion from the international system, both politically and economically, can create critical junctures that force the state to look for new means for survival. In the case of North Korea, this survival has been guaranteed through the institutionalization and complete co-option of criminal activities by the state.

Venezuela

For much of the 20th century Venezuela was considered to be a model of democracy and stability in Latin America. It was a country rich in oil which was used to fund successive development and modernization projects across the nation (Tinker Salas 2009). All governments in Venezuela have been highly dependent on oil to fund state-led activities. Thus, the oil shocks of the 1970s and 1980s combined to create an ongoing environment of political and economic crisis within the South American nation. By the late 1990s, the population was seeking a reprieve from the traditional party politics that had defined the country's democratic experience during the previous four decades. Hugo Chávez Frías initially appeared to be an unlikely candidate for president, but his charismatic demeanour and unorthodox approach to campaigning made him stand apart from other candidates and helped him to win the 1998 presidential election.

Early in his presidency Chávez implemented sweeping changes to Venezuela's governmental system which included larger roles and responsibilities for the Venezuelan military in relation to national and localized social initiatives (Polga-Hecimovich 2019). Chávez also doggedly pursued an agenda that sought to reform policies related to private property rights, agriculture, hydrocarbon industries and the most important state-owned oil company Petróleos de Venezuela S.A. (PDVSA). A divisive environment emerged in which senior leaders within PDVSA and the trade unions began to mobilize in opposition to the government. In response, Chávez chose to sack the most vocal of the dissenters. This led to members of the Venezuelan business community, the trade unions and certain elements within the armed forces to form a coalition that sought to directly challenge the authority of President Chávez. This triggered a 72-hour political crisis in the form of an attempted *coup d'état* that briefly removed Chávez from power. This event proved to be a critical juncture that 'created the necessary conditions for divergence from past trajectories to occur in future decision-making matters, particularly in relation to internal security, the role of the armed forces and other state institutions' (McCarthy-Jones and Turner 2022, 1204).

This was compounded by further challenges to President Chávez and his government in the form of a nationwide strike that included PDVSA employees. The cost of the strike was considerable as oil production plummeted from three million barrels per day before the strike commenced to around 200,000 barrels per day during the crisis (Johnson 2018). To stem the economic fallout and regain control of the company, President Chávez chose to sack 18,000 PDVSA employees. The PDSVA workforce, especially senior management, were replaced with loyalists to President Chávez – many of whom had no experience of working in the hydrocarbons field. Over time, this decision drastically changed the efficiency and profitability of Venezuela's most important industry and led to oil production in Venezuela declining year-on-year from 2003 (Cheatham and Cara Labrador 2021). It also had a negative effect on government revenue which had few significant sources beyond the oil industry.

The pattern of stifling dissent, replacing specialists with loyalists in key positions related to political, economic and military affairs, was designed to increase presidential and state control over the economy and society. This system appeared to work for a decade, mostly because the changes coincided with Venezuela's largest oil boom to date. However, by 2013, critical new junctures emerged that led to the unravelling of the system Chávez had built. In March 2013, President Chávez died, after battling cancer for the previous two years. Nicolás Maduro Moros became interim President of Venezuela until new elections were held in April 2013 which he won by a narrow margin. However, the conditions in which Maduro would govern were markedly different to those of former President Chavez. In early 2014, small protests sprang up across the country, fuelled by increasing dissatisfaction with the declining economic and security conditions within Venezuela (Taylor 2019).

The Venezuelan government deployed a series of repressive measures to quell the protests. These included a preference to rely on irregular security groups, known as *colectivos*, and the military to control protestors. Further exacerbating the crisis for the Maduro government was the sudden decline in the price of oil. For example, the price of oil dropped from US $115 in 2014 to just under US$ 30 per barrel in 2016 in the continuing context of declining output (Cheatham and Cara Labrador 2021). The economy more generally went into freefall and shrank by roughly three-quarters between 2014 and 2021. Debt soared, hyperinflation was endemic, poverty grew to unprecedented levels, government services collapsed and, in 2014, seven million of Venezuela's population of 30 million left the country. State revenue was drastically reduced but Maduro and his supporters clung to power using increasingly authoritarian measures and seeking alternative sources of revenue to fund their activities, especially to maintain the loyalty of the coercive forces of the state. Illicit business thus became a major pillar supporting regime survival.

Under Maduro's leadership, the Venezuelan state has demonstrated a proclivity to oscillate from passive involvement to large-scale regulation and coordination of criminality. For example, in relation to the *colectivos,* the Venezuelan government has adopted a passive approach that enables the *colectivos* to operate their small-scale criminal enterprises within their localized neighbourhoods without interference from the state (InSight Crime 2018). This passivity is a low-cost policy designed to engender ongoing loyalty to the state while simultaneously affording these groups income streams from micro illicit business activities that are of no interest to the state.

In contrast, other illicit businesses in Venezuela display a very different relationship with the Venezuelan state. For example, over the last decade numerous reports have referred to a Venezuelan criminal organization known as the Cartel de los Soles (Cartel of the Suns) as being one of the largest players involved in drug trafficking activity in Venezuela. The Cartel of the Suns is no ordinary drug trafficking organization. It has direct links to current and former officials from the Venezuelan government and military. For example, former

Vice President Tarek al-Aissami and former President of the National Assembly Diosdado Cabello are considered key members of the organization (DOJ 2020). Moreover, the nephews of President Maduro's wife, Celia Flores, were convicted of trafficking cocaine in the United States in 2016 and Flores's son has been the target of international investigations related to trafficking activities (InSight Crime 2018; DEA 2016).

In 2020, US authorities stated that Venezuelan President Nicolás Maduro, his Minister of Defence Vladimir Padrino, Chief Supreme Court Justice Maikel Moreno and nine other Venezuelan government officials had been charged with narco-terrorism, drug trafficking and other criminal offences that had occurred over the previous decade (DOJ 2020). However, the narrative attached to the US indictment in 2020 that describes a large organizational structure with a distinguishable hierarchy belies the reality of the state-crime nexus in Venezuela. According to InSight Crime (2022, 1), 'the Cartel of the Suns has never been a drug cartel. Instead, it emerged as a fluid and loose knit network of trafficking cells embedded within the Venezuelan security forces, facilitated, protected, and sometimes directed by political actors.' This characterization is more closely aligned to the outcomes of past critical junctures. The attempted 2002 *coup d'état* became the catalyst for former President Chávez to incentivize loyalty – no matter the cost – from parts of the state apparatus that could potentially mount a challenge to his authority in the future.

This departure from the status quo set the foundation for new dynamics between the state and criminality in Venezuela. Rather than operating as a monolith with centralized leadership like the Medellín Cartel under Pablo Escobar, the Cartel of the Suns is an umbrella network presiding over multiple illicit networks. In this system the state operationalizes its resources, especially the military, to protect the illicit activities and the income they generate. This in turn creates loyalty from members of the armed forces who derive economic benefits from their participation, loyalty from criminal groups that thrive in the permissive conditions provided by the state, and finally provides another income stream for the state in times of economic decline. In these unique circumstances, illicit activities become a panacea for many problems confronting the state. As McCarthy-Jones and Turner (2022, 1208) point out,

> the relationship between the state and crime in Venezuela is dynamic, opportunistic and mostly defined by the interests of the state. The state seems to pick and choose its involvement in certain criminal enterprises … and then simply ignore other aspects of criminality such as the activities of the *colectivos* which form important support bases for the regime.

The Syrian Arab Republic

Syria has been controlled by the al-Assad family since 1971, when Hafiz al-Assad became president. Upon seizing power, Hafiz al-Assad set about restructuring the functions of the Syrian state as well as the Syrian Regional Branch of the ruling Ba'ath Party. Most of the restructuring occurred along sectarian lines which favoured members of the Alawite population, a religious minority in Syria to which the al-Assad family belonged (Droz-Vincent 2014). The implementation of these changes was designed to consolidate al-Assad's power as president through the establishment of patronage networks based on kinship (Phillips 2015).

Under al-Assad's leadership, Syria developed into an 'ethnically dominated autocratic regime' that aimed to restrict any power held by competing ethnic or religious groups in the country (Mazur 2021, 40). For example, members of Syria's Sunni population and other non-Alawite communities were prevented from holding senior positions in areas related to economic, intelligence and miliary and security affairs, and instead were only afforded figurehead positions in political institutions. Viger (2018, 387) has described this thus:

> [The] repatrimonialization or reprivatization of Syrian politics was consolidated by Hafiz Al-Assad's corrective movement, which managed to isolate the radical factions of the party. The repression of class struggle favored this consolidation and allowed for the gradual creation of a new ruling class. This new ruling class acquired its power through the primitive accumulation of state resources, which acted through a reconfiguration of personalized networks of influence.

Over three decades, Hafiz al-Assad created a highly centralized system that placed his family at the apex of all power in Syria. Initially, Hafiz al-Assad considered his brother Rifaat to be his successor (Drysdale 1985). However, conflict between Hafiz and Rifaat and the unexpected death of Hafiz's eldest son, Basil al-Assad in 1994 paved the way for Bashar al-Assad to be named as his father's successor. Bashar al-Assad became President of Syria in 2000 following the death of his father (van Dam 2011).

Bashar al-Assad's ascent to power was at first met with optimism within Syria and by the international community. He came across as a progressive reformer, familiar with Western values and open to implementing social change in Syria (Zisser 2004). Initially, Bahar al-Assad displayed an openness towards policy reforms in diverse areas such as the banking, health and welfare sectors. However, the combination of political inexperience and poor policy development led to problems early in his presidency. Instead of mediating these problems, Bashar al-Assad demonstrated a willingness to clamp down on detractors and enact strategies aimed at preserving the regime and his role as an autocratic president. His popularity continued to decrease as problems of poverty and insecurity became more acute.

In the late 2000s, the internal problems in Syria were a microcosm of broader issues impacting many countries in the Middle East – especially those that had experienced uninterrupted authoritarian rule spanning decades. In early 2011, spontaneous protests against entrenched authoritarian rule in Tunisia and Egypt swiftly gained widespread domestic support and led to the rapid removal of authoritarian leaders in each country (Stepan and Linz 2013). Inspired by the early success of Tunisia and Egypt, populations across many Middle Eastern and North African countries began to publicly protest against declining living standards, the lack of economic opportunities and the perceived incompetence or apathy of their authoritarian rulers. This pan-continental movement became known as the Arab Spring.

Like many of its regional neighbours, Syria also experienced the spillover effects of the Arab Spring. However, the Assad regime's brutal response to protestors set the course for a protracted civil war, alienation from the international community and Syria's incremental transformation into a mafia state. During 2011, the harsh and often ruthless repression of peaceful anti-government and pro-democracy protests mobilized many citizens to take up arms against the regime (Josua and Edel 2015). The situation rapidly evolved whereby insurgent groups such as the Free Syrian Army established fronts against the government and by the following year Syria was engaged in a civil war. During the civil war, the Assad regime utilized a range of tactics against its population including sieges, sectarian massacres, torture and starvation as a form of collective punishment as well as the deployment of barrel bombs, chemical weapons, airstrikes and foreign mercenaries (Kozak 2015). In response, most Arab nations severed ties with the Syrian regime and the international community agreed to place sanctions on the Syrian government as well as high-ranking individuals including President Assad.

The United States, the United Kingdom and the European Union account for the majority of the sanctions imposed on the Syrian government, its officials and related parties. Industries involved in the development and production of technology, oil and gas as well as the Syrian business and banking sectors have been the focus of sanctions in Syria (Human Rights Watch 2023). During the first five years of the war, the Syrian government struggled to maintain control of the conflict. Despite the sanctions, by 2017, the Assad government had regained control of much of the country.

The protracted civil war in Syria destroyed large amounts of critical infrastructure and the cumulative impact of over a decade of economic sanctions decimated the Syrian economy and its population. The European Parliament (2023, 1) has estimated that 'half of the country's 22.1 million population is internally or externally displaced and 15.3 million people – nearly 70% of Syrians – are in need of humanitarian assistance.' Yet the Assad regime has continued to function and increase its control over the country. While traditional sources of trade and financing have been inaccessible to the regime for over a decade, new illicit industries have emerged, providing the regime and its supporters with a new means of survival. Due to the early implementation of sanctions, smuggling networks and black markets proliferated across all parts of Syria as access to legal goods became almost non-existent. However, it is the commercial production and trafficking of an amphetamine-type stimulant known as Captagon that has become the backbone of the Syrian economy and the regime's main revenue raising activity.

Captagon, often laced with caffeine, was used by armed groups in the civil war to boost their fighters' courage (Bubalo 2023). Post-war, the demand for counterfeit Captagon has rapidly increased in the Gulf countries and the broader Middle East. Multiple reports accuse the Syrian government of orchestrating the production of Captagon as far back as 2011 and engaging in large-scale production from 2017 (Nader 2023; Bubalo 2023; Schwaller 2023). The impact of economic sanctions, especially in relation to Syria's oil and banking industries, acted as a push factor for the regime to explore new sources of revenue that were immune to such measures (Walsh 2020). It is also no coincidence that the increase in Captagon production coincided with the period in which the Assad regime made significant gains against its enemies and turned the tide in the civil war. When the Syrian state reclaimed vast amounts of its territory it also reclaimed the means of production of illicit goods.

According to Nader (2023), members of the Syrian state and military apparatus, affiliates of Hezbollah and a mixture of OCGs in the Middle East work together to manufacture and traffic huge quantities of Captagon. For example, 13 metric tons of Captagon with a value of US $1 billion were seized in the United Arab Emirates in September 2023 (Bubalo 2023). The Assad family is considered to be central to the Captagon network. The president's brother Maher al-Assad is the commander of the Fourth Division, a special operations group within the Syrian defence force. The Fourth Division operates as a protector, facilitator and enforcer of the regime's interests and therefore plays an indispensable role in coordinating, transporting and protecting large shipments of Captagon from Syria (Neal 2020). The proceeds from the illegal trade in Captagon are estimated to be worth between US $10 billion and US $50 billion annually making it the largest foreign currency earner for the Assad regime (France 24 2022; Daly 2022). Over the past decade, the state-co-option of drug trafficking in Syria has been almost unprecedented. To put this into context, Syria currently produces 80% of the world's supply of Captagon. The scale of these state-led illicit activities is so significant that the UK government (2023, 1) has estimated that 'trade in the drug is a financial lifeline for the Assad regime – it is worth approximately 3 times the combined trade of the Mexican cartels.'

Conclusion

Understanding the relationship between criminality and the state holds significant explanatory power in relation to the causes and types of illicit business activities carried out in diverse regions of the world. As we previously discussed, conventional thought on this topic often assumes that criminal groups adopt a predatory or parasitic role in their relations with the state. However, as this chapter has demonstrated, in certain circumstances this relationship becomes symbiotic, meaning that the state opts to play a role, albeit to varying degrees, in illicit activities. In its most extreme manifestation, state-led illicit business can become so entrenched or institutionalized that a mafia state emerges. But what causes a state to take such drastic measures? In each case study, critical junctures in the form of political, economic and policy failures or crises were the precursors to each country's adoption and in some cases total co-option of illicit business activity.

During the Cold War, the North Korean regime's inability to service foreign debt, its isolation from the international community and declining financial support from its former allies, the Soviet Union and China, forced the regime to seek new ways to generate foreign currency. In Venezuela, the death of Hugo Chávez closely followed by the collapse of oil prices in 2014 fundamentally changed the political and economic landscape. The longest oil boom in Venezuela's history had come to an end and the new and deeply unpopular Maduro government was under pressure to find a new means to finance the reward system for loyalists previously set up by Chávez. In Syria, the spillover effects of the Arab Spring created unexpected upheavals across a range of societal groups. The Assad regime's brutal approach to quelling protestors in the early months of the Arab Spring led to the mobilization of the citizenry into armed groups, thus creating the onset of civil war. Moreover, all three case studies demonstrate that as each government progressively became more authoritarian (and, in the case of North Korea, totalitarian), their willingness to use violence and repression against their citizens increased.

Another common feature that can be discerned is that each country has been the subject of longstanding sanctions. The sanctions applied by other states in the international system are intended to pressure each country's political regime by severely limiting their capacity to conduct business and trade in the global market. While sanctions may achieve this objective, they also open the door for these countries to heavily invest and integrate themselves in illicit economies as a means of survival. As each case shows, illicit business activities become the panacea for a range of problems confronting these states, and thus the institutionalization of state-led illicit business and in its extreme form, the emergence of a mafia state, is all but guaranteed.

References

Andreski, S. (1968) *The African Predicament: A Study in the Pathology of Modernisation.* London: Joseph.

Armstrong, C.K. (2005) 'Fraternal socialism: The international reconstruction of North Korea, 1953–62.' *Cold War History* 5 (2) 161–187.

Bechtol, B.E. (2018) 'North Korean illicit activities and sanctions: A national security dilemma.' *Cornell International Law Journal* 51 (1) 57–94. Available at https://scholarship.law.cornell.edu/cilj/vol51/iss1/2.

Breuker, R.E. and van Gardingen, I. (2019) 'Tightening belts: Two regional case studies on corporate social responsibility.' Leiden Asian Centre. Available at https://www.universiteitleiden.nl/binaries/content/assets/geesteswetenschappen/lias/onderzoek-

breuker-ea—tightening-belts—two-regional-case-studies-on-corporate-social-responsi
bility.pdf.

Bubalo, M. (2023) 'Captagon: UAE seizes billion dollar amphetamine haul.' BBC, 14
September. Available at https://www.bbc.com/news/world-middle-east-66810832.amp.

Capoccia, G. (2016) 'Critical junctures.' In O. Fioretos, T. Falleti and A. Sheingate (eds)
The Oxford Handbook of Historical Institutionalism, pp. 89–106. Oxford: Oxford
University Press.

Carney, M. (2018) 'Defector reveals secrets of North Korea's Office 39, raising cash for
Kim Jong-un.' ABC News, 6 January. Available at https://www.abc.net.au/news/
2018-01-06/north-korea-defector-reveals-secrets-ofoffice39/9302308#Drugs,%20Weap
ons%20and%20Fake%20Cash.

Cheatham, A. and Cara Labrador, R. (2021) 'Venezuela: The rise and fall of a petros-
tate.' Council on Foreign Relations, 22 January. Available at https://www.cfr.org/ba
ckgrounder/venezuela-crisis.

Daly, M. (2022) 'Is the Syrian regime the world's biggest drug dealer?' *Vice*, 15 December.
Available at https://www.vice.com/en/article/v7v8k8/syria-captagon-pills-drug-trade.

Droz-Vincent, P. (2014) 'State of barbary (take two): From the Arab Spring to the return
of violence in Syria.' *Middle East Journal* 68 (1) 33–58.

Drysdale, A. (1985) 'The succession question in Syria.' *Middle East Journal* 39 (2) 246–257.

Drug Enforcement Administration (DEA) (2016) 'Former top leaders of Venezuela's anti-
narcotics agency indicted for trafficking drugs to the United States.' Available at https://
www.dea.gov/pressreleases/2016/08/01/former-top-leaders-venezuelas-anti-narcotics-agen
cy-indicted-trafficking.

Eberstadt, N. (2015) 'How North Korea became the world's worst economy.' *Wall Street
Journal*, 31 December. Available at http://www.proquest.com/newspapers/how-north-
korea-became-worlds-worst-economy/docview/1752538388/se-2.

European Parliament (2023) 'Impact of sanctions on the humanitarian situation in Syria
(briefing).' Think Tank European Parliament, 5 June. Available at https://www.
europarl.europa.eu/thinktank/en/document/EPRS_BRI(2023)749765

France 24 (2022) 'Captagon connection: How Syria became a narco state.' 3 November.
Available at https://www.france24.com/en/live-news/20221103-captagon-connection-
how-syria-became-a-narco-state.

Global Initiative Against Transnational Organized Crime (GI-TOC) (2017) 'Diplomats
and deceit: North Korea's criminal activities in Africa.' September. Available at http
s://globalinitiative.net/wp-content/uploads/2017/09/TGIATOC-Diplomats-and-Deceip
t-DPRK-Report-1868-web.pdf.

Human Rights Watch (2023) 'Questions and answers: How sanctions affect the humanitarian response in Syria.' 22 June. Available at https://www.hrw.org/news/2023/06/
22/questions-and-answers-how-sanctions-affect-humanitarian-response-syria#q2.

Huntington, S.P. (1968) *Political Order in Changing Societies*. New Haven, CT: Yale
University Press.

Hurst, C. (2005) 'North Korea: A government-sponsored drug trafficking network.'
Military Review 85 (5) 35–74.

InSight Crime (2018) 'Is Venezuela a mafia state?' Available at https://www.insightcrime.
org/wp-content/uploads/2018/05/Venezuela-a-Mafia-State-InSight-Crime-2018.pdf.

InSight Crime (2022) 'Beyond the Cartel of the Suns.' 2 May. Available at https://
insightcrime.org/investigations/beyond-the-cartel-of-the-suns/.

Johnson, K. (2018) 'How Venezuela struck it poor.' *Foreign Policy*, 16 July. Available at
https://foreignpolicy.com/2018/07/16/how-venezuela-struck-it-poor-oil-energy-chavez/.

Josua, M. and Edel, M. (2015) 'To repress or not to repress: Regime survival strategies in the Arab Spring.' *Terrorism and Political Violence* 27 (2) 289–309.

Kan, P.R., Bechtol, B.E. and Collins, R.M. (2010) *Criminal Sovereignty: Understanding North Korea's Illicit International Activities.* Carlisle, PA: United States Army War College Press. Available at https://press.armywarcollege.edu/monographs/349.

Katzeff Silberstein, B. (2023) 'The complicated truth about sanctions on North Korea.' East Asia Forum, 5 July. Available at https://www.eastasiaforum.org/2023/07/05/the-complicated-truth-about-sanctions-on-north-korea/.

Kim, H.M., Lee, J. and Pak, R. (2022). 'North Korean cryptocurrency operations: an alternative revenue stream.' Policy Brief, Belfer Center for Science and International Affairs. Available at https://www.belfercenter.org/publication/north-korean-cryptocurrency-operations-alternative-revenue-stream.

Kozak, C. (2015) 'An army in all corners: Assad's campaign strategy in Syria.' Middle East Security Report 26. Institute for the Study of War. Available at https://understandingwar.org/sites/default/files/An%20Army%20in%20All%20Corners%20by%20Chris%20Kozak%201.pdf.

Lankov, A. (2022) 'North Korea: A hermit kingdom again.' East Asia Forum, 4 January. Available at https://www.eastasiaforum.org/2022/01/04/north-korea-a-hermit-kingdom-again/.

Lupsha, P.A. (1996) 'Transnational organized crime versus the nation-state.' *Transnational Organized Crime* 2 (1) 21–48.

Magyar, B. (2016) *Post-communist Mafia State: The Case of Hungary.* Budapest: Central European University.

Martin, P. (2024) 'North Korea is behind cyberattacks worth $US3 billion and is stealing cryptocurrency to fund weapons programs, UN report finds.' ABC News, 22 March. Available at https://www.abc.net.au/news/2024-03-22/north-korea-stealing-cryptocurrency-to-fund-nuclear-weapons/103618152.

Mazur, K. (2021) *Revolution in Syria: Identity, Networks, and Repression.* Cambridge: Cambridge University Press.

McCarthy-Jones, A. and Turner, M. (2022) 'What is a "Mafia State" and how is one created?' *Policy Studies* 43 (6) 1195–1215. doi:doi:10.1080/01442872.2021.2012141.

Migdal, J.S. (1988) *Strong Societies and Weak States: State-Society Relations and State Capabilities in the Third World.* Princeton, NJ: Princeton University Press.

Myrdal, G. (1968). *Asian Drama: An Inquiry into the Poverty of Nations.* New York: Pantheon.

Nader, E. (2023) 'Syria: New captagon drug trade link to top officials found.' BBC, 27 June. Available at https://www.bbc.com/news/world-middle-east-66002450.

Naím, M. (2012) 'Mafia states: Organised crime takes office.' *Foreign Affairs* 91 (3) 100–111.

Neal, W. (2020) 'Assad regime implicated in massive captagon bust.' Organized Crime and Corruption Reporting Project, 13 July. Available at https://www.occrp.org/en/daily/12736-assad-regime-implicated-in-massive-captagon-bust.

Pattisson, P. (2020) 'UK sourced PPE from factories secretly using North Korean slave labour.' *The Guardian*, 21 November. Available at https://www.theguardian.com/globaldevelopment/2020/nov/20/uk-sourced-ppe-from-factories-secretly-using-north-korean-slave-labour.

Phillips, C. (2015) 'Sectarianism and conflict in Syria.' *Third World Quarterly* 36 (2) 357–376.

Polga-Hecimovich, J. (2019) 'Organized crime and the state in Venezuela under Chavismo.' In B. Bagley, J. Chabat and J. Rosen (eds) *The Criminalization of States: The*

Relationship Between States and Organized Crime, pp. 189–207. London: Rowman and Littlefield.

Rotberg, R. (2004) *When States Fail: Causes and Consequences*. Princeton, NJ: Princeton University Press.

Schwaller, F. (2023) 'Captagon: The little white pill fuelling Syria's drug trade.' *Deutscher Welle*, 19 September. Available at https://www.dw.com/en/captagon-the-little-white-pill-fueling-syrias-drug-trade/a-66814328.

Stepan, A. and Linz, J.J. (2013) 'Democratization theory and the "Arab Spring"' *Journal of Democracy* 24 (2) 15–30.

Taylor, L. (2019) 'Maduro turns to violent "mercenary" colectivos to maintain order.' *Global Post*, 25 April. Available at https://www.pri.org/stories/2019-04-25/maduro-turns-violentmercenarycolectivos-maintain-order.

Tinker Salas, M. (2009) *The Enduring Legacy: Oil, Culture, and Society in Venezuela*. Durham, NC: Duke University Press.

UK Government (2023) 'Tackling the illicit drug trade fuelling Assad's war machine – press release.' Foreign, Commonwealth and Development Office and Lord (Tariq) Ahmad of Wimbledon, 28 March. Available at https://www.gov.uk/government/news/tackling-the-illicit-drug-trade-fuelling-assads-war-machine.

United Nations Department of Economic and Social Affairs (UNDESA) (2023) *The International Trade Statistics Yearbook 2022, Vol. 1: Trade by Country*. Available at https://desapublications.un.org/publications/2022-international-trade-statistics-yearbook-vol-i-trade-country.

United States Department of Justice (DOJ) (2020) 'Nicolás Maduro Moros and 14 current and former Venezuelan officials charged with narco-terrorism, corruption, drug trafficking and other criminal charges.' 26 March. Available at https://www.justice.gov/opa/pr/nicolas-maduromoros-and-14-current-and-former-venezuelan-officials-charged-narco-terrorism.

United Nations Security Council (UNSC) (2021) 'Final report: Panel of experts (North Korea) S/2021/211.' 4 March. Available at https://www.securitycouncilreport.org/atf/cf/%7B65BFCF9B-6D27-4E9C-8CD3-CF6E4FF96FF9%7D/s_2021_211.pdf.

Van Dam, N.V. (2011) *The Struggle for Power in Syria*. London: I.B. Tauris.

Viger, J. (2018) 'Class, political power, and nationalism in Syria: A historical sociology of state-society relations.' *Dialectical Anthropology* 42 (4) 373–389.

Walcott, J. (2020) 'Cash, yachts, and cognac: Kim Yo-Jong's links to the secretive office keeping North Korea's elites in luxury.' *Time*, 29 April. Available at https://time.com/5829508/kim-yo-jong-money-office-39/.

Walsh, M. (2020) 'What is the drug captagon and how is it linked to the Islamic State Group and a drug bust in Italy?' ABC News, 2 July. Available at https://www.abc.net.au/news/2020-07-02/italy-drug-bust-captagon-how-is-it-linked-to-islamic-state/12414804.

Zartman, I. (1995) *Collapsed States: The Disintegration and Restoration of Legitimate Authority*. London: Lynne Rienner Publishers.

Zisser, E. (2004) 'Bashar al-Asad and his regime: Between continuity and change.' *Orient*, 45 (2) 239–256.

10

DIGITAL ILLICIT BUSINESS

Introduction

The digitization of modern technology has revolutionized the way business, both licit and illicit, is conducted. The opportunities for greater efficiency, productivity and profit created by advances in technology are dual purpose, meaning that they are just as valuable to an illicit business as they are to a normal business operating in the legal economy. These technological developments have enabled a range of criminal actors to operate in cyberspace and to develop cyber capabilities to augment their illicit businesses and broader criminal activities. Umbrella terms such as 'cybercrime' and 'cybercriminal' are often used to describe a rich tapestry of criminal acts and actors that in some way adopt and shape aspects of cyberspace to achieve their goals. However, the organizational arrangements, motivations and even the modus operandi of these actors can vary considerably.

To demonstrate these differences this chapter begins by examining definitions of cybercrime which form the fundamental building blocks for understanding the way in which digital illicit businesses is carried out in the 21st century. The chapter is divided into two sections. In the first section, distinctions are made between non-state actors such as organized cybercriminal groups who operate only in the cyber realm, and traditional organized crime groups (OCGs) who still primarily operate in the real world but who have incrementally adopted elements of cyber strategies and capabilities into their illicit business models. The second section examines the use of digital and cyber capabilities in modern statecraft and, more specifically, instances whereby states have engaged organized cybercriminal groups to achieve their strategic goals. The activities of such groups can be classified as either state-sponsored or state-sanctioned acts of cybercrime and present national security threats to many nations in the world.

DOI: 10.4324/9781003293620-10

Cybercrime

Cybercrime is an umbrella term that encapsulates a diverse range of criminal activities. While there is no universally accepted definition of the term, there is some agreement as to what constitutes the most basic or fundamental elements of cybercrime. For example, it is defined by the role of information communication technology (ICT) in a criminal act and refers to crimes in which the 'perpetrator uses specialized knowledge of cyberspace' (Furnell 2002, 21; Holt et al. 2018). In a general sense an act of cybercrime contravenes the law and is committed by leveraging or exploiting ICT to target specific websites, attack networks and computer systems, steal commercial and personal data and/or facilitate a crime (Maras 2016). Voce and Morgan (2023) identify that these types of crimes can be further categorized as being 'cyber-dependent' or 'cyber-enabled' crimes. According to Voce and Morgan (2023, 8),

> Cyber-dependent crimes are those directed at computers or ICT and can only exist in the digital world. They include crimes such as ransomware, which relies on the use of malware to extort money from victims. Cyber-enabled crimes are traditional crimes that are committed using computers, computer networks or other forms of ICT, which enable the offender to increase the scale or reach of the crime. These include profit-motivated crimes such as online fraud and identity crime and misuse, as well as online abuse and harassment, online child sexual exploitation and technology-enabled forms of domestic and family violence.

These elements are what make cybercrimes distinct from traditional crimes. While the internet, cyberspace and other new technologies are creating endless possibilities for governments, businesses and populations around the world, they simultaneously offer openings for criminals to perpetrate new types of crimes or develop new ways to undertake traditional crimes. Bossler and Berenblum (2019, 495) argue that cybercrimes fall into four broad categories, including 'cyber-trespass (e.g., unauthorized system access), cyber-deception/theft (e.g., identity theft, online fraud, digital piracy), cyberporn/obscenity (e.g., child sexual exploitation materials), and cyber-violence (e.g., cyberstalking; cyber terrorism).'

The frequency and complexity of cybercrimes continue to increase and pose a serious existential threat to individuals, businesses and governments around the world (Curtis and Oxburgh 2023). In cyberspace, crimes committed may traverse multiple borders in a matter of seconds and are able to victimize a significant number of targets at the same time. A cybercriminal's business model can be considered efficient and effective because their operations draw on resources which are already considered legitimate in most people's day-to-day lives. The ease of accessibility to the internet, peer to peer file-sharing and data encryption in most parts of the world have acted as key enablers of cyber-based crimes (Phillips et al. 2022). These resources allow cybercriminals to be uninhibited by traditional obstacles to crime such as physical or geographical borders and boundaries. Central to the exponential growth of cybercrime is the simple fact that it can be conducted with fewer resources, greater anonymity and greater speed than traditional forms of crime (Maras 2014).

Digital Illicit Businesses

ICT has transformed both legal and illicit business strategies. The very advantages that ICT has provided to legal businesses – expansion into global markets and access to international supply chains to support production and distribution – have been mirrored by illicit business. ICT has enabled criminal organizations to engage in a wider range of activities and to enhance various aspects of their existing ones. ICT now performs a vital role for traditional OCGs in activities such as money laundering, drug trafficking, human trafficking, counterfeit products, pharmaceuticals, identify theft, corporate theft, extortion, fraud, online scams and even kidnapping for ransom. The *2023 Official Cybercrime Report* published by Cybersecurity Ventures estimated that in 2024 the global cost of cybercrime would exceed US $9 trillion (Cybersecurity Ventures 2023).

The dark web hosts a range of online illicit marketplaces – also known as cryptomarkets – that connect buyers to sellers in a virtual setting. These online marketplaces deal in a large variety of illicit products but most notably have hosted businesses selling illegal narcotics. Broséus et al. (2016, 7) highlight that virtual marketplaces mirror some aspects of legitimate business because 'they share many structural features with popular marketplaces such as eBay or Amazon, with searchable listings of products for sale and buyers being able to leave feedback on their purchases.' To enhance consumer confidence and protect businesses operating in this space, online illicit markets use cryptocurrencies such as Bitcoin instead of cash transactions, communicate through encrypted messaging systems and can only be accessed by using the proxy browser The Onion Router (Tor) to reach the dark web (Holt et al. 2018). The use of these features in conjunction with one another obscures the identities of buyers and sellers and creates a higher level of trust in individual transactions. The Silk Road is the best-known example of an online illicit marketplace (see Box 10.1).

BOX 10.1 THE SILK ROAD

The Silk Road was an online marketplace that provided a platform for individuals and groups to buy and sell illicit products. It operated as a virtual host for online illicit businesses, particularly businesses selling illegal drugs. The Silk Road could only be accessed via the dark web and utilized a range of tools such as the Tor browser which hides a user's IP address and cryptocurrencies to protect the identity of its users. The site administrator was known by the pseudonym Dread Pirate Roberts. Although it operated for just two years, the Silk Road hosted over 4,000 illicit businesses and claimed to serve over 150,000 customers. It is estimated that the Silk Road generated over US $1 billion in revenue before US law enforcement agencies successfully shut down the site in October 2013, and subsequently charged Ross William Ulbricht (aka Dread Pirate Roberts) with a range of offences, including computer crimes such as hacking as well as money laundering and drug trafficking.

Sources: Lacson and Jones (2016, 43) and Holt et al. (2018, 7).

Beyond illicit online marketplaces, criminals, OCGs and even members of the public can access, with relative ease, cyber services that support the efficiency and profitability of criminal activities in a terrestrial and virtual setting. For example, OCGs are now able to take advantage of pre-packaged cyber products to augment their business activities. This is known as 'Cybercrime as a Service' (CaaS). Akyazi et al. (2021, 1) argue that 'the overall impact of CaaS is to make cybercrime more accessible to new criminals, as well as to support business models for advanced criminals via specialized business-to-business services.' This is an example of 'supply and demand' whereby the development of specific illicit businesses that sell pre-packaged cyber services (supply) is the result of the cyber needs (demand) of other illicit businesses. Some of the services offered include, but are not limited to, MaaS (Malware as a Service), MLaaS (Money Laundering as a Service), MMRaaS (Money Mule Recruitment as a Service) and RaaS (Ransomware as a Service).

In recent years, RaaS has become a particularly popular pre-packaged cyber product. Baker (2023) describes RaaS as the result of the relationship between a ransomware operator and its customers or clients. The type of customer in need of RaaS requires ransomware to support their own illicit activities. However, by and large these customers are usually time-poor or have insufficient knowledge of ICT to create ransomware unassisted. RaaS operators bridge this gap by providing pre-fabricated forms of ransomware that can be easily deployed without the need for expert knowledge of ICT. Similarly to legal businesses, RaaS operators advertise their services, albeit on the dark web, and their sites usually employ similar business strategies such as promotional offers, product reviews and competitive pricing. According to Baker (2023, 1), 'the price of RaaS kits ranges from $40 per month to several thousand dollars – trivial amounts, considering that the average ransom demand in 2021 was $6 million.' RaaS groups based in the Russian Federation, such as REvil (an abbreviation of ransomware and evil), have been linked to a range of large-scale ransomware attacks on organizations and companies in the United States, Europe and Australia. For example, in 2022, Medibank, a private health insurance provider in Australia, was subjected to a vicious cyber-attack from a Russia-based group with links to REvil. During the attack, hackers were able to steal large amounts of personal information including private health records from 9.7 million Medibank customers. The cyber criminals demanded a large ransom to be paid within a matter of days. When the ransom had not been paid by the specified time, the cybercriminals released the data on the dark web (Goldsmith 2022). In January 2024, the Australian government announced that it had placed sanctions on a Russian individual named Aleksandr Ermakov who was identified by the Australian Signals Directorate and the Australian Federal Police as being one of the key individuals responsible for the 2022 attack on Medibank (Crowley 2024). Such personal identification and sanctioning of cyber criminals may well be adopted by other jurisdictions as a means of deterrence.

The commercialization of ICT for illicit purposes has led to a significant increase in its availability and use, most notably in relation to ransomware. Ransomware seeks to infect a computer by encrypting its files or restricting the user's access to essential parts of the computer's operating system. The criminal uses this methodology to coerce the victim into paying a ransom – usually in cryptocurrency – in order to regain access to their computer (Beaman et al. 2021). In some cases, the criminals may use other ploys such as fear or shame rather than denial of access to data to pressure the victim into paying. For example, the ransomware may include features that send messages to the victim alleging that the computer has been commandeered by an authority. The messages might contain benign accusations that the victim has been identified as the user of counterfeit software or they might be more serious accusations relating internet searches for illegal content such as child pornography (Holt et al. 2018).

In recent years, businesses and organizations rather than individuals have become key targets of ransomware attacks (Beaman et al. 2021). In the case of a large organization or business, the financial losses incurred because of an attack can far outweigh the cost of paying the ransom. For example, over a short period of time in 2023, two major US gambling organizations, Caesar's Entertainment and MGM Resorts, were both subjected to significant cyberattacks involving ransomware. However, each business chose to respond to the attacks in different ways. The attack on Caesar's Entertainment involved the theft of confidential information by a cybercriminal group known as Scattered Spider (Kelleher 2023). The group threatened to disclose the information if the ransom was not paid. Due to the nature of the information and the damage that disclosure might have caused, Caesar's Entertainment chose to pay Scattered Spider US $15 million, although the original demand was estimated to be closer to US $30 million (Cybersecurity Ventures 2023). A few weeks later, MGM Resorts experienced an almost complete stoppage of its computer systems due to a cyberattack involving ransomware from a group known as Black Cat. The ransomware attacks disabled hotel reservations, digital room keys, credit card processing, cash withdrawal facilities, paid parking machines and casino gambling machines (Cybersecurity Ventures 2023; Kelleher 2023). Despite the significant disruption to its business operations, MGM Resorts decided not to pay the ransom.

These two examples demonstrate an important assumption that is factored into the business model of cybercriminals who use ransomware: the cybercriminal does not need, nor expect the ransomware to be successful every time it is used. Rather, it is a numbers game whereby the cybercriminal can deploy the product on a range of victims with the knowledge that it may only need to work once in order to generate a significant financial reward. In an age where most individuals, businesses and organizations are heavily reliant on computer systems to undertake their work, it is highly likely that there will always be victims willing to pay the ransom.

Virtual Kidnapping

Virtual kidnapping is a cybercrime that uses ICT to simulate a traditional crime (kidnapping) as a distraction to the real crime that is occurring. In fact, a virtual kidnapping is not a kidnapping, but a cover for an extortion scheme (FBI 2017). According to Maras and Arsovska (2023, 163), 'virtual kidnapping is a form of cyber-enabled fraud, whereby perpetrators use a myriad of deceptive and/or misleading tactics to obtain money, goods, services, or other gains.' These schemes operate by emotionally manipulating the victims in relation to a valued asset which in this case is usually a close family member. In short, victims are convinced into paying a ransom to free a loved one because they have been led to believe that their loved one is being threatened with violence or death. However, a virtual kidnapping does not involve the physical act of kidnapping a person (Chang et al. 2023). Instead, using phone and internet technology, specific deceptions such as fake photos in conjunction with threats are used to coerce victims to pay a ransom in a short period of time before the scheme can be uncovered. The cybercriminals take advantage of significant geographical distances between the victim and their loved ones. Physical distance creates great difficulties for victims to be able to quickly verify the safety of their loved one which makes this factor central to the success of these types of schemes.

During the COVID-19 pandemic, virtual kidnappings involving international students studying in Australia occurred with greater frequency. In 2023, the Australian government reported that virtual kidnappings across the country had increased sharply, and victims of virtual kidnapping schemes were overwhelmingly Chinese-speaking university students based in Australia (AUSTRAC 2023). The schemes usually begin via an unsolicited phone call to the victim by cyber criminals who impersonate 'authority figures' such as members of the Chinese military, police or government (Evans 2023). The 'authority figures' deceive their victims into believing that they have been implicated in a crime and that the only way to avoid arrest or deportation from Australia is to pay a 'fine.' This tactic is particularly effective with members of the Chinese diaspora as 'Chinese students are normally educated to be obedient and to follow the instructions of the authorities (Chang et al. 2023, 111). In order to avoid interference from law enforcement, the criminals will 'use technology to conceal their physical locations and persuade victims to continue communicating through encrypted applications like Skype, WeChat, and WhatsApp' (Evans 2023, 1). If the initial victim cannot raise the ransom, the cyber criminals will then persuade the victim to 'fake their own kidnapping, so the scammers can demand a ransom from their family for their safe return' (AUSTRAC 2023, 1). These types of digital extortion schemes use ICT to take advantage of geographical distance, communication barriers, cultural norms, fear and social and familial isolation. Moreover, these schemes are cheap to perpetrate but can deliver large paydays for the cybercriminals. In two separate events, cybercriminals targeting Chinese students in Australia received ransoms of A $500,000 and A $2 million (Chang et al. 2023; AUSTRAC 2023).

The Digitization of the Crime-Terror Nexus

In Chapter 4, we explored examples of a range of interactions between OCGs and terrorist groups in what has become known as the crime-terror nexus (Makarenko 2004). The nexus describes the way these two groups cooperate and exchange knowledge to enhance and develop their capabilities. One of the key drivers of the nexus has been particular skills and services drawn from conventional OCGs which have proven to be extremely valuable to terrorist organizations.

According to Choo and Grabosky (2014), ICT techniques that enable identity theft, immigration fraud, online scamming and the production of forged items are precursor crimes used by terrorist groups as part of revenue raising efforts to further their political or ideological goals. For example, one of the leaders of the 2002 Bali bombing plot in Indonesia, Imam Samudra, mounted a recruitment drive in the months prior to the attacks. However, he was not recruiting individuals to participate in the logistical planning and operational aspects of the attacks. Instead, this recruitment drive was specifically for the purposes of sourcing a small labour force with ICT skills to commit credit card fraud to fund the necessary training and equipment for the bombings (Prabowo 2012; Choo and Grabosky 2014). In 2011, the Surakarta Church in Indonesia was bombed. When the Indonesian police arrested five suspects in 2012, one of the suspects, Rizki Gunawan, an ICT expert, admitted to hacking activities that raised almost US $300,000 for extremist groups in Indonesia (Lakshimi 2022).

The importance of reliable and effective fundraising activities continues to be a key concern for modern terrorist groups. While previously these roles would have been performed by individuals considered to have specialized skills in ICT as was the case with Gunawan, according to Lakshimi (2022, 1),

[a]t the height of IS' so-called caliphate in 2016, a prominent Indonesian jihadist, Bahrun Naim, who had forged close links with IS Central from his base in Syria, wrote manuals on his websites providing basic training for cybercrimes such as hacking and carding. The manuals also included advice on fund-moving techniques involving various new digital payment methods, such as PayPal, Western Union and cryptocurrencies.

Given that cybercrime continues to be a key source of funding, ICT skills and a sound knowledge of cyberspace will be a key characteristic of a terrorist organization's membership profile. Beyond using ICT to support terrorist financing, over the past two decades, these groups have mastered the use of ICT to augment their communications, disseminate their promotional material/propaganda and act as one of the key methods of recruitment. According to Kapsokoli (2019), terrorist groups such as Al Qaeda, Hamas and Islamic State in Iraq and the Levant have all used aspects of ICT to raise funds to support their ideological objectives through the online sale of propaganda. Usman and Owubokiri (2023, 87) further argue that in the past the jihadists had to physically seek recruits themselves thus exposing them to capture by state operatives. However, the internet provides anonymity, takes much less time, can furnish more information and allows for information to be quickly shared through social media sites such as Facebook, Instagram, You-Tube and WhatsApp. The use of ICT and its co-option by radicalized groups has been considered as an important variable in the global recruitment drive that became known as the foreign fighters phenomenon (Windsor 2020; Hegghammer 2010). More recently, we have seen perverse examples of far-right extremists co-opting social media platforms to supercharge the impact of their terrorist attacks by reaching a global audience. For example, during the 2019 Christchurch mosque shootings in New Zealand, the lone wolf gunman Brenton Tarrant used the Facebook platform to live-stream during the terror attacks in which over 50 people lost their lives (Besley and Peters 2020). ICT and advanced cyber capabilities have become central components of the business models used by OCGs and terrorist organizations alike. Modern terrorist organizations have shown significant innovation through the development of digital criminal acumen that supports both their financial needs and their ideological goals, thus demonstrating the digitization of the crime-terror nexus.

Organized Cybercrime Groups and Statecraft

Over the past decade, cybercrime groups have also become closely associated with activities used in modern statecraft. This is because most states have adopted cyber capabilities as increasingly important parts of their statecraft. Cyber capabilities provide two options from which a state can choose to pursue its interests: namely the carrot or the stick. The 'carrot and stick approach refers to a policy of offering a combination of rewards and punishment to induce the adversary behavior' (Shiva et al. 2010, 2). Cyber carrots refer to strategies that favour investment in the development of cyber infrastructure. These investments enable states to disseminate important information and reach populations located at home and abroad. These carrots are influential tools that provide important scaffolding to project a state's interests through a low-cost platform. However, cyber capabilities are dual purpose and can be deployed as cyber sticks.

When opting for the stick approach, cyber capabilities can take the form of intense propaganda campaigns, censorship of specific and/or sensitive matters, and in extreme cases offensive cyber-attacks on other nation states, institutions or companies. These types of approaches are available to almost every cyber-capable country in the world. Jensen (2017, 168) states that 'cyber coercive campaigns are online political warfare. They work in an indirect and additive manner to coerce rivals and signal resolve.' The use of these capabilities as sticks rather than carrots was identified in the *2018 Worldwide Threat Assessment* as being favoured by the People's Republic of China, Iran, the Democratic People's Republic of Korea (North Korea) and Russia (Coats 2018). This has prompted the introduction of 'responsible cyber power,' an idea that advocates for rules and ethically based considerations to be used in the deployment of cyber power (Willett 2023). But the low cost of cyber capabilities means that they are likely to be deployed as an important element of statecraft. States will increasingly draw on the skills and expertise of cybercriminal groups to achieve their political and strategic goals.

2007 Cyber-Attacks on Estonia

One of the earliest examples of cyber statecraft was the 2007 Russian cyber-attacks against Estonia. In 2007, the Estonian government decided to relocate a Russian war memorial statue from the centre of the capital, Tallin. The decision by the Estonian government proved to be significant because the statue was symbolic of two things: Russian occupation and oppression of Estonia as well as the sacrifice of Russian soldiers against Nazi invaders during World War II. The problem was that the former represented the Estonian government and its citizens' perception of the memorial and the latter represented the perspective of the large ethnic Russian population living in Estonia. This decision triggered a series of protests by the Russian-speaking population in Estonia which led to the arrests of more than 1,300 protestors (Holt et al. 2018). The conflict moved into online spaces which eventually culminated in a cyber-attack against a nation-state on an unprecedented scale (Herzog 2011).

Starting on April 27, the cyber-attacks on Estonia lasted for 22 days and systematically disabled Estonia's critical internet infrastructure. The attackers targeted a range of organizations and government services, including Estonian media organizations, national and private banks, internet service providers and information systems and domain name services, and the ICT infrastructure of various Estonian government departments (Herzog 2017). The significance of this event is that it constituted the first distributed denial-of-service (DDoS) cyber-attack against a state actor. Russia has consistently denied its involvement in the attacks, despite evidence that pointed to Russian involvement. For example, the initial cyber-attacks were identified as originating from computers linked to the Russian government. Further investigations found that Russia-based internet forums and sites (hosted anonymously) had posted instructions and user guides for the coordinated launch of a DDoS attack (Pernik 2018). Importantly, evidence emerged that these guides were intended to be used by thousands of individuals from a range of locations around the world.

The impact of these events has fundamentally transformed the way states understand and respond to cyber-attacks. Following the attacks, Estonia has focused its international diplomacy on highlighting the need for an international cyber agenda. Importantly, Estonia was actually the first country to raise the alarm about Russian cyber power. Estonia has become a cyber norm entrepreneur and has been integral to the creation of Cooperative Cyber Defence Centre of Excellence operated by the North Atlantic Treaty Organization (NATO). Estonia continues to use powerful organizations such as NATO as platforms to raise awareness of the threats posed by nefarious cyber groups and their state sponsors (Herzog 2017). In more recent years, certain cyber groups are known to maintain close links to specific states. These groups can be categorized as either state-sponsored or state-sanctioned cyber groups.

State-Sponsored versus State-Sanctioned

State-sponsored cyber groups are funded and controlled by a state and undertake cyber operations that pursue the particular interests of their sponsor. The behaviour of an archetypal state-sponsored cyber group involves activities and specific operations that unequivocally promote a state's strategic goals. These activities include, but are not limited to, acts of espionage, information warfare, sabotage and theft that are carried out in cyberspace. In contrast, state-sanctioned cyber groups operate with a greater level of autonomy from the state they serve. The activities of these groups are tolerated by a state because some of their operations may align with the state's interests, even though most of their work is not done at the behest of the state. We will now turn to some examples of organized cybercrime groups and their known or alleged links to specific nation-states.

China

Cyber groups operating on behalf of the Chinese government have become a defining feature of China's statecraft in the 21st century. One of the longest running operational cyber groups is a formalized contingent of the People's Liberation Army known as Unit 61398 or Advanced Persistent Threat (APT) 1. The impact of Unit 61398's operations has been central to debates on cyber warfare and state-sponsored hacking. This unit has been implicated in a range of cyber activities that extend beyond conventional military operations. Mandiant (2013) published a report that released evidence linking APT1 to key sections of the Chinese military apparatus. In the report the authors argued that:

> We believe that APT1 is able to wage such a long-running and extensive cyber espionage campaign in large part because it receives direct government support. In seeking to identify the organization behind this activity, our research found that People's Liberation Army (PLA's) Unit 61398 is

similar to APT1 in its mission, capabilities, and resources. PLA Unit 61398 is also located in precisely the same area from which APT1 activity appears to originate.

(Mandiant 2013, 3)

Since the release of the report, Unit 61398 has continued to expand its activities and the sophistication of its cyber techniques. Meanwhile, another state-sponsored cyber actor connected to China, a group known as Volt Typhoon, has been active since 2021. Volt Typhoon specializes in espionage and information-gathering operations and leveraging stolen credentials with a specific focus on critical infrastructure organizations in the United States, including Guam. This is why, in 2023, the US Office of the Director of National Intelligence (2023, 10) stated that 'China probably currently represents the broadest, most active, and persistent cyber espionage threat to U.S. Government and private-sector networks.'

Russia

Like China, Russia is also a key sponsor of cyber groups that are used to undertake operations in cyberspace to advance Russian political and economic interests. One of the most well-known is a group that calls itself Fancy Bear but is also known as APT 28. Fancy Bear is considered to be part of Russia's foreign military intelligence agency. It is known to employ methods such as phishing and credential harvesting via spoofed websites to launch attacks in cyberspace. However, it does not seek out financial information nor does it seek to profit from such information unlike other known Russian cybercriminal groups (CrowdStrike 2019; Jensen et al. 2019). Fancy Bear has attacked European military organizations, US political organizations, international sporting organizations, Eastern European governments, and most recently the Ukrainian government. Since the Russian invasion of Ukraine in 2022, cyber groups such as Fancy Bear have systematically attacked Ukrainian government and military infrastructure (Dark Reading 2023).

Wizard Spider is a Russia-based, state-sanctioned cybercrime group. As a state-sanctioned group, Wizard Spider's activities may overlap with the objectives of the Russian state, but its actions are not explicitly directed by the state. For example, most of its operations are financially motivated. Wizard Spider specializes in financially motivated cyber activities such as large-scale ransomware campaigns that victimize a range of targets including large organizations, banking institutions and hospitals. Wizard Spider has also been responsible for deploying malware such as Ryuk, Conti and the malicious banking Trojan virus 'Trickbot' (PRODAFT 2022; Lakshmanan 2022). Trickbot was originally developed as malware, but over time it evolved into a digital suite of malware tools used to target businesses and individuals. Spider Wizard has stolen personal and financial information from millions of people and the organization is considered to hold assets worth hundreds of millions of dollars (PRODAFT 2022; Baker 2023).

North Korea

The North Korean government is a prolific sponsor of cybercrime operations. In particular, the Lazarus Group (also known as Guardians of Peace or Hidden Cobra) and its operations have been directly attributed to the interests of the North Korean state (Haggard and Lindsey 2015). The group has been active for well over a decade and has been implicated in a number of events beginning with 'Operation Troy' which was a damaging DDoS attack against South Korea 2009. The cyber-attacks on Sony Pictures in 2014 by a group claiming to be Guardians of Peace attempted to pressure Sony Pictures to retract the upcoming release of a satirical comedy called 'The Interview' that centred on a plan to assassinate the leader of North Korea, Kim Jong-un (Sharp 2017). Ultimately Sony Pictures did not lose a significant amount of revenue from the attacks. However, 'the reaction of the US government was unprecedented, resulting in the first-ever attribution of a cyber attack to a nation state by a US president' (Haggard and Lindsey 2015, 2).

A couple of years later, the 2016 Bangladesh Bank heist was also linked to the work of the Lazarus Group and other actors operating on behalf of the North Korean state (Mazumder and Sobhan 2020). In early 2015, approximately 12 months prior to the attack, the cyber criminals gained access to the Bangladesh Bank's computer systems via a phishing email. However, the hackers did not launch the attack on the bank until almost a year later. In February 2016, acting as representatives of the Bangladesh Bank, the cyber criminals sent instructions to the Federal Reserve Bank of New York (which held an account for the Bangladesh Bank) to make 35 separate transfers which totalled approximately US $1 billion (White and Lee 2021). Only five transactions were successfully completed before the Federal Reserve Bank flagged the remaining 30 transactions as suspicious and placed a block on their completion. Even so, the successful transactions meant that the cybercriminals had managed to steal US $81 million (White and Lee 2021). In the Philippines, the group used a combination of fake bank accounts, charities, casinos and a wide network of accomplices to support the sophisticated scam. Bank accounts in Manila transferred the money to a casino in Manila. The money was 'cleaned' in a Manila casino and eventually funnelled to Macau which is 'an important financial conduit between North Korea and the outside world' (Hammer 2018, 1). Most of the money sent to the Philippines has never been recovered.

Finally, the Lazarus group is also said to have been responsible for the 2017 release of the WannaCry ransomware (Orcutt 2020). WannaCry targeted the Windows operating system by exploiting a weakness that enabled the malware to infect compromised computers, encrypt the data and then demand a ransom to be paid in Bitcoin. Over a period of three days, WannaCry malware spread to over 300,000 computers around the world. In particular, the malware impacted thousands of National Health Scheme (NHS) hospitals and surgeries in the United Kingdom. Kaspersky (2024) estimated the cost of the attack to be approximately £92 million, with the total cost of the WannaCry global cyber-attack estimated at US $4 billion. In 2023, Seongsu Park, Lead Security Researcher at Kaspersky Global Research and Analysis Team, observed that 'the Lazarus group's continued activity is a testament to their advanced capabilities and unwavering motivation. They operate on a global scale, targeting a wide range of industries with a diverse toolkit of methods' (Park quoted in Kaspersky 2023, 1.)

Conclusion

The digitization of illicit business has allowed criminals to develop new ways to perpetrate old crimes and has created opportunities for new crimes. OCGs can use ICT to enhance their terrestrial activities or create new markets. Cyber-related crimes can be conducted with greater speed and efficiency because cyber capabilities are low cost, flexible and accessible. They can be adopted and easily adapted to the user's needs regardless of the size, location, motivation and type of activities that they might be used for. The modern universal need for at least some ICT or cyber capabilities and skills means that these tools are as useful for criminal and terrorist groups as they are for nation-states. Moreover, the development of CaaS and the use of cyber tools as a form of statecraft means that the use of cyber products to commit a range of crimes in cyberspace for financial or ideological reasons has significantly increased in the past decade.

References

Akyazi, U., van Eeten, M. and Gañán, C.H. (2021) '*Measuring cybercrime as a service (CaaS) offerings in a cybercrime forum.*' Workshop on the Economics of Information Security (WEIS), 28–29 July, pp. 1–15. Available at https://weis2021.econinfosec.org/wpcontent/uploads/sites/9/2021/06/weis21-akyazi.pdf.

Australian Transaction Reports and Analysis Centre (AUSTRAC) (2023) 'Our work to combat virtual kidnappings.' November. Available at https://www.austrac.gov.au/our-work-combat-virtual-kidnappings.

Baker, K. (2023) 'Ransomware as a service (RaaS).' *CrowdStrike*, 30 January. Available at https://www.crowdstrike.com/cybersecurity-101/ransomware/ransomware-as-a-service-raas/.

Beaman, C., Barkworth, A., Akande, T.D., Hakak, S. and Khan, M.K. (2021) 'Ransomware: Recent advances, analysis, challenges and future research directions.' *Computer Security*, 111, 102490. Available at https://doi:10.1016/j.cose.2021.102490.

Besley, T. and Peters, M.A. (2020) 'Terrorism, trauma, tolerance: Bearing witness to white supremacist attack on Muslims in Christchurch, New Zealand.' *Educational Philosophy and Theory* 52 (2) 109–119.

Bossler, A.M. and Berenblum, T. (2019) 'Introduction: New directions in cybercrime research.' *Journal of Crime and Justice* 42 (5) 495–499. Available at https://doi.org/10.1080/0735648X.2019.1692426.

Broséus, J., Rhumorbarbe, D., Mireault, C., Ouellette, V., Crispino, F. and Décary-Hétu, D. (2016) 'Studying illicit drug trafficking on darknet markets: Structure and organisation from a Canadian perspective.' *Forensic Science International* 264, 7–14. Available at https://doi.org/10.1016/j.forsciint.2016.02.045.

Chang, L.Y.-C., Zhou, Y. and Phan, D.H. (2023) 'Virtual kidnapping: Online scams with "Asian characteristics" during the pandemic.' In R.G. Smith, R. Sarre, L.Y.-C. Chang and L.Y.-C. Lau (eds) *Cybercrime in the Pandemic Digital Age and Beyond*, pp. 109–130. Cham: Palgrave Macmillan. Available at https://doi.org/10.1007/978-3-031-29107-4_6.

Choo, K.R. and Grabosky, P. (2014) 'Cybercrime.' In L. Paoli (ed.) *Oxford Handbook of Organized Crime*, pp. 482–499. Oxford: Oxford University Press.

Coats, D.R. (2018) 'Worldwide threat assessment.' Office of the Directorate of National Intelligence, 13 February. Available at https://www.dni.gov/files/documents/News room/Testimonies/2018-ATA—Unclassified-SSCI.pdf.

CrowdStrike (2019) 'Who is FANCY BEAR (APT28)?' 12 February. Available at https://www.crowdstrike.com/blog/who-is-fancy-bear/.

Crowley, T. (2024). 'Russian man identified as Medibank hacker, hit with sanctions by Australian government.' ABC News, 23 January. Available at https://www.abc.net.au/news/2024-01-23/australian-government-sanctions-russian-over-medibank-data-leak/103377976.

Curtis, J. and Oxburgh, G. (2023) 'Understanding cybercrime in 'real world' policing and law enforcement.' *Police Journal*, 96 (4) 573–592. Available at https://doi.org/10.1177/0032258X221107584.

Cybersecurity Ventures (2023) '2023 official cybercrime report: Cybercrime to cost the world $9.5 trillion USD annually in 2024.' *Esentire*. Available at https://www.esentire.com/web-native-pages/cybercrime-to-cost-the-world-9-5-trillion-usd-annually-in-2024?utm_medium=email&utm_source=pardot&utm_campaign=autoresponder.

Dark Reading (2023) 'Russia's "Fancy Bear" APT targets Ukrainian energy facility.' 7 September. Available at https://www.darkreading.com/cyberattacks-data-breaches/russia-fancy-bear-apt-ukrainian-energy-facility.

Evans, J. (2023) 'Alarm raised over "virtual kidnapping" scams targeting international students.' News.com.au, 18 October. Available at https://www.news.com.au/national/crime/alarm-raised-over-virtual-kidnapping-scams-targeting-international-students/news-story/da63fdf52c34b58ccd54e010cbc6d2c4.

Federal Bureau of Investigation (FBI) (2017) 'Virtual kidnapping: A new twist on a frightening scam .' *FBI News*, 16 October. Available at https://www.fbi.gov/news/stories/virtual-kidnapping.

Furnell, S. (2002) *Cyber Crime: Vandalizing the Information Society*. London: Addison Wesley.

Goldsmith, A. (2022) 'Russian ransomware gang likely behind the Medibank cyber attack?' *The Conversation*, 11 November. Available at https://theconversation.com/what-do-we-know-about-revil-the-russian-ransomware-gang-likely-behind-the-medibank-cyber-attack-194337.

Haggard, S. and Lindsey, J. (2015) 'North Korea and the Sony hack: Exporting instability through cyberspace.' *Asia Pacific Issues*, 117 (May).

Hammer J. (2018) 'The billion dollar bank job.' *New York Times*, 3 May. Available at www.nytimes.com/interactive/2018/05/03/magazine/money-issue-bangladesh-billion-dollar-bankheist.html?action=click&module=MagazineModule&pgtype=Article&contentCollection=Magazine&region=Header.

Hegghammer, T. (2010) 'The rise of Muslim foreign fighters: Islam and the globalization of Jihad.' *International Security* 35 (3) 53–94.

Herzog, S. (2011) 'Revisiting the Estonian cyber attacks: Digital threats and multinational responses.' *Journal of Strategic Security* 4 (2) 49–60.

Herzog, S. (2017) 'Ten years after the Estonian cyberattacks: Defense and adaptation in the age of digital insecurity.' *Georgetown Journal of International Affairs* 18 (3) 67–78.

Holt, T.J., Bossler, A.M. and Seigfried-Spellar, K.C. (2018) *Cybercrime and Digital Forensics: An Introduction*, 2nd edition. New York: Routledge.

Jensen, B. (2017) 'The cyber character of political warfare.' *Brown Journal of World Affairs* 24 (1) 159–172.

Jensen, B., Valeriano, B. and Maness, R. (2019) 'Fancy bears and digital trolls: Cyber strategy with a Russian twist.' *Journal of Strategic Studies* 42 (2) 212–234.

Kapsokoli, E. (2019) 'The Transformation of Islamic Terrorism Through Cyberspace: The Case of ISIS.' Proceedings of the 18th European Conference on Cyber Warfare and Security, University of Coimbra, Portugal, 4–5 July. Available at https://www.researchgate.net/publication/342354032.

Kaspersky (2023) 'A cascade of compromise: Kaspersky exposes Lazarus' new campaign exploiting legitimate software.' 27 October. Available at https://www.kaspersky.com/about/press-releases/2023_a-cascade-of-compromise-kaspersky-exposes-lazarus-new-campaign-exploiting-legitimate-software.

Kaspersky (2024) 'What is WannaCry ransomware?' Available at https://www.kaspersky.com/resource-center/threats/ransomware-wannacry.

Kelleher, S.R. (2023) '2 casino ransomware attacks: Caesars paid, MGM did not.' *Forbes*, 14 September. Available at https://www.forbes.com/sites/suzannerowankelleher/2023/09/14/2-casino-ransomware-attacks-caesars-mgm/?sh=7dcff11c402d.

Lacson, W. and Jones, B. (2016) 'The 21st century darknet market: Lessons from the fall of Silk Road.' *International Journal of Cyber Criminology* 10 (1) 40–61.

Lakshimi, S. (2022) 'Terrorism financing in Southeast Asia: Transformations, continuities and challenges.' S. Rajaratnam School of International Studies. Available at https://www.rsis.edu.sg/ctta-newsarticle/terrorism-financing-in-southeast-asia-transformations-continuities-and-challenges/#_edn22.

Lakshmanan, R. (2022) 'Notorious TrickBot malware gang shuts down its botnet infrastructure.' *Hacker News*, 22 February. Available at https://thehackernews.com/2022/02/notorious-trickbot-malware-gang-shuts.htm.

Makarenko, T. (2004) 'The crime-terror continuum: Tracing the interplay between transnational organised crime and terrorism.' *Global Crime* 6 (1) 129–145.

Mandiant (2013) 'APT1 exposing one of China's cyber espionage units.' Available at https://www.mandiant.com/sites/default/files/2021-09/mandiant-apt1-report.pdf.

Maras, M.H. (2014) *Computer Forensics: Cybercriminals, Laws, and Evidence*. Sudbury, MA: Jones and Bartlett.

Maras, M.H. (2016) *Cybercriminology*. Oxford: Oxford University Press.

Maras, M.H. and Arsovska, J. (2023) 'Understanding the intersection between technology and kidnapping: A typology of virtual kidnapping.' *International Criminology* 3, 162–176. Available at https://doi.org/10.1007/s43576-023-00091-4.

Mazumder, M. and Sobhan, A. (2020) 'The spillover effect of the Bangladesh Bank cyber heist on banks' cyber risk disclosures in Bangladesh.' *Journal of Operational Risk* 15 (4) 53–76.

Office of the Director of National Intelligence (2023) 'Annual threat assessment.' 13 February. Available at https://www.dni.gov/files/documents/Newsroom/Testimonies/2018-ATA—Unclassified-SSCI.pdf.

Orcutt, M. (2020) 'How the North Korean hackers behind WannaCry got away with a stunning crypto-heist.' *MIT Technology Review*, 24 January. Available at https://www.technologyreview.com/2020/01/24/276082/lazarus-group-dragonex-chainalysis/.

Phillips, K., Davidson, J.C., Farr, R.R., Burkhardt, C., Caneppele, S. and Aiken, M.P. (2022) 'Conceptualizing cybercrime: Definitions, typologies and taxonomies.' *Forensic Sciences* 2 (2) 379–398.

Pernik, P. (2018) 'The early days of cyberattacks: The cases of Estonia, Georgia and Ukraine.' In N. Popescu and S. Secrieru (eds) *Hacks, Leaks and Disruptions: Russian Cyber Strategies*, pp. 53–64. Paris: European Union Institute for Security Studies. Available at https://www.jstor.org/stable/pdf/resrep21140.9.pdf?refreqid=fastly default%3A082df560c14c7bbe73d138f268d0c8ac&ab_segments=&origin=&initiator=&acceptTC=1.

Prabowo, H.Y. (2012) 'Terrorist financing, cybercrime and the underground economy.' *The Jakarta Post*, 9 July. Available at https://www.thejakartapost.com/news/2012/07/09/terrorist-financing-cybercrime-and-underground-economy.html.

PRODAFT (2022) 'Wizard Spider in-depth analysis.' 20 March. Available at https://25491742.fs1.hubspotusercontenteu1.net/hubfs/25491742/%5BWS%5D%20Wizard%20Spider%20Group%20In-Depth%20Analysis.pdf.

Sharp, T. (2017) 'Theorizing cyber coercion: The 2014 North Korean operation against Sony.' *Journal of Strategic Studies* 40 (7) 898–926.

Shiva, S.G., Roy, S. and Dasgupta, D. (2010) 'Game theory for cyber security.' Cyber Security and Information Intelligence Research Workshop (CSIIRW) Proceedings of the Sixth Annual Workshop on Cyber Security and Information Intelligence Research, April, Article No. 34, pp. 1–4. Available at https://doi.org/10.1145/1852666.1852704.

Usman, I.A. and Owubokiri, T.F. (2023) 'International terrorism in the age of information and communication technology.' *Jurnal Ilmu Pemerintahan dan Sosial Politik UMA (Journal of Governance and Political Social UMA)* 11 (2) 86–99.

Voce, I. and Morgan, A. (2023) 'Cybercrime in Australia 2023.' Statistical Report no. 43. Canberra: Australian Institute of Criminology. Available at https://doi.org/10.52922/sr77031.

White, G. and Lee, J. (2021) 'The Lazarus heist: How North Korea almost pulled off a billion-dollar hack.' BBC, 21 June. Available at https://www.bbc.com/news/stories-57520169.

Willett, M. (2023) 'Offensive cyber and the responsible use of cyber power.' International Institute for Strategic Studies, 2 March. Available at https://www.iiss.org/online-analysis/online-analysis/2023/03/offensive-cyber-and-the-responsible-use-of-cyber-power/.

Windsor, L. (2020) 'The language of radicalization: Female internet recruitment to participation in ISIS activities.' *Terrorism and Political Violence* 32 (3) 506–538.

11
CONCLUSION

Illicit Business is Big Business

This book has explored organized crime's involvement in illicit economic enterprises from a business perspective. While it has drawn on literature from criminology, legal studies and other disciplines the object of our endeavours has been to examine a wide range of organized criminal enterprises as businesses. The book has provided an introduction to a variety of illegal money-making activities that have been set up in a systematic and structured way by criminals. They are designed for the economic production of goods and services in exchange for payment, just like legal businesses. However, unlike legal businesses, illicit businesses operate outside of the law.

From the chapters of this book it is evident that our opening assertion that 'illicit business is big business' has been confirmed many times over. Illicit business does not entail a minor set of criminal activities. It accounts for a significant proportion of the world's gross domestic product, although the hidden nature of the illegal activities undertaken by organized crime groups (OCGs) makes it extremely difficult to measure. Illicit businesses are also diverse, ranging across drug, arms and people trafficking to wildlife poaching, money laundering, digital scamming, and more. They thrive on demand and therefore need markets which already exist but are also boosted or created through promotion by the criminals operating in the supply chain. The enterprises must also be profitable and worth the risk for the numerous participants in the global supply chains that have increasingly come to characterize the illegal activities. The markets are segmented into different broad categories of demand – for example, drugs, fish and counterfeit goods – and within each category there is further segmentation – for example, cocaine, squid and Gucci handbags. It is a complex world of illicit networks devoted to the procurement

DOI: 10.4324/9781003293620-11

of particular products and transporting them for sale to the end users, all the while trying to keep out of sight of law enforcement agencies while being accessible to other actors in the global supply chain right down to the buyers at the end of the chain. Sometimes there may even be overlap or cooperation between networks. Despite the obvious complexity and diversity of illicit business types and practices revealed in the chapters of this book we are still able to make some general observations about illicit business in the contemporary world.

Similarities with legal businesses: Ultimately, illicit businesses are de facto businesses and as such they share important similarities with their legal counterparts. Obviously they are driven by the need to make a profit and will fail if they do not earn that profit. They also have organizational structures that divide up and coordinate the work and enable them to pursue their business strategies. Both types of business operate in organizational environments made up a of a multiplicity of actors, forces and events. This environment is ever-changing and can be highly volatile. This means that businesses, both legal and illegal, must understand and constantly monitor their environments and adapt to changing threats and opportunities to survive and perhaps thrive. They try to control as much of the environment as possible to increase the predictability of their economic activities. In contemporary business jargon, they must be nimble, agile and build capabilities that can manage change. Entrepreneurial talents are highly valued by both types of business as they are deployed to identify new opportunities and to work out how to exploit them to produce more profit. These entrepreneurial skills have often been linked to technological change. In recent decades, the most significant technological changes have been the development and adoption of information and communications technology (ICT). Both licit and illicit businesses have embraced ICT as it has opened up new opportunities for profit-making and increasing organizational efficiency and effectiveness. These common characteristics of licit and illicit businesses have been evident throughout the book and point to shared capitalist imperatives that play major roles in shaping business organizations in a globalizing world.

Differences from legal businesses: While illicit and licit businesses may share many characteristics and are subject to market forces, there are some profound differences between them. The most obvious one is that illicit businesses deliberately break the law. Their enterprises are established in the full knowledge that they are legally proscribed. In some cases, there may be legal businesses operating in the same fields such as fishing or the wildlife trade. But many types of illicit business are wholly illegal such as drug or people trafficking. The state sets rules and regulations for the governance of economic activities. They dictate what can be done and what cannot. This is not to say that some legal businesses break the law, but they were not set up to do so. A second major difference that we have consistently observed is that illicit businesses frequently develop a capacity for violence and utilize that violence as a component of their business strategy – both offensively and defensively. For example, people traffickers employ violence or the threat of it as a central element of their business operations. Different illegal enterprises may deploy violence against each other to enhance their competitiveness. Thus, Mexican drug cartels have waged war against each other in the pursuit of greater market share. They also intimidate local populations to secure their acquiescence. This helps to make their business environments more predictable. The third major difference between illicit and licit businesses is their need to avoid the attention of law enforcement agencies. The latter's goal is to terminate illicit businesses. They are mostly set up and managed by the state although some are international in nature. They cooperate and coordinate their activities, not always successfully, to combat illegal businesses. While legal businesses must abide by the laws and regulations of the state or face the consequences, the organizational environment of illicit businesses contains official agencies that are dedicated to their elimination.

Globalization and the rise of network structures: All organizations have structures through which they divide up and coordinate their activities. These structures display different configurations according to their organizational strategies and capabilities and the preferences of their leaders. In a globalizing world economies and economic actors have increasingly created inter-connections for production, transport and marketing that can criss-cross the entire globe. These linkages can be seen in terms of networks of actors providing specialized services that contribute to the achievement of mutual goals. Actors in the illicit economy have followed this trend and as we have demonstrated can be best seen in terms of networks. We have identified network structures for most of the illicit businesses delineated in this book. They have been adopted for several reasons. Unlike traditional hierarchical structures, networks spread risk among multiple actors. They are flexible and can be reconfigured when there is network disruption, for example when law enforcement agencies arrest participants. Criminal networks have demonstrated resilience. They provide access to markets and suppliers across international boundaries and are the reason why transnational crime has become such an enormous enterprise. Members of networks can have relationships which range from the loosely coupled to the tightly coupled, while within a network different participants may have different internal structures. One ubiquitous and critically important network actor that has been evident in our analyses of illicit business operations ranging from drug trafficking to the illegal wildlife trade has been the broker. Their role is to span the structural holes; that is, to link actors who would be otherwise disconnected. The broker is a boundary spanner on whom the network depends. As such, law enforcement agencies are able to inflict the maximum damage to a network when they apprehend brokers.

Ambiguity and the role of the state: As we learned earlier, the state is a centralized political organization that wields the authority and power to establish the rules which prescribe citizens' behaviour within the state's geographical boundaries. A major responsibility is to maintain law and order. To perform this and other functions the state generally seeks a monopoly of violence within its territory. This puts the state in direct opposition to OCGs as the latter deliberately set out to break the rules decreed by the state. Agencies of the state seek to apprehend and prosecute the participants in illicit business. However, this idealized picture of state versus illicit business is not always manifested in practice. Occupants of state offices may cooperate with illicit business and states may depart so far from the ideal that they become 'mafia states' where illicit business and leading state officeholders work together for their own personal benefit. Corruption has been found to have an insidious effect on the motivation of state officials in many countries, from humble clerks to cabinet ministers, to enforce the law on illicit businesses. The latter use corruption to make their organizational environments more predictable, so that they know that illegal shipments will not be identified or confiscated, that inadequate documents will be accepted, and that officials will be told to 'look the other way.' Beyond corruption, there is also the problem of inadequate state ability to deal with the operations of illicit businesses within national borders. Developing countries in particular lack the resources to be effective enforcers. Thus, although the state is the entity that should ideally combat organized crime and disrupt criminal networks, some of its officials may well be working against this objective and bringing adverse consequences to the state's citizens.

The threat to security: We should not only look at illicit businesses exclusively in terms of crime. Rather, in recent decades, international bodies and state organizations have increasingly come to view the operations of organized crime as security threats. The threats can be manifested in several domains – to livelihoods, to law and order, to the environment, to food supplies, to personal safety, and more. Illicit business networks undermine peace, development, governance and the environment. Examples are unfortunately not hard to find. In Africa, arms trafficking has fuelled civil wars and led to population displacement, loss of life, exploitation of children, economic decline and human misery. Wildlife trafficking and illegal, unregulated and unreported fishing have plundered the environment, thus threatening ecosystems and biodiversity on which the sustainability of the planet depends. Drug trafficking cartels have sowed terror in their use of violence and have undermined state efforts in socioeconomic development and effective governance. It is important not to dissociate illicit business from the wider effects it has on society and the environment. Illicit business is not simply a criminal matter. It poses an existential threat to our desired way of living and its sustainability.

Cooperation and technology in countering illicit business: Many commentaries and analyses on combating illicit business have emphasized the need for cooperation and coordination between state law enforcement agencies and international bodies devoted to the same objectives. But, despite the proliferation of organizations and the huge volume of laws and regulations directed against organized crime, enforcement cooperation often remains weak despite the huge gains that could be made. It is evident that transnational crime organizations do not respect national borders. Indeed, they thrive on their networks that span continents and multiple jurisdictions. Thus, it requires coordinated efforts among different agencies in different geographical locations to increase the efficiency and effectiveness of law enforcement agencies targeting illicit business. This is not to say that cooperation does not happen. It most certainly does and there is much evidence to show how effective it can be. However, more needs to be done to increase the rate of arrest and trial of actors in illicit business networks. In addition, there needs to be increased deployment of advanced technology that can facilitate and enhance the work of those working in law enforcement. Coordinated action by multiple law enforcement agencies that can utilize advanced technological tools should make inroads into the activities of transnational organized crime. But the achievement of this desirable state of affairs requires political will and adequate resourcing, neither of which appear to be readily available. They will perhaps become more available when citizens and governments fully appreciate the enormity of the threats to economy, society and environment posed by illicit business.

INDEX

Note: Italic page numbers refer to figure; Bold page numbers refer to table

Printed in the United States
by Baker & Taylor Publisher Services